Rural Industry in India

Policy Perspectives, Past Performance and Future Options

G. K. Chadha

South Asia Advisory Team (SAAT)
International Labour Organization
New Delhi

First Published 2003
ISBN: 92-2-111913-0

Printed in India

Preface

The ILO has been engaged, for well over a decade now, in a technical co-operation programme on rural industrialization with a view to examining the potential of rural industries to create gainful employment and decentralized development in India. While the experience of other countries, particularly those in East Asia, indicated that the rural sector has a vast potential of creating worthwhile job opportunities as well as decentralized development, the pattern of development in post-Independence India, which did contribute to the creation of a modern industrial base in the country, did not help in creating jobs in any significant manner for the larger rural masses. This underscored the need for a new look at finding alternative strategies for creating gainful employment in the agrarian sectors as well as for the new entrants to the labour force.

The ILO programme, funded by SIDA, was conceived in this backdrop and aimed at conducting a number of well researched studies to arrive at concrete conclusions for public policy. The overall responsibility for this essentially research oriented programme rested with ILO-SAAT. The programme ran over two phases. In Phase I, ten papers were commissioned on various aspects of rural industrialisation in India, largely based on existing literature and secondary/published data. These papers were discussed in an ILO-SAAT seminar in August 1994, primarily to take stock of the existing position, and to consider further course of action. It was felt at that stage that the efforts underlying Phase I could not throw up much light on the nature and working of this sector, and that more information and analysis were needed to arrive at meaningful policy conclusions. Thus came Phase II.

In Phase II, it was decided that (limited) sample survey should be conducted to collect primary data for developing a better understanding of some crucial aspects of rural industries, such as productivity, technology, employment and environment. This survey was conducted in select districts of Karnataka and West Bengal at the level of enterprises as well as workers. A total of four papers came forth under Phase II.

The two rounds of papers generated sufficient evidence on the strengths and weaknesses, especially on the policy front, of the rural industrial sector in India. To concretize ideas and frame suitable policy recommendations for fostering a healthy growth of rural industries, especially to generate an expanding employment base for the rural job aspirants, an expert group seminar on "Rural Industrialisation in India: Issues and Policies" was organised by the ILO-SAAT at Manesar-Haryana on August 25-26, 2000. The seminar attracted a wide public participation encompassing academic and research institutions, central, state and local governments, international development agencies, NGOs, in fact, all categories of stake holders. The presence of Dr. K.C. Pant, Deputy Chairman, Planning Commission, Mr. I.P.Anand, Member, ILO Governing Body, Dr. S.P.Gupta and Dr. D.N. Tewari, Members, Planning Commission, among many other distinguished participants, clearly demonstrated the importance that the ILO and the Government of India attach to the growth of rural industries, and employment and welfare stakes of people involved in them. The Manesar seminar threw up many suggestions which needed to be put in perspective, especially in the context of the changing economic regime, partly under the changing domestic policies and partly coming in from the external economic environment.

The present volume puts together all available evidence on the policy and working of the rural industrial sector in India, based on the papers commissioned by the ILO-SAAT under Phases I and II of the programme, discussions at the Manesar seminar, and the latest policy changes announced/effected during 2000 and 2001. Actually, the volume looks at the whole gamut of issues that has been impinging upon the pace and pattern of rural industrial development in India. The manuscript was prepared by Prof. G.K. Chadha, at the instance of the ILO-SAAT, New Delhi. The ILO thanks him for his keen interest in the subject and academic input which has indeed brought the issue of rural industrialisation as the central focus of policy discussion. Many other people have also contributed, in their own way, to the present volume, the foremost among them is Dr. A.S. Oberoi, former-Director, ILO-SAAT, New Delhi, who not only initiated the study but also nursed its progress with utmost keenness and interest. I must thank him for taking continous interest in this area which bears great significance to ILO's own policy and research agenda. Other ILO colleagues who made their respective contributions in the preparation of this manuscript are Ms. Mary Johnson, former-Director, ILO Area Office, New Delhi, Mr. I.P. Anand, Member, ILO Governing Body, Dr. S. Acharya, Subject Specialist, Mr. M.L. Nandrajog, ILO consultant, Ms. Amrita Mehrotra, Mr. Ravichandran, and Mr. Gopi Krishna. We gratefully acknowledge their assistance. Thanks are also due to the individual paper writers, and the participants in the August-1994 and August-2000 seminars who made valuable contribution towards clarifying many issues, and providing useful insights on others. The contribution made, during Phase I of the programme, by Dr. Rizwanul Islam, and Dr. Ajit Ghosh, then from ILO-SAAT, New Delhi, helped in giving a concrete direction to the programme during the post-1995 phase. Lastly Mr. P.P. Sahu, Doctoral Student working with Prof. G.K. Chadha at JNU rendered excellent research support.

HERMAN VAN DER LAAN
Director,
ILO Area Office/SAAT

New Delhi
March 2003

Contents

List of Tables

1

Significance of Rural Non-farm Sector

It is a pity that till recently, the significance of non-farm employment and income to rural households, especially the weaker sections among them, did not receive adequate attention. Undoubtedly, this was partly due to excessive preoccupation of most development economists and policy administrators with the two-sector growth model under which the steadily expanding modern industrial sector would show an uninterrupted capacity of taking on the surplus labour from the backward agricultural sector (Lewis, 1958; Ranis-Fei, 1961). For all practical purposes, the rural-urban linkages would be forged through the mechanism of labour transfer from agriculture to industry, and the industrial sector would hold the central stage. Implicit in the two-sector model is, *inter alia*, the assumption that employment growth in the modern, capitalist sector would be proportional to the rate of capital formation. This did not happen in actual development process. Both capital formation and output expansion occurred, in varying form and content, but employment grew at a much slower pace.

1.1 Disenchantment with Two-Sector Model

Two aspects need to be underlined in this regard. First, for a fairly long period after the commencement of the development process, industrial growth in most developing economies did not reflect any remarkable performance and accordingly, its capacity to generate incremental employment opportunities for rural job aspirants has been rather limited, even if we keep aside the constraints of technical skills and educational deficiencies of rural labour force in general, and a fairly high growth rate of labour force itself in particular. Second, and of more crucial significance, is the reality of ever rising levels of incremental capital:labour ratio in the modern industrial sector, to effectuate technological improvements to meet competitive urges, on the one hand, and to ward off labour cost hikes and 'labour troubles', on the other. By the close of the 1960s, the operational weaknesses of the dual sector approach, especially the painful consequences of increasing rural under-employment, became obvious. Policy makers started looking for solutions inside rural areas themselves. The necessity for expanding the network of non-farm activities for rural development, improvement of employment, productivity and earnings, and poverty reduction, thus gained a high policy significance in the developing world, and what was earlier looked at as a passive side-route for employment growth became the central plank of rural development strategy (Ho, 1986:1).

Keeping aside the disenchantment with the employment consequences of the two sector model, the case for non-farm employment in the developing economies, especially the more populous ones amongst them, such as China, India and Indonesia in Asia, stood on its own. It is now fully recognized that in peasant economies, typically characterised by population pressures, an ever-declining land:man ratio, small and fragmented holdings, highly inequitous land distribution structures, etc. agriculture alone could not provide the ultimate solution for rural un- and under-employment. Non-farm avenues of employment and earnings are a must.

1.2 Rural Non-Farm Sector is a Must

Guided by world-wide development experiences, as a part of long-term strategy of employment for the rural households, it is both illogical and inadvisable to keep too much reliance on agriculture alone. The inadvisability stems from the fact that, in the life history of every developing economy, agriculture is bound to witness a relative decline, *inter alia*, because of the inevitable and continuing process of demand restructuring. Colin Clark and Simon Kuznets persuasively remind us of the ever declining share of agriculture in national income and employment as the tempo of development picks up. While the wider implications of the demand-borne sectoral restructuring need not be spelt out here, nonetheless, it needs to be underlined that a developing economy must strive to expand its non-agricultural sectors, and thereby facilitate the transfer of workforce out of agriculture, on an enduring basis.

Theoretically, the income and employment restructuring can occur in varying combinations but the most common empirical experience is that agriculture's share in national income declines sizeably but the proportion of work force does so much less proportionately. A natural corollary of this development is that per worker earning of those staying back in agriculture keeps on sliding in relation to that of those getting absorbed in diverse, and upcoming, non-farm activities. A glaring example of this comes from India's own development experience. On a rough counting, the ratio of per worker earning in non-agricultural sectors to that in agriculture was about 2.0 in 1950-51 which gradually increased to 3.3 in 1990-91; during the 1990s, it rose at a much faster pace and stood as high as 5.0 in 1999-2000. This is reported to be an important reason for a near-halt in the pace of rural poverty decline that the Indian economy had been witnessing until about the close of the 1980s. In any case, compared with the rest of the economy, the relative squeeze in agriculture's share in national income and work force is an empirical reality through which most of the currently advanced economies have lived, in varying form and proportion, and this is what is inextricably linked with the inherent nature of low income elasticity of demand for agricultural goods and the fairly wide range of elasticity values for non-agricultural goods and services. If non-agricultural base of the rural economy remains narrow, the country is in for trouble on employment, earning, and poverty fronts.

It may not be inferred from the foregoing analysis that there are no real possibilities of enhancing on-farm labour absorption through suitable technological, institutional and organizational improvements (Ishikawa, 1986; Vyas-Mathai,1978; Oshima, 1982; Edgren-Muqtada, 1989). Undoubtedly, for a long- time to come, on-farm employment will remain a major source of income for the rural households, and it is in the fitness of things that such avenues are strengthened and fully made use of. Nevertheless, the moot point that needs to be underlined is that "even if such technical possibilities are realized, the agriculture sector in some of the land-scarce countries will be unable to fully employ the rural labour force that is (or will be) available" (Islam,1987: 1). This is especially so in the developing countries where, *inter alia*, the age-composition of the population is skewed more in favour of the younger members while the level of fertility is not showing much diminution. These elements exasperate further the problem of land-scarcity.

The advocates of agriculture-led growth theories *also* visualise an important role for the rural non-farm sector in stimulating agricultural growth through inter-sectoral linkages. A modern agriculture is based on strong forward and backward linkages with industry and other non-agricultural sectors some of which may partly be available in the rural areas themselves (Mellor, 1976: Ch. VII). But then, the converse is equally true; the prospects of non-farm growth also critically hinge on the performance of their agriculture (Hazell-Haggblade, 1991 : 515). The farm non-farm linkages can be visualized in three different ways. First, increase in farm incomes stimulates demand for a wide variety of consumer goods, some of which might be produced by the rural non-farm (RNF) sector itself. Second, a growing agriculture demands production inputs that are either produced or distributed by local non-farm enterprises. Third, rising agricultural productivity and wages raise the opportunity cost of labour in non-farm activities, inducing a shift in the composition of non-farm activities out of very labour-intensive, low-return activities into more skilled, higher investment, high-return activities (Hazell-Haggblade, 1991: 519).

It must also be kept in mind that, in some cases, through a conscious state policy, many industrial and related commercial activities are located in the rural areas. These policies will have their own impact on boosting local people's employment and earnings. Put in different words, the question of non-farm development then becomes a part of the general question of state's approach to rural development. If rural development is accorded due priority in the very beginning, crucial elements of agricultural infrastructure (e.g. irrigation, power, roads, education, research and extension, and so on) are adequately provided for, agricultural output, employment and incomes grow apace, and by the same token, much success is pre-assured for the development of the non-farm sector. Still more crucially, a well-developed infrastructural network may attract a variety of non-farm activities from outside, greatly enhancing the two-way flow of economic activities between rural and urban areas. Who can deny that 'rural industry' made tremendous success in Japan, South Korea, and Taiwan-China primarily because, *inter alia*, rural infrastructure was strong, and rural development stood high in their development priorities.

1.2.1 Multifarious Effects of RNF Sector

Apart from the significant role that a dynamic rural non-farm sector plays towards agricultural development, many other theoretical arguments can also be adduced in its favour. **First**, rural non-farm activities utilize local talent and local 'slack' resources, which could not be easily transferred and utilised in urban, modern industry. **Second**, a planned strategy of rural non-farm development may prevent many rural people from migrating to urban industrial and commercial centres. In the face of the growing social and economic problems associated with urban expansion, it is increasingly realized that the network of rural non-farm activities could play an important role in containing large-scale urban-ward migration of rural job seekers. Thus, through localizing employment in the rural areas themselves, the rural non-farm activities could contribute in easing urban congestion and reducing the pressures on scarce urban infrastructural facilities (e.g. housing, water, sanitation, transport, education, etc.). Undoubtedly, labour exodus from rural areas, which is the main breeding-ground for urban slums and a host of socio-economic problems, gets intercepted which works to the benefit of both rural and urban economies (Islam, 1987: 2).

Third, the rural-urban economic gaps, and many other aspects associated with life and aspirations of people, are bound to get narrower when the economic base of the rural economy extends itself beyond agriculture. It is much more likely, *ceteris paribus*, for the rural people to see, assimilate and adopt urban work patterns and higher earning expectations when their own non-farm sector is expanding than otherwise. **Fourth**, rural industries are generally less capital-intensive and more labour absorbing. The social objectives of deriving higher employment and output gains for every unit of capital invested is likely to be more readily fulfilled through a chain of rural industrial activities. **Fifth**, most of the empirical studies testify that rural income distribution is much less unequal in areas where a wide network of non-farm avenues of employment exists; the lower strata of the rural societies participate much more intensely in non-farm activities although their involvement is decidedly in less capital- and technology-intensive enterprises and is much less remunerative compared with that of the upper strata. **Sixth**, a real dent into rural poverty is reported to come more readily through a wide network of non-farm activities, most ostensibly because, in general, for people without a land base of their own, per worker productivity and earning are higher in non-farm than in farm employment.

> Finally, such activities and industries, which are usually labour and local-resource intensive, would be in line with the perceived comparative advantage of most developing economies. Furthermore, rural industrialisation policies also fit in well with the industrial location strategies being followed by multinational enterprises and national industrialists alike in a wide range of products of light industry...(Saith, 1992: 7).

1.3 RNF for Rural India

Going by the whole range of arguments set out above, the rationale for non-farm development in rural India, characterised as it is by population pressures, an ever-declining land:man ratio, small and fragmented holdings, and a highly skewed land distribution structures, etc. should be fairly obvious. Nonetheless, three points, perhaps in the specific context of the Indian rural economy, need to be reiterated. **First**, undoubtedly, for a long time to come, on-farm employment will remain a major source of income for the rural households, and it is in the fitness of things that, through suitable technological, institutional and organizational improvements, such avenues are fully explored by Indian policy makers, especially in regions where agriculture is still a drag on the local economy and rural poverty is still of a very high order. Yet again, it needs to be emphasized that agriculture alone cannot, and would not, provide the ultimate solution for rural un- and under-employment, and low level of earnings and poverty. A study conducted as far back as the early 1980s showed that a fairly big percentage of marginal and small farmers in the state of Punjab were living below the poverty line primarily because their reliance on agriculture was of a high order, although this is the state where most spectacular breakthroughs occurred in crop productivities, on-farm labour absorption witnessed a noticeable increase and agricultural wage rates did not register any real decline (Bhalla-Chadha, 1983). The question of adequacy of employment should not be seen independent of remunerativeness of employment if poverty is to be tackled on an enduring basis. We have another study from a similar, fast growing agriculture (District West Godavari, Andhra Pradesh,India) which clearly shows that with agricultural development alone, poverty cannot be completely wiped out (Chadha, 1994: 192-94). We have thus to reiterate that as a part of long-term strategy of employment for the rural households, non-farm avenues are, therefore, a must.

Second, the employment problem has continued to be the Achilles' heel of the Indian economy. Partly due to the failure of the modern industrial sector to absorb the expanding army of surplus agricultural workers and partly because, in many regions of the Indian economy, agriculture too cannot take on more working hands on an indefinite basis, rural non-farm expansion would have to be a logical way-out of the employment impasse. It is widely believed that one of the crucial preconditions for effectuating enhanced labour absorption in agriculture is to impose higher limits on ceilings on land holdings and create an egalitarian land distribution structure. Unluckily, the needed degree of political determination for making it a reality has neither been in sight in the past decades nor is it likely to emerge in the near future (Islam, *ibid*: 2). As a matter of fact, the recent economic pressures have been working for diluting the whole issue of ceilings on land holdings 'if we have to realize economies of scale in production and have to stay competitive in the open trade regime'. Interestingly, re-distributive land reforms have been steadfastly kept alive as a political propaganda by Indian government, yet these are essentially a closed option, in *de facto* if not in *de jure* terms. As an alternative, rural non-farm development may benefit all sections of the rural community and in terms of sheer political expediency, may be acceptable to one and all. There are studies to show that a much higher percentage of the landless and marginal farming households pursue non-farm activities, compared with higher categories of rural households and that the expanding network of non-farm jobs has the effect of mollifying the highly inequitable distribution of incomes arising out of farming and its related activities (Bhalla-Chadha, 1983: Ch.4; Chadha, 1994: Ch.8; Rosegrant-Hazell, 2000: 89-103).

Lastly, over time, the labour absorptive capacity of agriculture has been shrinking, as indeed the consistently declining employment elasticity with respect to aggregate agricultural output from 0.54 during 1972-73/1977-78 to 0.49 during 1977-78/1983, and further down to 0.36 during 1983/1987-88 readily testifies for the Indian case (Bhalla, 1994: 131). Since this trend is likely to continue, it is high time, reliance on agriculture is reduced and concrete policy measures are put in place for a steady expansion of the rural non-farm sector. The form and content of non-farm growth, as also the combination of farm and non-farm employment, has to be judiciously worked out, perhaps differently by different regions, on short, medium and long-run basis. Their short term choices, however, cannot ride over their long-run compulsions; in the long-run, each region must diversify its rural economy and its employment base.

1.4 About the Study

The present study relates to rural industry which is a dominant constituent of the rural non-farm economy. For example, in 1999-2000, rural manufacturing alone accounted for 25.52 per cent of rural non-farm employment and about 18.0 per cent of rural net domestic product originating in all non-farm activities put together. Another, and perhaps more telling, way of looking at the significance of rural industry is to look at its share in rural net domestic product and employment in the non-farm commodity sectors. Again, in 1999-2000, rural manufacturing accounted for as much as 50.18 per cent of income originating in the secondary sector of the rural economy; its share in employment was even higher at 57.94 per cent. From other perspectives also, such as inter-sector linkages, trade and technology flows, especially between the rural and urban economies, general development of rural areas, etc., rural industry is a more persuasive stake-holder on behalf of the rural non-farm economy. Hence, the importance of the study.

2

Policy Perspectives

Rural industry has a significant role to play in the Indian economy. The importance of this sector was never lost to the policy makers in India, and for reasons of social justice and political expediency, if not of economic efficiency, the general strategy of industrialization has always been spelt out side by side with rural industrial development policies and programmes. Although, the orientation and emphasis have been different between the two, yet the issue of rural industrialization has remained as much atop the agenda of policy makers as of industrialization in general. Over time, the organic link between the two has not only been fully recognized but also sought to be strengthened in more than one ways. In what follows, we give a brief narration of official policy on rural industrialization, followed by a look at the growth profile of this sector. Before we do that, we must, however, bring out the major thrusts in India's industrialization strategy in general so that the changing policy strands for rural industrial development are seen in a proper macro perspective.

2.1 General Industrialization Strategy in India

2.1.1 Industry that India Inherited in 1947

In 1947, India emerged as an extremely backward economy. A vast majority of its people lived in poverty and suffered from inadequate and unbalanced diet, primitive housing, lack of social security, health and educational facilities, widespread un- and under-employment, and so on. With the added effect of the Partition, what we inherited from the British Empire was a backward, stagnant, depleted and amputated economy. The lopsidedness of the then Indian economy can be gauged from the fact that in 1950-51, only 9.6 per cent of the gainfully employed population was engaged in manufacturing which contributed a mere 11.7 per cent to India's net domestic product (Shirokov, 1980: 13-14). Not only that, the Indian manufacturing sector was small and dominated by cottage and small-scale industries; the domination was indeed overwhelming in terms of persons employed. Accordingly, by international standards, productivity levels in Indian industry were very low. One can quote elaborate statistics to show backwardness of individual economic sectors but that is not needed. What needs, however, to be underlined is that building the national economy from the level we inherited in 1947 was an extremely challenging task. Besides contending with a not-so-helpful international environment, the policy makers had also to make room for divergent economic perceptions of sectional lobbies and regional claims. Tremendous deficiencies inherited from the colonial rule, the conflicting interplay of economic, political and social factors across regions and pressure groups, a bureaucracy not yet attuned to meet development demands, a democratic political regime which was yet fumbling towards institution-building, Indian masses which were as yet completely unfamiliar with the democratic polity of a newly emerging nation state, etc., all stood in the way of framing a widely acceptable development strategy. A strategy was nevertheless framed and put into operation.

Development strategy is too broad a concept to be discussed here. Expressly germane to our study, we take up the broad contours of industrialization strategy that was evolved in the initial years of planned economic development, modified later from time to time under political pressures or economic compulsions including the latest round of measures towards liberalization and globalization of the Indian economy, most ostensibly its industry. To put the record straight, since our discussion of the industrialization strategy must necessarily be intertwined with an analysis of rural industrialization policies and programmes, we would steer through only those aspects of industrialization strategy which, in our view, have some bearing on the growth of rural industry.

2.1.2 Case for Industrialization

When India gained political Independence in 1947, it had a strong case for industrialization. A large territory, big and growing population, a highly uneven distribution of national income with its implicit pressure on demand for consumer goods including consumer durables, a modest industrial base (although confined to light consumer goods industry) inherited from the colonial empire, the presence of a powerful national bourgeoisie, etc., all combined to justify India's claim towards industrialization (Shirokov, 1980: 9; Chakravarty, 1987: Ch.2). If one were to read the central message in debates and resolutions passed in the 1931 Karachi Session of the Indian National Congress, the 1938 Congress National Planning Committee's deliberations, the 1944 Bombay Plan, and the 1945 Statement of Industrial

Policy (SIP), one discovers that it was well recognized much before Independence that an important task that India would have to undertake after Independence would be to give a major thrust towards industrializing the economy (Inoue, 1992: 4-6; Paranjape, 1977 : 325). Perhaps, inspired by Lewis, Nurkse and Ranis-Fei, and the pioneering work of Kuznets followed by a number of empirical updatings, etc., the much greater forward and backward linkages as also the multiplier effects of investment in industry compared with, say, agriculture, the academic opinion in India also lent an overwhelming support to the case for industrialization. Although many analysts believe to the contrary, the high-track emphasis on industry was never supposed to be at the cost of agriculture. The agriculture-industry dichotomy vanishes if one takes a long-run view of development strategies and priorities emanating therefrom. It was widely accepted, therefore, that industry would be the leading sector. Opinions were, however, divided on how to industrialize.

2.1.3 Nehru-Gandhi Approaches to Industrialization

Two major schools of thought on the approach to industrialization stand out clearly (for three other viewpoints on industrialization, see Swamy, 1994: 44-46). While Nehru-Mahalanobis model favoured a strategy of building basic and key industries with the expectation of maximizing growth rates over the long-run, Gandhi did not think that large factories would be able to solve either the problem of un- and under-employment or that of providing Indian masses with their basic requisites (Chakravarty, 1987: Ch.2). As is well known, ultimately Nehru-Mahalanobis strategy prevailed over the Gandhian approach and the Second Plan embarked upon an ambitious programme of building a network of basic and key industries, whose gestation period was long, whose investment requirements were too heavy, and whose growth propelling effects were to flow only after big time gaps. Nevertheless, the merit of Gandhian philosophy was not completely lost to the Nehru-Mahalanobis school, and the ultimate shape in which India's industrialization strategy emerged did provide for boosting the modern industrial growth at the same time that it sought to support the traditional village industries. India thus chose to 'walk on two legs', and this core element of industrialization strategy has stayed on till today.

Let us take a close look at the two positions. The core of the Nehru-Mahalanobis strategy was to take a long-run perspective of the economy: invest heavily today so that production capabilities expand tomorrow, and a high growth regime follows as a consequence. It was essential to build, in the initial period, the *investment goods sector*, through a concentrated investment effort, that would lead to a more rapid rate of growth of investment over the long-run. In other words, the most strategic pre-requisite for a sustained process of industrial growth was the rapid development of basic and heavy capital goods industries in the initial years of industrialization. The development of capital goods sector in the transitional period would, however, involve a deficit balance of payment. The machinery, technical know-how, basic raw materials and other commodities necessary for building the capital goods industry had to be imported. India's major exports at that time (tea, jute, cotton textiles, etc.) did not possess much scope for expansion and, therefore, there was no way in the immediate future of increasing export earnings fast enough to match the rise in demand for foreign exchange. This led to an emphasis on the development of import-saving industries. The essential idea was that capital goods which were to be imported initially should ultimately be produced at home. India should be self-sufficient in her production of capital equipment and basic raw materials. *In the transitional period, reliance on external assistance was necessary because of the gap between requirements and earnings.* Ultimately, however, the development which took place as a result of this external assistance would itself remove the need for such assistance.

Planning has both social and economic objectives. The social objectives may not be obtained by growth maximisation alone. Some conflict between the achievement of economic and social objectives is conceivable in most cases. Nonetheless, we discover a number of elements in our pre-Independence industrial development strategy which sought to reconcile the possible conflict between economic and social objectives. In this regard, an extremely crucial post-Independence element was the development of a mixed economy under which there would be a public sector coexisting and interacting with the private sector. It was clearly foreseen that, left to itself, industrialization of India's backward and multi-structural economy would run into a series of problems (e.g. shortage of financial and material resources, dependence on the world market and foreign technical know-how, a narrow and lopsided domestic market, etc.). Hence government's active participation in crucial areas of infrastructural development was an indispensable pre-requisite. Also, the government would be the best agency to develop many heavy industries. The private sector would also play an important role in setting up new industries, relying both on the national and foreign capital.

In this perspective, government's economic functions had to be considerably extended to include: direct entrepreneurial activities within the more backward sectors of the economy; assisting the private sector in industrial construction, as also to protect it from foreign competition; co-ordination and regulation of development among various branches of the private sector and organizing an effective interaction between the private and public sectors. Clearly, the idea of industrialization in India was closely tied up with the concept of sweeping state-capitalist measures and industrialization was conceived as the direct offshoot of government intervention and participation (Shirokov, 1980: 200). Looked from the other angle, this would prevent undue concentration of resources in private hands, which brought us nearer the objectives of the Directive Principles.

Against the Nehru-Mahalanobis strategy of rapid industrialization with priority for basic and heavy, urban-based industry, the Gandhian ideology pleaded for restoration of 'village economy'. This ideology could not conceive of India imitating the West in its economic and industrial growth. To conceive of Indian industrialization largely in terms of mechanized units was, to Gandhi's mind, both impractical and undesirable. A labour-intensive production, based on local labour and materials, could cater more effectively to local needs. Gandhi advocated for self-employment rather than wage labour, the latter being rejected as an expression of exploitation of workers by employers.

> Industrial activities should be carried out to the extent possible, in cottages but the provision of raw material and the marketing of the finished products should be organized along cooperative lines in order to eliminate the harmful role of middlemen. Mechanization was to be permitted only if it did not lead to displacement of labour. Finally, there was a strong aversion of foreign technology and of imported goods (Haan, 1980: 1).

The two economic ideologies were not altogether incompatible. The early policy makers, therefore, struck a pragmatic compromise between the two and the blue-print of the declared industrialization strategy, appearing first under the Industrial Policy Resolution (IPR) of 1948 and then under its counterpart of 1956, clearly demonstrated that traditional rural industries too had a crucial role to play. For example, while heavy industry was given priority, it was duly recognized that the village and small industries had a great potential for labour absorption. These industries were expected to restrain the inflationary tendencies inasmuch as they could increase their production with minor capital outlays, not only because of their presumed lower capital-output ratio but also because of a widespread underutilization of the existing capacity (Haan, 1980: 2). A high point of the reconciliatory strategy was, therefore, to assign the production of a large range of goods, most notably consumer goods, to village, cottage and small-scale industries. To quote freely from the 1948 Industrial Policy Resolution:

> These industries are particularly suited for the better utilisation of local resources and for the achievement of local self-sufficiency in respect of

certain types of essential consumer goods like food, cloth and agricultural implements. The healthy expansion of cottage and small- scale industries depends upon a number of factors like the provision of raw-materials, cheap power, technical advice, organised marketing of their produce, and where necessary, safeguards against intensive competition by large-scale manufacture, as well as on the education of the worker in the use of the best available technique ...

...It will be examined, for example, how the textile mill industry can be made complementary to rather than competitive with the handloom industry, which is the country's largest and best organised cottage industry. In certain other lines of production, like agricultural implements, textile accessories, and parts of machine tools, it should be possible to produce components on a cottage industry scale and assemble these into their final product at a factory. It will also be investigated how far industries at present highly centralized could be decentralized with advantage.

Again, quoting extensively from the 1956 Industrial Policy Resolution:

The state has been following a policy of supporting cottage and village and small-scale industries by restricting the volume of production in the large scale sector, by differential taxation, or by direct subsidies. While such measures will continue to be taken, whenever necessary, the aim of the State policy will be to ensure that the decentralised sector acquires sufficient vitality to be self-supporting and its development is integrated with that of large scale industry. The State will, therefore, concentrate on measures designed to improve the competitive strength of the small- scale producer. For this it is essential that the technique of production should be constantly improved and modernised, the pace of transformation being regulated so as to avoid, as far as possible, technological unemployment. Lack of technical and financial assistance, of suitable working accommodation and inadequacy of facilities for repair and maintenance are among the serious handicaps ... The extension of rural electrification and the availability of power at prices which the workers can afford will also be of considerable help. Many of the activities relating to small-scale production will be greatly helped by the organisation of industrial co-operatives. Such co-operatives should be encouraged in every way ...

2.1.4 1977 Policy Turn under Janata Regime

The industrialization strategy outlined above, with its one leg in the modern factory sector and the other in the rural and cottage industries, endured itself in plan after plan, till Janata Government arrived at the scene in 1977. In the mean time, the tardy growth of industrial sector, in spite of a high investment rate, an increasing support from public sector and a highly protected domestic market for a wide range of industrial products, etc. became a matter of public concern. The capital-output ratio witnessed a continuous increase in plan after plan (Chakravarty, 1987: 55) which militated against the Nehru-Mahalanobis case for a capital intensive way of production; against 'half a bread today but two breads tomorrow' what the nation was getting was 'half a bread today and again half a bread tomorrow'. Moreover, with tardy industrial growth, the 'gleaming future' shifted too far ahead "especially for agricultural workers, small peasants, workers in household industries, etc., as these groups have to bear the main burden of a postponed increase in the level of consumption" (Haan, 1980: 3).

The Janata government had, therefore, some justification to question the congress strategy of heavy industrialization. The 1977 SIP said for cottage and village industries what the 1948 or 1956 IPRs said for basic and heavy industries: a near reversal of the earlier positions. The Janata government loudly alleged that the emphasis of industrial policy so far had been mainly on large industries neglecting cottage industries completely and relegating small industries to a minor role. The primacy of village and small industry was to be the prime goal of the new industrial strategy since employment was no more to be given a short shrift.

Let us see what the Janata government thought of large industry in its 1977 SIP:

> In addition to small and village industries, there is also a clear role for large industry in India. However, the Government will not favour large scale industry merely for demonstration of sophisticated skills or as monuments of irrelevant foreign technology. The role of large scale industry will be related to the programme for meeting the basic minimum needs of the population through wider dispersal of small scale and village industries and strengthening of the agricultural sector. In general, areas for large scale industry will be: (a) basic industries which are essential for providing infra-structure as well as for development of small and village industries, such as steel, non-ferrous metals, cement, oil refineries; (b) capital goods industries for meeting the machinery requirement of basic industries as well as small scale industries; (c) high technology industries which require large scale production, and which are related to agricultural and small scale industrial development such as fertilizers, pesticides, and petro-chemicals etc; and (d) other industries, which are outside the list of reserved items for the small scale sector, and which are considered essential for the development of the economy such as machine tools, organic and inorganic chemicals.

2.1.5 1980 Policy Re-thinking by Congress

With the return of the Congress to power in 1980 things started changing fast, although only on an incremental basis. The economy had grown fairly satisfactorily for most of the 1970s yet the 1979-80 oil price shock alone upset the balance of payment situation in a big way. It was now getting clear that India could no longer afford the luxury of a highly protective industrial policy regime. To promote domestic industries as an alternative to imports, productivity and quality aspects could not be ignored. For raising productivity, the whole range of bottlenecks had to be removed; the restrictive and complex features of the industrial licensing policy were, *inter alia*, held responsible for production bottlenecks in many areas. In brief, many policies and procedures needed to be changed. It is understandable, therefore, that the July 1980 SIP was an interesting mingle of political statements aimed to demonstrate government's eagerness to attain social justice in economic development (largely to countervail the strong anti-Congress propaganda set out in the 1977 Janata government declarations) and, at the same time, covertly supporting the resumption of the country's uninterrupted growth through optimum utilization of existing capacity as well as expansion of industries (Inoue, 1992: 92-94).

Among the many objectives set out under the 1980 statement, higher employment generation, promoting economic federalism and preferential treatment to agro-based industries, need to be underlined in particular. The new idea of economic federalism was introduced as a counter to Janata Government's artificial division between small and large industry. As if to reiterate its 1956 position which did not see any real conflict between large and small industries, the Congress government's economic federalism proposed setting up of a few "nucleus plants" in each district identified as industrially backward. Such "nucleus plants" would generate a spread-out network of small-scale and cottage industrial units. Each nucleus plant would concentrate on assembling the products of the ancilliary units falling within its orbit, on producing the inputs needed by a large number of smaller units, and on making adequate marketing arrangements. Thus, the 1980 SIP sought to link small and ancillary enterprises with large industries,

> but it fell into the same trap that previous policies did when it said that the nuclei would also ensure a widespread pattern of investment and employment and would distribute the benefits of industrialization to the maximum extent possible. It failed to set forth a logical and feasible policy for creating employment opportunities and spreading industrialization into industrially backward areas in accordance with overall development policy. The role of creating larger employment and attaining more equitable distribution were again turned over to the small and ancillary enterprises without regard for the capabilities and effectiveness of these industries (Inoue, 1992: 95).

A few other notable changes occasioned by the 1980 SIP were: (1) excess production capacity in certain areas including mass consumption goods industries was allowed; (2) large industrial groups and foreign companies were no longer barred from entering the fields of production hitherto restricted to small-scale enterprises on the condition that such production would promote exports, and (3) the backward areas industrial development programme was intensified through investment, subsidies and infrastructural improvements. The programme of industrial development of backward areas was especially welcome by state governments who vied with one another in promoting industries in districts which were not necessarily remote or industrially disadvantaged but were industrially promising. This served to increase, rather than decrease, the regional unevenness in industrial development.

2.1.6 Incremental Reforms and Economic Restructuring

Then, in December 1989, came the World Bank report on the need for economic restructuring, liberalization and globalization of the Indian economy. The report had something to suggest practically for each segment of the Indian economy, including its industrial sector. In regard to the industrial sector, the report reiterated the necessity of dispensing with industrial licensing; complete phasing out of all forms of capacity licensing for industry over the medium term; restructuring public sector enterprises including price tariff and protection supports; raising asset-limit for MRTP companies in the short-run and phasing out MRTP investment and production clearances over the long-run; the gradual tapering off of industrial subsidies including those to small-scale units to prevent non-optimal use of resources often witnessed under the highly subsidized production regimes; de-reservation of products from the small-scale sector simultaneously with raising their asset limits; in the context of backward area industrial development programme, replacing investment subsidies and the use of licensing controls with temporary production subsidies or excise/sales tax concessions which would reduce the bias in favour of capital intensive production and would keep inter-state competition in offering concessions within bounds, and so on.

2.1.7 Restructuring under 1991 Reforms

It is true that despite a decade of incremental reforms, India at the end of 1980s still had a tightly regulated manufacturing sector. In July 1991, as a part of economic restructuring and liberalization programme, a new industrial policy was announced by the newly installed Congress government. Many of the World Bank recommendations were forthrightly implemented. For example, industrial licensing was completely abolished; licensing for capacity expansion by existing units was also abolished for all except 18 industries which accounted for only 20 per cent of the manufacturing output; the number of industries reserved for public sector investment was drastically reduced from 17 to 8; the MRTP Act was amended to lend a free hand to big firms for expansion, diversification and merger; most importantly, administrative and regulatory barriers to entry, expansion and modernization by industrial units were also drastically reduced. Until the close of the 1980s, foreign direct investment was a mere trickle. The new industrial policy sketched out an elaborate list of industries in which ownership up to 51 per cent, by both existing and new foreign companies, was freely permitted. Private domestic and foreign investment in oil, gas and power industries was also welcome. Clearance for technological collaborations could be almost taken for granted (Cassen-Joshi-Lipton, 1993: 172-73).

Public sector too faced big changes. Under the new regime, it was expected to:

(1)   strengthen its managerial autonomy and show concrete 'economic results';

(2   face increased domestic private sector competition in productivity and return to investment and international competition in tradable goods through reduction of protection;

(3)   absorb gradual elimination of budgetary support from government to meet enterprise losses;

(4)   partially dis-invest equity in selected enterprises to inject a greater degree of accountability and performance-consciousness; and

(5)   effect restructuring or closure of patently unviable enterprises while mitigating the social cost of adjustment by instituting a social safety net, and so on (Cassen, et al., 1993: 175).

It really seemed that the old paradigms were on their way out. The public-private sector dichotomy, so much hammered out in the early days of planning, was getting blurred. Big industry could grow as much bigger as it wished. Multinationals were now welcome in diverse fields. Foreign direct investment started increasing. The whole economic landscape looked vastly different than what it was even a few years earlier; and the process seemed irreversible. The march towards the change was so fast, and so formidable, that the government was hard put to explain, with a tinge of apology, that the basic economic institutions, assiduously nurtured since the Nehru-Mahalanobis days, were not being thrown to winds. See, for example, the following:

> India stands totally committed to a policy of mixed economy as propounded
> by Nehru and other founding fathers under which both the public sector

and the private enterprises co-exist and function, side by side. *But both need to be efficient.* It is this strong motive for inducting efficiency which has partially prompted the recent policy of partial disinvestment of the shareholding in the public sector enterprises...

The Industrial Policy Statement of July 22, 1991 has set out the broad outlines of the nation's industrial policy in the near-term future. *In many respects, it signifies a return to the 1956 Industrial Policy Resolution with only one major exception,* viz., the reduction of the industrial activities exclusively reserved for the public sector from 17 to 8 industries. Indian industry has developed a highly diversified structure, considerable entrepreneurship and a vastly expanded capital market. All this makes it possible for the public sector to vacate many areas hitherto exclusively reserved for it and throw them open to private sector initiative... (Eighth Five Year Plan, 1992-97: 104).

2.1.8 Indian Industry under WTO Regime

Then came the WTO on January 1, 1995 which would soon start changing the shape and structure of Indian industry in a big way. On a broad plane, the canvas of WTO agreements is spread over three compartments: goods, services and intellectual property rights. First, **Trade in goods** of all descriptions (agricultural, industrial and others) is to be governed under GATT re-formulations, effected under the Uruguay Round. Second, **Trade in Services** of all kinds (e.g. business services including professional and computer; construction and engineering; financial services such as banking and insurance; and transport services, is to be regulated under General Agreement on Trade in Services (**GATS**). Finally, **Trade Related Aspects of Intellectual Property Rights** (**TRIPs**) would set out the terms and conditions for the international flow of intellectual property. Consistent with the theme of the present study, we may better take note of some of the GATT agreements that would have direct or indirect bearing on domestic industry.

Under GATT, thirteen major agreements (on customs valuation, pre-shipment inspection, technical barriers to trade, sanitary and phytosanitary measures, import licensing procedures, safeguards, subsidies and countervailing measures, anti-dumping, trade-related investment measures, textiles and clothing, agriculture and rules of origin) have been signed. It should be evident that a number of these agreements directly relate to or impinge upon domestic industry, while others are intertwined with domestic industry through the diverse cob-web of inter-sectoral trade and technological linkages. That the structure of India's foreign trade, both export- and import-wise, is now overwhelmingly biased in favour of manufactured products, supports the former, while the immensely increased agriculture-industry-service linkages in the domestic economy, especially since the beginning of the 1980s, lends weight to the latter point. A few of these, viz. Agreement on Textiles and Clothing (**ATC**), and Agreement on Antidumping Measures (**ADP**) attract our pointed attention given the structure of India's external trade, the employment stakes involved in **ATC**, and the hurt that these agreements are likely to cause to the Indian economy. Under the **ATC**, the restrictions hitherto maintained by the developed countries on import of textiles, clothing and ready-made garments from the developing economies, are to be progressively phased out by 2005. Under the **ADP**, if a country exports a product at a price lower than the one it normally charges in its domestic market or if it sells it at less than the cost of production, it can be complained against for dumping activities; retaliatory measures can be instituted. *The serious implications of anti-dumping activities for small producers can be easily visualised.*

So far, India has done reasonably well in observing its commitments to WTO, say, in removing quantitative restrictions and tariff restructuring, simplification of customs procedures, evolving international standards in trade and industry (in compliance with the Agreement on Technical Barriers to Trade and that on Sanitary and Phytosanitary measures), Textiles, Anti-dumping Measures and Safeguards, and so on. India's handling of the most contentious issue of the conversion of non-tariff barriers into equivalent tariff barriers and the reduction in the base tariff structure, needs to be understood in perspective. This process had been initiated, in right earnest, even under the pre-WTO GATT commitments. The regime of industrial protection that prevailed prior to the signing of the WTO agreements, through a high tariff wall as well as a rigorous import licensing regime, was getting dismantled around the time that we stepped into the WTO regime. Till 1997, Quantitative Restrictions (QRs) on imports, notified to the WTO on Balance of Payment (BoP) grounds, were operative only for 2714 tariff lines; in March 2000, their number had come down to 1429, including 685 tariff lines under special import license. In compliance with the tariffication commitment, QRs on 714 (out of 1429) tariff lines stood withdrawn with effect from April 1, 2000, while those on the remaining lines were lifted on April 1, 2001. Moreover, all the items on which QRs were maintained on BoP grounds, except 36 canalized items, can now be freely imported. Furthermore, *as many as 643 of the 812 items reserved for small scale industry, that were earlier protected through QRs, are already put under OGL.* This aspect alone may create serious problems for India's small scale industrial sector which, under the existing economic dispensation, cannot compete with cheap imports; the adverse impact may get magnified once the effect of the end-of-transition-periods in WTO Agreements (e.g. TRIMs, TRIPs and tariff bindings) is felt in the near future.

Let us look at the track record of the developed world. While the developing world was cajoled to remove non-tariff barriers to smoothen out the international trade environment, the developed world has been consistently expanding the network of their non-tariff measures and imposing various trade impediments including the latest outcry of environmental concerns, labour standards, child labour, and so on. For example, going by the 1998 UNCTAD estimates, as many as 22 non-tariff barriers were operative in Japan, as many as 16 in the EU, 9 in Australia, 4 in the USA, and so on (Panchamukhi, 2000: 61). The story about tariff reduction, and binding, is perhaps more depressing.

For us, as also for the rest of the developing world, nothing could be more damaging than to live under an illusion that the WTO agreements would affect only those involved in international trade, importing or exporting something, and would not affect those who are producing and selling domestically. For example, even petty farm operators, producing exclusively for the domestic market, will get linked with the international movement of input prices, just as their brethren engaged in tradable commodity production may face more severe earning swings under the new and volatile price regimes. Similarly, even a small scale, family-based industrial enterprise in a village may face a decline in its economic fortune just because the demand for its product is declining now that cheaper substitutes are available through imports, or else, its production efficiency may improve now that raw material costs are lower under the open trade regime or else, it is now ancillarized to an urban-based, modern industrial enterprise, and so on. The fact is that those in international trade might have already started feeling the pinch, in a variety of ways. And, for those engaged in other sectors, shocks are soon to follow. Small and rural industry is most certain to face the worst (FISME, 1999: 1).

Admittedly, the precise impact on domestic industrial structure, more pointedly the junior partner of rural industry, is difficult to spell out at this stage. We are nonetheless sure that under the new dispensation, production efficiency would be the touchstone for survival and growth, ancillarizations and integrations would expand, public sector would have very little to support the 'survival philosophy' of production units including government-aided rural industrial activities, and so on. To what extent and which branches of rural industry are able to chip off the benefits of technological updatings, industrial hook-ups and ancillarizations, market expansions, etc. is still an open question. After all, rural industry has had its own profile of successes and failures and, on that basis, one can imagine some positive effects of the new industrialization strategy for one bunch of rural industry just as one has reasons to foresee a difficult time for others. To frame a plausible conjecture of what is likely to happen, we must look back. Perhaps, a critical assessment of what has been going on in the realm of rural industrial policy is extremely essential for this purpose. This follows now in Section 2.2 below.

2.2 Policy Strands for Rural Industrial Development

Basing oneself on a variety of policy documents, one readily discovers that during the five decades of planned economic development, there has been no dearth of policy pronouncements on the significant role that rural industrialization has to play in India. In plan after plan, one discovers adequate emphasis on the need, rationale and concern for accelerating the growth of rural industry (Kurien, 1978: 457). The ambit of institutional support, most notably subsidized loans and marketing concessions, has been expanding ever since the inception of the planning era. It almost appears to an outside observer that the government wanted to take upon itself each aspect of rural industrial development, and if one were to follow in letter the declared intentions, the government certainly seems to have been 'overdoing'. In any case, it never 'hesitated' to impose product-line demarcations, most ostensibly to obviate competition between 'weak' rural units and 'strong' urban industries. Special institutions and organizations came up to take care of diverse problems of specific groups of rural industries or producer groups. Attention was also fixed on technology upgrading and product improvement, and so on. In brief, it would appear from official documents that the rural/ village industry in India has been the recipient of a well thought-out policy and a wide range of state patronages. Yet, an objective assessment of its track record shows that it has not yet come of age; many problems especially those concerning technology-in-use, product-quality, marketing and price disadvantages, are still afflicting a large part of rural industry.

2.2.1 Rural Industry Policy in Early Plans

As far back as 1948, the first industrial policy resolution emphasized better utilization of local resources and achievement of local self-sufficiency in respect of certain essential consumer goods such as food, clothing and agricultural implements as the most suitable characteristics of cottage and small industries (Papola, 1982: 20). It thus appears that from the very beginning, the policy for small-scale industries was intended to be closely related to rural development, and the responsibility for creating job opportunities was entrusted to small-scale and rural industries (Inoue, 1992: 67). In reality, much of the rural demand itself spilled over beyond such industries.

The First Five Year Plan drew a distinction between cottage and small-scale industries in that the former were to play a central role in coping with the problem of un- and under- employment. Cottage industries were treated synonymously with traditional artisanal crafts. Again, small-scale industries were perceived to be largely located in urban centres, producing goods with partially or wholly mechanized equipment employing some outside labour while the cottage industries mostly involved manual operations, carried out primarily through family labour (First Plan, 1952: 162). Finally, a common production programme was proposed for those cottage and factory industries which were producing the same products. The crucial element in the First Five Year Plan was that rural industrial development was conceived largely in isolation of the rest of the economy (Haan, 1980: 23). In the Second Plan, their scope was widened considerably and they were seen as an integral component of the national economy. The 1956 IPR visualized the role of cottage, village and small-scale industries as under:

> They provide immediate large scale employment; they offer a method of ensuring a more equitable distribution of the national income and they facilitate an effective mobilization of resources of capital and skill which might otherwise remain unutilized. Some of the problems that unplanned urbanization tends to create, will be avoided by the establishment of small centres of industrial production all over the country (Haan, 1980: 25-26).

The 1956 IPR supported a protective policy for the cottage, village and small-scale sector by restricting the volume of production in the large-scale sector, by differential taxation, and provision of subsidies. At the same time, it did emphasize the necessity of improving the competitive strength of small-scale producers and their self-supporting capacity (Inoue, 1992: 72).

During the Second Plan, primary focus was fixed on basic and key industries and the production of a large variety of consumer goods was expected to come from the cottage and small-scale industries sector. The Mahalanobis model was criticized on this account. There was confusion in policy as well as industry circles, especially because, as in the First Plan, cottage and small-scale industries were lumped together as far as investment versus consumption goods debate was concerned. And then, the plan over-stressed the employment side rather than the production side; consequently, vertical relationships in the industrial sector remained undefined or unelaborated.

The issue of industrial dispersal suffered confusion of a different kind. The plan did acknowledge that some of the small-scale industries were ancillaries to large industries and, in the interest of their operational efficiency, had to be located in urban or semi-urban areas. However, in its perception, the process of development of village and small-scale industries in general was to graduate from traditional village industries to 'modern' small industries; by implication, this rural-oriented approach lent only a marginal push to industrial dispersal into the rural areas. Finally, to forge stronger links between agriculture and rural industry, 26 pilot projects, intended to promote cottage and small-scale industries in rural areas through coordinated activities in the selected community development blocks, were launched towards the end of 1950s (Jain, 1980: 48).

The Third Five Year Plan, drawing upon the working experience of these pilot projects, formulated an extended Rural Industries Projects (RIP) Programme. The goal of this programme was to promote village and small-scale industries primarily to achieve a balanced regional development and to reduce the tendency of concentration of industry in large urban areas. It was realized that by locating large industries in specified regions, the problem of uneven regional development could hardly be tackled. Instead, village and small-scale industries could spread all over the country, and could trigger off the process of balanced regional development. Thus, it was for the first time that sectoral policies were sought to be integrated with the area development approach.

2.2.2 Rural Industry under Backward Area Development Plan

During the Fourth Plan, emphasis was laid on growth centres for rural industrialization under the auspices of Backward Area Development Programme (Papola, 1982: 21). These growth centres, in small towns or rural areas, were expected to serve as nuclei for more widespread development. Following the recommendations of the Pande and Wanchoo Working Groups, a programme of giving financial, fiscal and other supports (e.g. store purchase facilities, price preferences, quality control, marketing assistance, convenient location of raw material depots, etc.) to private entrepreneurs for locating industrial units in backward areas, was introduced. The Backward Area Development Programme became instantly acceptable to state governments who, in fact, vied with one another in extending the ambit of concessions so that their range and coverage differed widely from state to state and within the state, from area to area. It was natural, therefore, that the programme made a better impact in those 'backward' areas "which had access to such factors as markets, a skilled labour force, materials and better infrastructure. For those backward areas with preferable conditions, there was often a rush to establish new firms while quite a few other backward areas were ignored due to the lack of industrial facilities" (Inoue, 1992: 80).

Although the wisdom of spreading limited resources over various regions, in the name of balanced regional development, has been challenged by some analysts (Harris, 1977: 142-43), yet political pressures and strategic choices of the central government (*a la* Indira Gandhi's post-1969 counter-fights) did not allow the government to consider such reasoning. A more equal development across regions was a programme that would sell politically, and would indirectly add to employment/earning network of the poor people and the poorer regions. In actual effect, many things went by default.

The Fifth Plan broadened the RIP programme spatially under which the existing 49 RIP areas were extended to cover the entire districts, except towns with a population of more than 15,000 (1971 Census) and 100 new districts were to be included in the existing projects. From now onwards, the RIP programme was to be guided to rural areas while the Backward Area Development Programme would be oriented to urban centres with a population of more than 15,000. The Fifth Plan came to an abrupt end with the fall of Indira Gandhi government in March 1977. The Janata government that succeeded issued its SIP in December 1977. In this SIP, the focus shifted entirely to village and small-scale industries, and employment promotion became a political watchword of the times. It was a shrewd political calculation that inspired Indira Gandhi to carry over the central part of the Janata government's SIP of 1977 pertaining to cottage and rural industries as also the dispersal of industries into her own economic programme, when she returned to power in 1980. In the Sixth Plan that followed under the Congress regime, one therefore easily discovers many an echo of the Janata government's stress on rural industry.

2.2.3 Rural Industry under Extended Institutional Umbrella

The Sixth Plan put main emphasis on employment creation in the village and small-scale industries. Four new elements were directly connected with small-scale and village industrial development. Firstly, and most importantly, an effective integration of spatial development and sectoral policies was to be achieved through the creation of District Industries Centres. These centres were to assume the overall responsibility for promoting village and small scale industries and their functions would be as diverse as the provision of raw material, machinery and equipment, credit and marketing support, dissemination of market intelligence, and so on (Kurien, 1978: 457). Further, the Industrial Development Bank of India would have a special wing to deal exclusively with the credit requirements of small, village and cottage industries and this very wing would coordinate the entire range of credit facilities offered by other institutions for the small and cottage sector. Secondly, the number of products reserved for the small-scale sector was increased from 180 to about 500, under the motto that "whatever can be produced by small and cottage industries must only be so produced". Most of these items, however,were produced very largely by the urban-based small-scale units, and bore little significance for the rural sector. Thirdly, within the small-scale sector, special attention would be given to units in the `tiny` sector. Finally, the introduction of special legislation for cottage and household industries to ensure that these activities get due recognition in industrial development. However, the nature of these measures was not specified.

The Seventh Plan put further emphasis on improving productivity, enhancing product-quality, reducing costs and restructuring product-mix through upgradation of technology and modernization. At the same time, the need to strengthen the programme of ancillarization for a harmonious growth of the total industrial sector was given special importance. Institutional, financial and marketing bottlenecks facing the village and small industries were to be expeditiously dealt with, primarily through the aegis of the District Industries Centres. At the same time, financial constraints of the tiny sector were to receive special attention. For example, such units as had investment upto Rs. 2 lakhs were to be accorded preference for availing of concessions and facilities. In overall terms, the need for dispersing industries from urban concentrations to the less developed and rural areas was to command special attention. In this context, rural industrialization was to be given adequate attention so as to check the exodus of artisans to urban concentrations. Even the possibility of setting up a separate commission for village industries and handicrafts was hinted at (Seventh Plan, Oct. 1985: 98-100).

2.2.4 Policy Dilution in 1991 Economic Reforms

When Janata Dal took over in early 1990, and they made strong rural-oriented policy commitments, the rural analysts were looking forward to sweeping economic changes including a more comprehensive approach to rural industrialization. Fast political changes, however, occurred between 1990 and 1991 and policy statements during the interregnum could hardly assume a concrete shape. The Congress party returned to power in July 1991 and since then, the Indian economy has been changing its complexion, internally as well as internationally. Tremendous shifts took place in industrial policy. Most significantly, on the one hand, to demonstrate their concern for rural development matching the policy intentions declared by the Janata Government just a year ago, and, on the other, to let the small and tiny sector absorb the effects of new economic policies and opening up of the economy, the Congress Government announced, for the first time on August 6, 1991, separate policy measures for promoting and strengthening small, tiny and village industries. This was followed by minor policy tinkering, almost on a year-to-year basis till WTO came in.

Under the auspices of the August-1991 policy, many new things were introduced. For example, a distinction was now made between small-scale, ancillary, export-oriented, tiny, and industry-related service/business units. Investment limits in plant and machinery were raised to Rs.60 lakhs for small-scale units, Rs.75 lakhs for ancillary and export-oriented small units, Rs.2 to Rs.5 lakhs for tiny and service/business units. Tiny enterprises were to be the prime focus of special development programmes and official support. While small-scale sector would be mainly entitled to one-time benefits, tiny enterprises would be eligible for support on a continuing basis, including easier access to institutional finance, priority in government purchase programme, and so on. Single window loan scheme would be sufficiently enlarged. An extremely important change would be to shift focus from subsidized/cheap institutional credit to its adequate and timely availability; accordingly, banking sector would have to be roped in to meet the rising credit requirements. A legislation (**Prompt Payment Act**) to ensure prompt payment of bills to small and tiny enterprises and/or to impose penal interest for delayed payment was also enacted. To facilitate location of industries in rural/backward areas and to promote stronger linkages between agriculture and industry, a new scheme of Integrated Infrastructural Development for small-scale industries would be implemented soon. For marketing, hope was pinned again on co-operative and public sector institutions. Complementarity in production programmes of large/medium and small industries was yet another area of pointed focus (Govt. of India, Economic Survey, 1991-92: 88). In 1994, a Quality Certification Scheme was launched to improve the quality of the products of small scale industry which were to be assisted by awareness programmes and financial support to acquire ISO 9000 or similar international quality standards (Govt. of India, Economic Survey, 94-95: 116).

It is thus evident that government does not wish to give any impression of policy let-up or support withdrawal. In fact, the inventory of problems is well articulated in the Eighth Plan document (Govt. of India, 1992: 132-33). Nonetheless, when one looks, say, at the plan outlay for village and small industries, or concrete government-supported steps for industrial relocations and dispersals, or technological upgradation through public support, one clearly discerns that market-driven propensities would henceforth guide all policy outfits. The most striking features of the changing policy under-currents were a gradual elimination of input, price and marketing subsidies, a reduced dependence on the budgetary support, and an increasing reliance on private initiative and risk-absorbing capabilities. Adequate hints about such changing winds are available from what the Eighth Plan says:

In the new orientation to planning during the Eighth Plan, people's initiative and participation would be a key element in the process of development.

Greater emphasis will be laid on private initiative in industrial development. The public sector will become very selective in the coverage of activities and in making investment. Small enterprises in the village and small industries sector are, more or less, based on private initiative and entrepreneurship (p.133)

OR

In this context, it is necessary to increase the active involvement of banks in funding of KVI programmes and in this process to reduce their dependence on the budgetary support. It is also necessary to review the subsidies which are presently being provided for the development of khadi and village industries. The present policy of KVIC to advance loans for the development of village industries to the beneficiary organisations at 4% rate of interest also needs to be reviewed in view of the hike in the lending rates of commercial banks (p.136).

2.2.5 Untethering Policy Threads under WTO Regime

Through a sheer coincidence, all policy changes that came about since the establishment of WTO in January 1995, were under the auspices of non-Congress Governments, first United Front Government and then the NDA Government led by the BJP. In any case, the entire policy thrust for the Ninth Five Year Plan was evolved under the shadow of the WTO economic regime and policy preparedness needed for meeting the impending challenges of having to compete with freer imports or to pursue 'aggressive export drive', on the one hand, and the lessons learnt from the working of the liberalization and globalization policies that came up, under the previous Congress Government, during the first half of the 1990s, on the other. It is in this perspective that the definition of small scale sector was revised in 1997, enhancing the ceiling on investment in plant and machinery from Rs. 5 lakh to Rs. 25 lakh for tiny units and from Rs. 60 lakh to Rs. 300 lakh (subsequently, during 1999-2000, brought down to Rs. 100 lakh in the case of small scale and ancillary undertakings: Govt. of India, 2000: 127) for small scale units as a way of helping them to modernize and upgrade their technologies and facilitating them to expand/diversify for becoming more competitive. A number of product lines, most notably leather products, readymade garments, hosiery, hand tools, toys, packaging material, auto components, pharmaceuticals, and food processing, were expected to benefit from such enhancements. Further, credit up to 60 per cent under priority sector lending to small-scale industry (ssi) sector was earmarked for the tiny sector, for ensuring that it was not cornered by relatively larger units within the ssi sector. Still further, excise duty exemption limit for the small-scale sector, including tiny units, was also enhanced from Rs. 50 lakh to Rs. 100 lakh. In order to secure timely payments to ssi units for supplies made by them to large industrial units, the Interest on Delayed Payments to Small Scale and Ancillary Industrial Undertakings Act was suitably amended. It was now compulsory that the payments to ssi units be made within 120 days after which penal interest would be imposed.

Since mid-1990s, the policy on product reservation for the small scale sector attracted a lot of public debate; it was increasingly felt that in spite of the reservation umbrella extended to the sector for well over three decades, technological obsolescence of both products and processes, managerial, financial and marketing weaknesses, cumbersome rules, regulations and procedural hassles, etc. could not be tided over. It is against this background that in 1997 the Abid Hussain Committee recommended de-reservation, accompanied by appropriate assistance to small scale sector in terms of information base, availability of technology, technology transfer, improved credit availability and infra-structural and marketing support. Some of the recommendations of the Committee, especially those relating to de-reservation in areas which are critical for exports, have been accepted in principle. However, *except for the garments sector, the general policy of de-reservation is held in abeyance in view of the significant contribution that the small scale sector makes to employment, output and exports; decline in employment, especially in the tiny and rural industries, reported in recent years from different parts of the country, seems to have influenced this step.*

A small but important policy tinkering, introduced in 1999-2000, largely to increase the reach of banks to the tiny sector, was to enlarge the definition of priority lending by the banking sector; financial accommodation by banks to non-banking financial companies or other financial intermediaries, for expanding their lending to the tiny sector, was now brought under the ambit of priority sector lending (Govt. of India, Economic Survey, 99-2000: 127).

A special policy landmark that came up in 1999 was about the setting up of 100 rural industrial clusters every year under the umbrella of National Programme for Rural Industrialisation. In particular, to prepare the small-scale sector for the threat posed by the WTO-monitored multilateral free trade regime, a special cell was to be created in the office of the Development Commissioner to disseminate information to Small Scale Industrial Associations regarding recent developments, in and outside the Indian economy.

Special packages have been offered to the tiny sector, from time to time. For example, the National Small Industries Corporation started giving composite loans upto Rs. 25 lakh to the tiny sector at a heavily subsidized concessional interest rate of just one per cent; the Small Industries Development Bank of India started charging 10.5 per cent concessional rate of refinance from the tiny sector against 12 per cent from the ssi sector, and so on. Perhaps, in due recognition of the mounting difficulties surrounding the tiny and rural industry, especially after the WTO regime commenced in 1995, the government has thought it politically expedient to extend a few more institutional concessions to it. For example, the Prime Minister announced in August 2000 that from then onwards, preference would be given to tiny units for more loans for technology upgradation; more specifically, under the National Equity Fund Scheme, 30 percent of investment loans would be earmarked for the tiny units; under Integrated Infrastructure Development Scheme, 50 percent of the plots would be set aside for the tiny units; under the National Programme for Rural Industrialisation, the major beneficiaries of the cluster development programme would be the tiny sector units; the sponsoring organisation i.e. KVIC, SIDO or NABARD, for each cluster will be solely responsible for providing the design development, capacity building, technology intervention and consortium marketing, and so on (Govt. of India, 2000a:9).

2.3 Policy Synthesis

Looking back at the history of industrial development policy, it is clear that the strategy of 'walking on two legs' sought to encompass many aspects connected with rural industrialization in India. Although emphasis on different aspects changed from time to time, yet never ever an impression was given out that the rural industry was losing its relevance. This impression was kept in tact even after the arrival of economic reforms in 1991, although in the course of expanding pace of liberalization, privatization and globalization, rural industry might have faded into policy oblivion. Nonetheless, it must also be understood that the intensity of policy concern for rural industry in general, and its more employment-intensive traditional component in particular, that was unfailingly discernible during the 1960s and 1970s, was getting eroded; rural industry was no more a darling of our policy makers.

Our analysis of general industrialization strategy (Section 2.1) and policy strands for rural industrial development (Section 2.2) puts the broad policy threads together, and one can develop an idea of how rural industry were to be groomed to serve many socio-economic objectives, partly as an adjunct to the modern industrial development and partly in its own right. We do not wish to draft an exhaustive account of all that had been happening in the name of rural industrialization policy. Instead, only a few broad objectives underlying the chosen industrialization strategy are delineated, and in the light of the same, an assessment of the status and performance of the rural industrial sector is made in the subsequent chapters, with the available secondary data.

First, looking at the plethora of descriptions freely used in plan documents, one is justified to believe that the contours of rural industry have never been clearly defined, much less rigidly followed. While the rural locale has always been implicit in all policy assertions, the rural-urban linkage has never been denied either. Sometimes, rural industry implied a household or cottage enterprise using local material and catering to local market while at other times, it included modern industrial enterprises as well. Again, at one time, the dynamism for rural industrial expansion was envisaged to sprout from local buoyancies, at others, it was the dispersal of modern industrial activity into the countryside that used to underlie the policy stress on rural industrialization. Clearly, one could not operate with one concept or definition since, after all, all that was envisaged in the name of 'rural industrialization' was expected to promote general rural development also. In operational terms, therefore, *rural industry in India has meant a huge and heterogeneous conglomerate of industrial activities*; enormous variety of products, technology-in-use, scale of operation, market coverage, etc. has been discernible under the rubric of rural industry.

Second, policies expressly addressed to the needs of rural industries, especially the tiny segment, have been fewer and far between. In general, it has been, say, the composite assemblage of urban and rural small scale or tiny units that was covered by different policy packages. It has been only occasionally when political expediencies so demanded or there was a change of policy makers in strategic positions that rural industry in its purest manifestation attracted some attention. The most typical example of this is the persistence of a single official umbrella called VSI sector under which the traditional tiny or village industries have remained lumped with small industry a sizeable proportion of which did have a modern outfit. This generated wrong perceptions on the needs of the junior partners in the VSI sector. Although, it was occasionally felt that it would be more advantageous to treat each sub-sector independently, yet in all successive policy strands, the composite sector continued to be the focus of policy intervention (Inoue, 1992: 68,72). In official parlance, the composite 'VSI' sector has 'traditional village industries' as one part, important as it were in providing a lion's share of employment irrespective of the level of productivity, and 'modern small industries' as the other which accounts for a lion's share in output against a small share in employment. The teaming up of un-matching entities was thus bound to create a weak partnership, if it were ever in policy frame, and a relative sufferance of the former.

In effective terms, for every aspect of official support, the two constituents received 'unequal' treatment most ostensibly because of an understandable tilt in favour of the 'modern constituent' since 'impressive' outcomes of official dispensations could be shown only that way. For example, "the protection offered to some of the cottage and village industries has been without a firm commitment. Organized industry was allowed to violate the restrictions and employment in the cottage sector" (Jain, 1980:1748). Similarly, "even in government purchases, the small sector has price preference and organizational backup but not the cottage sector. The small sector also gets technical and organizational support through Small Industries Service Institutes, but there is no matching technical service for the village industries whose need is even greater" (*ibid*: 1748). An evaluation study on the working of the Rural Industries Projects revealed

> that there had been some deviations in the implementation of the programme to the extent that some part of the assistance was provided to relatively larger amongst the small scale units and also in towns which were excluded from the purview of the scheme. On the other hand, rural artisans did not receive adequate assistance, particularly in respect of technical advice, credit, training and marketing (Thakur, 1985: 39).

The hiatus and lopsidedness in policy attention grew sharper during the 1990s. With the establishment of the Department of Small Scale Industries and Agro and Rural Industries in early 1990s (since elevated to the status of a full-fledged Ministry, under the same name, in 1999), one would have expected a clear and an exclusive policy thrust for rural industrial development, through well-conceived policy initiatives. However, nothing of the kind happened primarily because economic reforms intervened in 1991-92, and policy attention got riveted to competitive market urges which rural industry, especially its traditional component, could hardly absorb. The small-scale industry became the 'favourite child' of the Department, summarily the same way that it was the policy makers' cynosure under the VSI sector. In all that was envisaged and publicly recorded, in plan documents, and policy pronouncements of the Department/Ministry, etc., exclusive attention to the problems of rural industry, most markedly its tiny and traditional components, was the last thing to be observed.

To the extent that small-scale industry exists in the rural areas also, the benefits of the new policy initiatives accrued to them as well just as they did to their urban counterparts. But then, small-scale industry is only a small part of the rural industrial sector; it is the tiny and household type enterprises that preponderate the rural scenario. It is an irony that the core competence of most of the tiny units, largely manifested in their flexibility and capacity to customise, remained outside the policy domain, primarily because small scale industry was more readily equipped to answer the urgent requirements of output growth, export expansion and technological updating. On the other hand, the tiny units have been allowed to assume the dimension of an endemic problem of technological obsolescence coupled with primitive business practices. The country's industrialisation process still has a long way to go and there will be a continuing need to foster new entrepreneurs for the foreseeable future. It is the new entrepreneurs starting tiny units today who could be the industrial titans of tomorrow (Hussain, 1997: 70)

Third, the most avowed objective of promoting rural industrialization has been *to provide expanding avenues of employment to rural labour force*. Reliance on rural industry was based on the expectation that the modern, capital-intensive industry would not be able to take on rural job-seekers beyond a point and that labour absorptive capacity of agriculture itself would dwindle in due course. According to general perceptions, *rural industries were expected to be less capital-intensive, and were, therefore, capable of creating a larger number of workplaces for a given amount of capital*. For a capital scarce economy, this was foreseen as a highly rational resource allocation strategy. The allied problems of product acceptability, technical capabilities of the rural workforce, rural-urban competition for the same product lines, etc. were not seriously dwelt upon. Employment expansion *per se* received the most heightened emphasis, ostensibly to accommodate the Gandhian strategy of rural development. In the case of many traditional village industries, self-employment in family enterprises seemed to readily fulfil these expectations. Any absolute accrual of incremental income to the household was welcome, irrespective of the number of working hands involved or the amount of human effort put in or price and quality considerations. Perhaps unconsciously, our policy administrators opted for employment gains whose multiplier effect remained extremely limited. It is only from Seventh Plan onwards that efficiency and productivity too gained a respectable consideration.

Fourth, the future of rural India could not be tagged with agriculture alone. *The labour absorptive capacity of agriculture gradually declines* because of continuing population pressure and ever-declining land:man ratio on the one hand, and the small and fragmented holdings and their highly skewed structure, on the other. Non-agricultural avenues of employment must gradually emerge for the rural population. Among non-agricultural activities, rural industry always stands out most robustly largely because of its strong forward-backward linkages. Implicitly, if not in words, rural industry was eulogized as an engine of structural transformation of the rural economy. For a number of industries, most notably agro-processing, rural locale is a natural choice. Moreover, the rural:urban gaps in earnings, levels of living, human capital formation, etc. could hardly ever be bridged through agriculture alone, howsoever fast it may grow or get commercialised. In one word, *the future of rural India lay in non-farm activities, and among them, in rural industry*.

Fifth, from Fourth Plan onwards, under the auspices of Backward Area Development Programme, *dispersal of 'modern' industrial enterprises into the countryside became the new operational strategy of boosting rural industrial development*. The ambit thus went beyond the traditional village industries. Inter-industry linkages would now rope in rural industries also. *Ancillarization was no more an alien concept to rural industrial units*. Many among the rural industries now started aping urban industrial sector, in style if not in content. The objective of modernizing, at least a part of the rural industrial sector, thus got firmly entrenched in our development strategy. `Modern' industrial units in the rural areas do face many operational difficulties, yet many among them are working in tandem with urban industries. The vertical industrial integration is tending to promote rural-urban integration also. In brief, the house of rural industry today is a conglomerate of heterogeneous product lines, technology-in-use, production scales, employer-employee relationships, marketing outfits, and so on, in a large measure, no different than its urban counterpart. The highly disparate composition not only entails divided policy attention but also an expanding arena of internal competition in which the very big lot of tiny enterprises at the bottom are always at the receiving end. A typical example of this comes through serious setbacks that the rural-OAME segment has suffered during the nineties compared with rural-DMEs (see Section 4.2 below). In the changing economic scenario, economies of scale do acquire a heightened significance, in a variety of product lines.

Sixth, an allied objective of fostering rural industrial development is *to keep rural-urban migration under check*. The problems unleashed by unregulated rural-urban migration became too serious in recent years, and economic interceptions in the nature of non-farm employment in general and rural or semi-urban industrial employment in particular attracted accelerated attention from all quarters. The urban development authorities, which have always been at the receiving end, cried out the most. In international circles too, the burgeoning urban slums and squatter settlements were openly decried as offshoots of rural economic backwardness. Thus, the case for rural industrialization gained eminence through enlightened self-interest of urban development authorities.

Seventh, through a series of development efforts, vertical linkages were sought to be built among the various strata of industrial enterprises. Specifically to the rural industry, growth centres in small towns or rural areas themselves were expected to serve as nuclei for more widespread development. These linkages encompassed only a small proportion of rural industrial enterprises. A vast majority of rural enterprises operated in an isolated island of their own; they used local raw materials, operated for local market, used outdated technologies, clung on to traditional products or product designs, and so on. Those which jumped on to the linkage opportunities, developed fresh avenues of growth and modernization. *The rural industry thus stands divided into two distinct camps: modern sector and traditional sector.* The dichotomy between the two has widened considerably over time; today the former shares most of the commercial virtues with its urban counterparts while the traditional village industries work almost like an appendage to the rural economy.

Eighth, government support has been extended in many different ways, to *protect a wide range of village industries, and to promote commercial viability of others.* Until recently, the traditional village industries have been operating under the expanding umbrella of official protection while the modern sector among the rural industries has been extended a variety of promotional support. Protection measures have naturally been more numerous and more costly, including more binding budgetary supports and more pervasive market interventions. Involvement of public institutions and public money has been the most important instrument of promoting/ protecting rural industry. *Under the new market-driven economic regime that came into existence in July 1991, and got intensified since January 1995 under India's obligations to the WTO, protection-promotion balance needed to be reworked.* The original objective of 'compulsorily' protecting the traditional village arts and crafts faced considerable policy dilution; rural industries too were now to be seen in terms of their development and modernization potential. Non-market considerations were necessarily to be kept aside while answering questions of product quality, productivity levels and cost efficiency.

Protection to rural industry, for that matter to small-scale industry as a whole, *inter alia*, took the shape of product reservation. For example, the number of items reserved for exclusive manufacture in the small-scale sector, which was 47 only in April 1967 gradually rose to 836 in July 1991 (Hussain, 1997: 102-03). Although, because of political expediency and the anticipated employment stakes, the number has summarily remained the same since 1991, yet for a variety of reasons, most noticeably the forceful plea for de-reservation made in 1997 by the Abid Hussain Committee, and reinforced by domestic organised industry lobby, the product reservation policy seems to be on its way-out. In more recent years, the WTO-inspired free trade regime seems to have hastened the process of de-reservation. The de-reservation in the garments sector has already been announced (The Economic Times, November 3, 2000:5); it may follow soon for other sectors. A sizeable proportion of rural industry awaits a beating.

Ninth, rural industry, in all its manifestations, has never been looked at from the points of view of workers' welfare, working conditions, occupational and health safety, productivity and earning levels, etc. as from employment angle; in fact, the near-exclusive fixture on employment promotion, irrespective of productivity levels or the quality of work environment or health status of workers, can be pointed out as a devastating failure of policy vision. For understandable reasons, employment in rural industry has largely been taken as an adjunct to employment in the main economic activity, namely agriculture, and the need for enforcing public safety standards and hygienic working conditions, or even to enforce simple labour laws, has never been considered to be an issue. Ironically, the partnership between public authorities and the rural industrial enterprises themselves, in maintaining a studied silence about such serious matters, is a shameful episode in the history of rural industrialisation in India.

The hiatus between the organised and the unorganised industry is rather glaring in terms of labour laws, industrial safety standards and pollution control measures; needless to reiterate that in rural areas, an overwhelming proportion of industrial enterprises belongs to the latter category. While, *legal provisions for protecting workers against a variety of occupational risks and other exploitations do exist and are applied, in varying form and content, to workers in organized industry, nothing of consequence exist for, and much less applied to, workers engaged in unorganized industry; as we have seen above, tiny and small rural industries in India nearly completely belong to the latter group and lend themselves to all kinds of exploitation, including self-exploitation and industrial abuses.* Occupational health hazards are even more serious for those employed temporarily on contract basis. It is a pity that acts such as *Workmen's Compensation Act, Employees State Insurance Scheme Act (ESI), Indian Factory Act, Industrial Disputes Act, Dangerous Machines (Regulation) Act, Fatal Accidents Act, Payment of Gratuity Act, and Employers Liability Act do not generally apply to casual and contract workers as well as those engaged in the unorganized sector.* (Anant-Sundaram-Tendulkar, 1999: 36-38). Even for those engaged in the organized sector, relief through these acts does not come that easily (Nihila, 1995:1485). A greater pity is that a few of these acts, e.g. Workmen's Compensation Act, and ESI, which are legally supposed to be applicable to all varieties of industrial workers, are observed more in breach in respect of those working in the unorganized sector, a very big proportion of which consists of rural industry. This is plainly so because, *inter alia*, there is negligible scope for organizing labour engaged in such tiny and geographically scattered enterprises as rural industries are. In a preponderant majority of such rural enterprises, no labour is hired from outside *a la* OAMEs; the family workers themselves act as employers as well as employees and in their case, the question of compensation or relief under most of these acts is, at best, an academic exercise.

Tenth, there has been no serious attempt, at the national level, to evolve a regional view of the rural industrial development policy. It is generally given out that a growing rural industrial sector has the potential to mollify the disparities in regional development. A national-level coordinated plan initiative to foster rural industrial development in different regions, has hardly been in evidence; for all practical purposes, individual states have been ploughing their lonely furrow, with occasional support from the centre only under some special schemes.

Finally, apart from policy changes and re-orientations directly connected with rural industry, new policy initiatives arising out of domestic compulsions or international commitments are also likely to indirectly affect its future. For example, the contemplated change in the ownership structure of the commercial banking sector, say, dilution of share holding by the state, is likely to affect the whole operation of priority sector lending by public sector banks; undoubtedly, the most pronounced credit squeeze would be faced by rural industrial enterprises in general, and the tiny units in particular. As a matter of fact, the axe has already started falling; the share of the ssi sector in priority sector lending witnessed a steep decline from 29 per cent in 1998-99 to 15 per cent only in 1999-2000 (EPW Editorial, 2000: 4068). Likewise, the subsidized or prioritized availability of electricity would disappear when the state electricity boards get revamped and privatization of electricity generation, transmission and distribution is increasingly resorted to. Still again, under increasing international pressures for environment concerns and labour issues in the days ahead, production regimes in the rural and tiny sectors would get more and more stiffened. It is abundantly clear that difficult times lie ahead of the rural and tiny industrial enterprises.

Keen analysts of India's development experience would testify that rural industry has witnessed a remarkable mingle of enlightened and obfuscated policy initiatives, of 'too-much-care' for some segments and 'too-little-attention' for others, of 'sustained garnering of growth propensities' for some and 'resuscitation through continual official props' for others, and so on. The government has not hesitated to intervene in a big way, through regulatory checks and promotional supports, and yet, as an opinion goes, "rural industries have remained ... an inefficient and unlinked appendage to the industrial structure of the country" (Papola, 1982: 25). In a single study, especially the one based on secondary data, it is rather difficult to see through the veracity of claims and disclaims. Nonetheless, in what follows, we put the available secondary data together, and look at the performance of rural industries so that the weaknesses and strengths, both at the policy and implementation levels, are thrown bare, in a fairly general way. First, however, a word about how to approach rural industry in terms of secondary data.

3

Approaching Rural Industry in India

3.1 Definitional Complexities

In India, the term 'rural industry' lends itself to varying interpretations. On a broad plane, location in or linkage with rural areas are the two main criteria to identify a rural industry from its urban counterpart (Saith, 1992:16). In a straightforward interpretation, all industrial enterprises located in the rural areas, irrespective of their size of operation either in terms of volume of output or employment, technology-in-use, range of market operation, etc., are entitled to be called 'rural industries'. Going by this criterion alone, we will have, under the umbrella of 'rural industry', a variegated mix of industrial activities ranging from those that are traditionally routed in the socio-cultural and economic life of the village community (often carrying the tag of traditional, household-based tiny 'village industries'), on the one extreme, and large-scale, factory-based manufacturing units, on the other. Rural-located activities such as village arts and crafts, pursued as independent economic entities or in collaboration with urban trade and commercial interests, easily fall under rural industry just as modern, small, medium and large enterprises can also do.

The locational approach does not pay attention to the organic connections between the industrial unit and the life of the rural population. On a broad plane, this approach has two major limitations. First, in the typical Indian situation, many rural areas get re-designated as urban areas in due course, primarily because of dynamics of population growth. Many rural industrial units may get re-classified as urban units, without involving any physical re-location. In a formal accounting sense, the number of rural industrial units may decline in such re-designated areas, yet reading a real decline in the economic fortune of the rural population would be highly misleading. Second, the reverse might as well be happening in many cases where urban congestion, increasing stress on infrastructure, environmental hazards (e.g. polluting effluents and dangerous industrial by-products) might prompt conscious policy initiatives to shift industries, including large and medium enterprises, from the densely populated urban to thinly populated rural areas.

As we see a little later, a pattern very commonly observed in India is that, for a number of reasons, industries of all sizes, including the most capital- and technology-intensive ones, get located, usually in clusters, at places just outside the municipal limits of the cities and industrial towns. Definition-wise, these are classified as 'rural industries' but for all practical purposes, these are part and parcel of urban economic system. If we were to go by location criterion alone, this would elevate rural industrialization to highly pleasing levels but, as can be easily imagined, the reality is quite different.

The second approach puts premium on organic linkages between the industrial enterprise and the rural people (Saith, 2000: 7-9). Here, rural-ness of the industrial unit owes itself, *inter alia*, to employment linkages with the rural people. Clearly, in this interpretation, the subtle distinction between *industrialization of the rural areas* and *industrialization for the rural areas* is of no significance since the prime consideration is the availability of industrial employment to rural job seekers. According primacy to employment does not imply that factors such as the origin of entrepreneurship or industrial ownership, the nature of technology in use, the sources of demand, etc., are not important or relevant; in fact, a variegated rural-urban mix of the above features, as also a rural-urban mingling of industrial workers, are to be expected when we take recourse to such a broad definition.

It is thus clear that, conceptually, there is no simple way of identifying 'rural industry' in our country. While the location of industry in rural areas is important for its general development, the relevance of employment linkages that rural people may have with units located in the semi-urban and urban locales, cannot be trivialized or dismissed at hand. Besides, if one is working with published reports or secondary data, finer classifications are not possible. For example, in official surveys of industrial enterprises, say, those organized by the National Sample Survey Organisation, rural areas are usually defined in terms of population census criteria and the surveyed industrial units are accordingly assigned to rural and urban locales of their operation. In surveys on employment and unemployment, the very same organization does not go by location criterion; rural workers engaged in industrial enterprises, irrespective of locale of production of such enterprises or the geographical proximity between the place of residence and locale of work, automatically become a part of the industrial workforce. If we were to constrict rural industry only to rural locales, the degree of under-estimation of employment in general, and of non-farm employment in particular, for the rural households, would obviously be high. In sum, the Indian reality cannot be understood if we go singly either by location or linkage criterion. Both criteria are relevant in their own right. At this stage, it is in the fitness of things that we try to understand, *albeit*, in tentative and conjectural terms, the types of location-linkage outfits that are dotting the industrial landscape of our economy.

3.2 Location-Linkage Outfits

Anybody familiar with the changing structure of India's rural economy would testify that its base today goes much beyond agriculture and its allied activities. In particular, the network of industrial activities stretches itself far beyond the traditional handicrafts, household and cottage industries that used to be the mainstay of its non-farm economy some 2-3 decades back. A large part of the rural industry today is a part of the total industrial sector of the Indian economy, and it certainly chips off some, *albeit very small*, share of growth and employment benefits. As an adjunct to the general phenomenon of higher industrial growth during the late seventies and eighties, many small-scale and tiny industrial units got located in the rural areas under the pressure of push and pull factors, varying significantly from state to state. Quite naturally, ancillarization and sub-contracting too have been growing in many industrial lines. Going by the variety of industrial activities, technologies in use, market linkages etc., the present-day house of rural-located industries is perhaps as heterogeneous as its urban counterpart.

Two crucial differences between rural and urban industrial sectors need, however, to be underlined. First, household, cottage and tiny enterprises dominate the rural industry far more overwhelmingly than is the case with the urban industry. This makes them more vulnerable, especially after the onset of the free trade regime since mid-90s. Second, the hierarchical structure of rural industry, from the viewpoint of its location and dispersal within a given geographical area, say, a taluka/tehsil or a district, adds its own complex dimensions to its functioning and growth. In plain terms, the urban linkages of rural-located industries are far more numerous, tedious and fragile than the rural linkages of urban-located industries.

3.2.1 Conceptualizing Location-Linkage Outfits

What can be the nature of semi-urban and/or urban linkages of rural-located units? And which of them are of prime interest to us? One can think of a long chain of linkages that encompasses practically each aspect of the existence and functioning of the rural industry. For example, sources of technology, machinery and skills, social origins of entrepreneurship and the life-view of entrepreneurs, and sources of investment funds and capital, could be one set of linkages (Saith, 2000: 10). The rural-urban partnership under which rural units act as ancillaries or sub-contracting nodes to urban or semi-urban enterprises refers to another set of linkages. In many product lines, commercial linkages between the rural and urban enterprises are fairly common for raw materials and other input supplies. Finally, the rural population could be linked with the semi-urban and urban economies for the purpose of employment, just as it could be true the other way round also, *albeit*, on a much smaller scale and under different set of circumstances. Although, each category of linkage is important in its own right yet, from the perspective of well-being of the rural people, it is the employment linkage that should receive greater attention.

Extending Saith's formulation, the cob-web of location-linkage outfits can be conceptualized in the form of a 3x3 matrix (Saith, 2000: 8-9). Three production locales and three linkage points are set out, in a rather abstract form; no geographical tag is attached to the semi-urban and urban areas. We are visualizing each production locale to have three types of linkages: For example, rural-location showing linkages with rural areas themselves, with semi-urban and then with urban areas, represented respectively by Cells (11), (12) and (13), in the first row of the matrix. The reverse process can be read through Cells (31), (21) and (11), starting from bottom upwards in the first column. Going by the full matrix, we can work out the location-linkage outfits in nine different ways. That is not needed in the present case. Our basic interest is in the rural economy and rural industry. The first row and the first column of the matrix should suffice to throw open all varieties of linkages that rural areas can have with semi-urban and urban areas, or vice versa. Let us begin with the first row.

Cell (11) constitutes the heart of rural industry, especially when seen from an evolutionary rural point of view. These are the enterprises that are closest both in spatial and socio-economic terms to the rural population and have a strong connection with their various livelihood strategies. As individual enterprises, most of these industries rely more upon human skill, manual power, local resources and traditional tools, and, from every conceivable angle, are run as household enterprises, either in the direction of supplementing agricultural incomes or independently as traditional village crafts or artisanal activities, a wide range of agricultural processing enterprises, and so on. Industries in cell (11) suffer from numerous handicaps, the most restrictive of which is the sluggish pace of demand expansion, and in many product lines even a declining demand prospect because of demand switch-over to cheaper substitutes, largely coming from urban areas.

Rural-located industries having links with semi-urban and urban areas, under cells (12) and (13) respectively, have also been a reality of Indian industrialization experience; the recent years have witnessed a sizeable expansion of these types of linkages. We can visualize many possibilities for such linkages to exist. First, under a conscious policy of pushing out certain categories of industrial enterprises away from the urban congested areas, existing and prospective enterprises are encouraged to re-locate themselves in the rural areas, largely to overcome the danger of environmental pollution and unhealthy by-products that these product-lines commonly generate. The most typical example comes from the on-going effort to shift out many thousand industries from the congested and non-conformable areas of urban Delhi, under the Supreme Court orders. In some cases, the easy and cheap availability of natural resources, low land prices, fiscal incentives (most importantly, tax exemption and/or relief for a number of years, subsidized availability of power and other inputs), cheap and assured availability of local labour, minimum fear of labour trouble, etc. may pull many industrial enterprises to the rural areas. This has been a popular strategy of fostering rural industrialisation in many states of India where an inter-state competition in terms of fiscal incentives, financial support, infrastructural back-up offered to the prospective rural industrialists has been at work. In a number of states, this took the form of rural industrial estates where a cluster approach has been followed, industrial infrastructures, including the rural-urban link roads, have been built by the state governments, and some kind of partnership has been forged between the public and private sector units.

Location- Linkage Outfits

Location/Linkage	LINKAGE		
	Rural (1)	Semi-urban (2)	Urban (3)
Location Rural (1)	(11)	(12)	(13)
Semi-urban (2)	(21)	(22)	(23)
Urban (3)	(31)	(32)	(33)

The rural-urban linkages explicated above under the first row of the matrix have, sometimes, a definitional caveat attached to them. It is fairly well known that the process of rural-ward movement of urban industrial enterprises, does not occur in a haphazard or *ad hoc* manner; it has a definite and market-driven pattern. The most common pattern is to shift exiting units from the heart of the city and to re-locate them, most commonly, along a metalled road, in 'rural locations' that begin just where the municipal limit ends. A kind of industrial corridor comes up in the 'rural areas', located along the main road running between a city and a town, or even between two cities/towns.

Gradually, the corridor expands away from the specified city/town towards the neighbouring town and acquires the character of an industrial cluster that would accommodate diverse product lines, reflect a variety of production technologies and market linkages, and most importantly, employment linkages with the rural areas, in varying form and content.

Without the risk of abstracting too much from the main theme of the study, we briefly sketch out two of the numerous Indian experiences. The first one relates to the industrial city of Ludhiana in the State of Punjab (Figure 1). Ludhiana is one of the renowned bristling industrial city of India which could not absorb the fast pace of its industrial expansion inside its municipal limits. Industries started coming up, very close to the outer limit of the city, on as many as five roads that connect Ludhiana to Phillaur-Phagwara-Jalandhar, Samrala-Chandigarh, Khanna-Gobindgarh-Rajpura, Malerkotla-Dhuri, Jagraon-Moga in five different directions. Figure 1 roughly caricaturizes the present status of such 'rural industrial clusters' around Ludhiana. For example, the cluster in village Bhatian along the Ludhiana-Phillaur roads starts a few meters away from the outer limit of the city, and stretches itself out upto about 8 kms, bordering on villages Quatewal, Hussainpura and Bahaderke.

The other experience comes from Warangal city of Andhra Pradesh which too has 'rural industrial clusters' very close to its outer limit (Figure 2), in as many as four directions. For example, just where the municipal limit ends on the Warangal-Hyderabad road, Rampura industrial estate begins which accommodates a wide variety of product lines such as steel processing, granite industries, rice mills, pesticide units, pipe manufacturing, and so on.

The examples of industrial corridors have a few messages for policy planners. First, it must be understood that all that is reported in official surveys such as NSS reports on manufacturing, most expressly its organized segment, under 'rural industrial sector', needs to be accepted only in a qualified manner. As we have seen, many of such industries, irrespective of their scale of production and the product lines in which they are involved are rural in definition; for all operational purposes, they are semi-urban or urban enterprises. An unqualified interpretation of such units as rural enterprises may look highly pleasing inasmuch as the rural industrial sector would appear to encompass flourishing units of all sizes, technologically up-to-date and market-savvy along side the most traditional and languishing household and cottage enterprises in the villages. Understandably such a pleasure is partly a fiction and needs to be toned down. Nonetheless, such examples reinforce our earlier contention that the question of rural industrialization should not be seen in isolation of what is going on in the semi-urban and urban areas; it is the urban-semi urban-rural continuum that enables us to grasp the wider connotations of rural industrialization processes.

Second, it cannot be denied that employment linkages for the rural people are real, and often substantial, especially when technical and skill capabilities of the rural job seekers are kept in mind. To give an example, again from our survey around Ludhiana city, in a medium-sized paper mill located in Village Bhatian, along the Ludhiana-Phillaur-Phagwara road, nearly 40 per cent of the local (Punjabi) floor workers come from the surrounding villages; in this mill, as in most others in Punjab, employment of migrant workers from other states is also a common phenomenon. If we go by an extended definition of the 'rural catchment area' that encompasses not only the local rural areas but also those outside Punjab, the example of the Bhatian paper mill clearly shows that 70-75 per cent of the workers are from the rural areas. To go by one more example, in a truly rural-located industrial enterprise that employs nearly 550 workers, (namely, GIS Ltd.), located in Village Akbarpura nearly 23-24 kms. away from Ludhiana, on the Ludhiana-Malerkotla road, the catchment area goes as far away as 35 kms. deep into the countryside; the company provides to and fro transport facilities to the lady workers; has built living quarters for nearly 200 workers inside the factory premises; is accessible by bicycle to a large number of rural male workers, and so on.

Finally, in some cases, the scale, product and technological diversities underlaying such 'on-the-border-located' industrial enterprises create production and marketing linkages with rural areas, especially when the possiblities of sub-contracting and ancillarization are forthcoming. In many cases, these are not trivial and *ad hoc* types of exchange relations; perhaps, some select categories of rural artisans, especially those engaged in handicrafts and local skill-based artistic items, and other educated and enterprising self-employing persons, could benefit from such linkages.

Let us now briefly look in the reverse order, *a la* cells (31) and (21). Three distinct possibilities can be visualized for such linkages to operate. First, the units currently located in the urban- or semi-urban areas might have had rural origins, but relocated themselves into smaller semi-urban centres, or urban areas, as a consequence of needs and implications of an expansion of their scale of operations. Second, in some cases, due to a sizeable expansion of their population, rural areas themselves get re-classified as semi-urban, and later full-fledged urban areas, and with that, the erstwhile rural units automatically get re-classified as urban units, without any physical relocation.

Figure 1:
Industrial Clusters Around Ludhiana
Punjab : September 2000

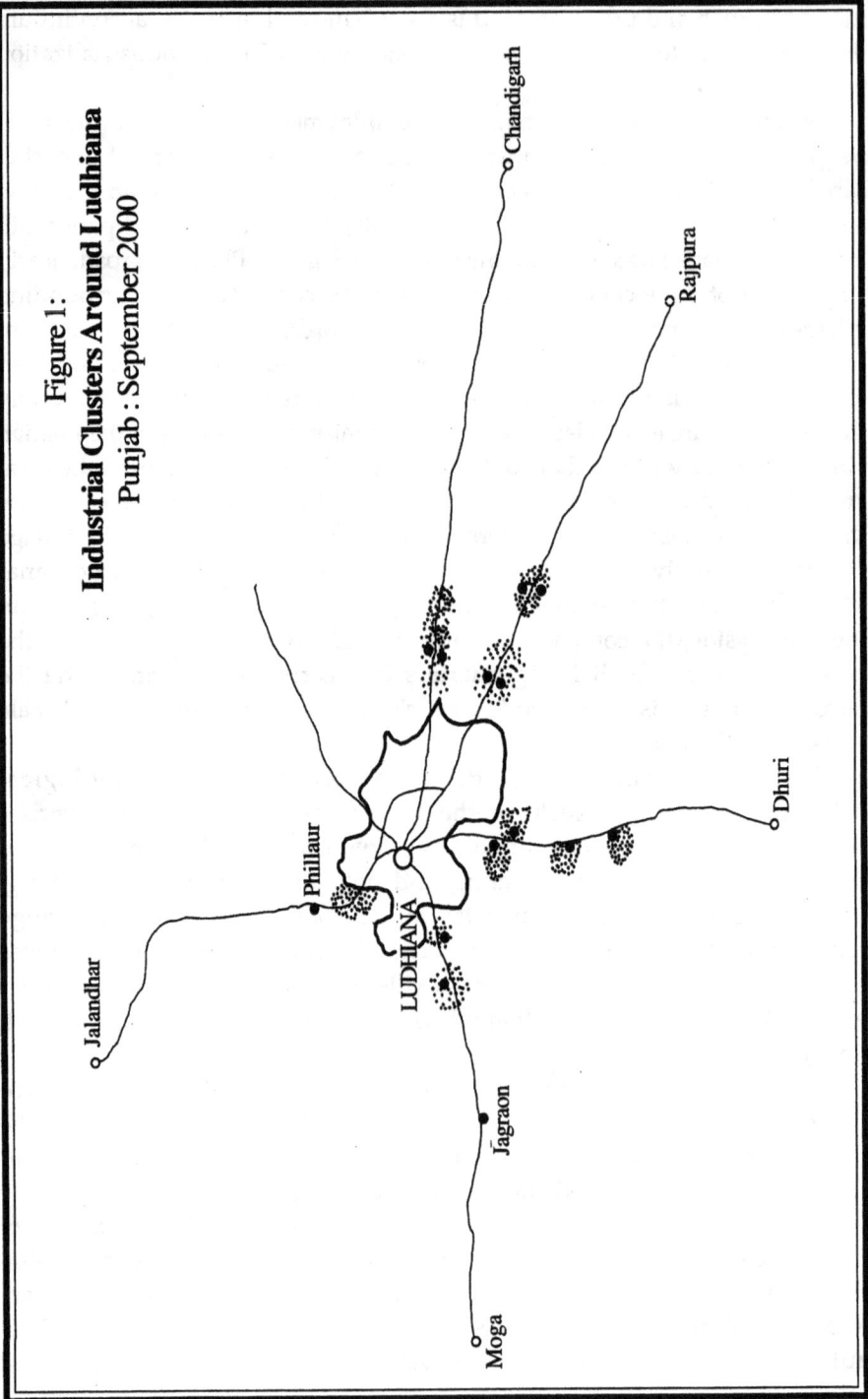

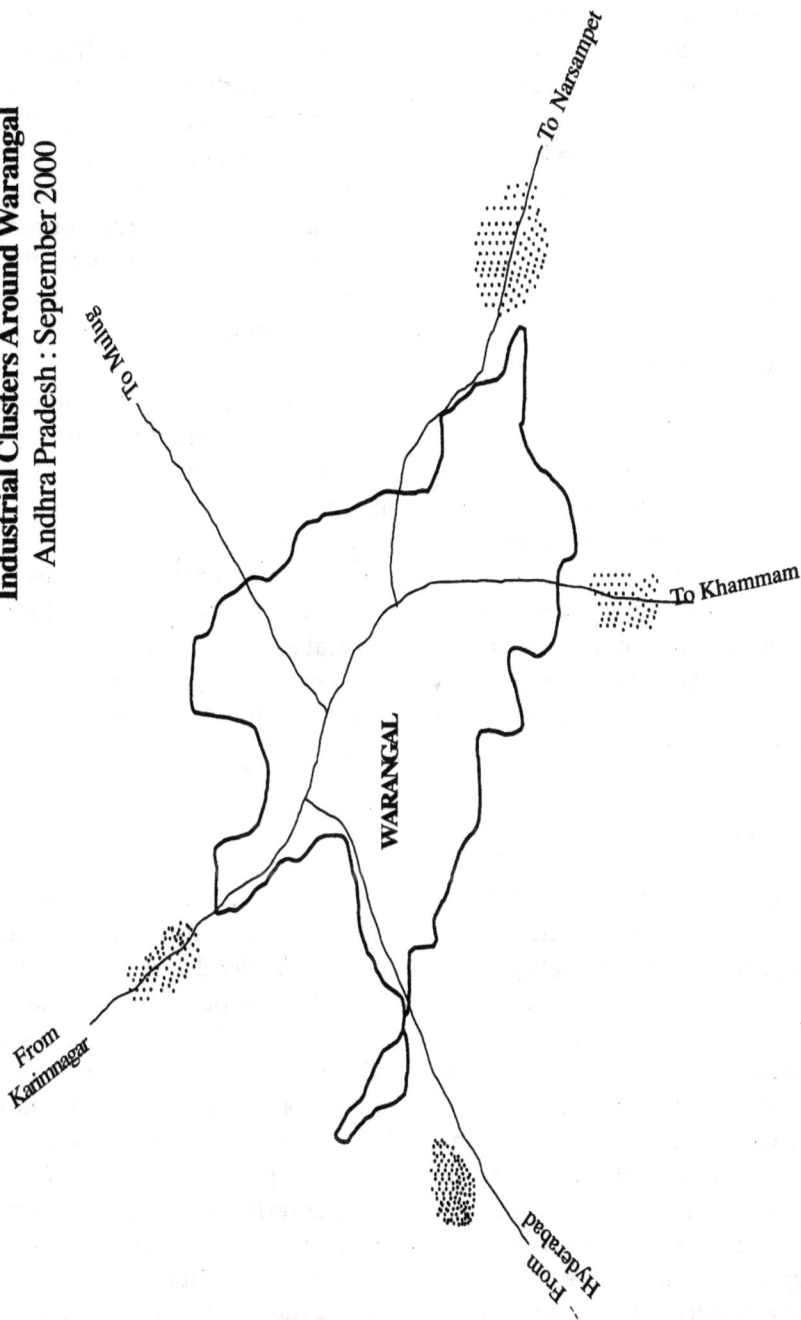

Figure 2 :
Industrial Clusters Around Warangal
Andhra Pradesh : September 2000

Third, one more form in which cell (21) or (31) type relationship may operate is through sub-contracting between rural industries, most commonly the household and cottage enterprises, and urban enterprises. In many product lines, e.g. transport equipment and parts, machines and machine parts, metal based products, leather-based products, textiles, etc., sub-contracting operates rather commonly. Interestingly, in some cases, the chain of sub-contracting runs from urban enterprises to semi-urban or directly to rural enterprises, and, sometimes between semi-urban and rural enterprises. There are studies to show that rural industry benefits in more ways than one through such sub-contracting arrangements, the most ostensible being technology up-gradation and more and better employment for its workers (Chadha, 2001b).

It needs to be pointed out that, in numerous cases, the intermediate category of semi-urban locales, are more akin to the rural than to the urban socio-cultural and economic environment. These are the areas that have graduated themselves out of the rural setting and, for a fairly long time to come, their links with the rural areas would not undergo any organic transformation. The Indian experience of urbanization testifies to the expanding economic and commercial status of the semi-urban settlements. Their most important linkage with the rural areas, via the structure of their industrial activities, is in the area of agro-processing. This category should thus occupy a place of central importance in the rural-semi urban-urban continuum.

3.3 Hierarchy of Rural Industry

As should be evident from the above analysis, in the Indian context , 'rural industry' is a conglomerate of diverse economic activities that satisfies, *inter alia*, different location-linkage specifications. Naturally, the term carries different meanings to different analysts. We need not involve ourselves in these diverse perceptional descriptions. In our view, there are two broad angles from which we can look into the problems of 'rural industry' in India. For example, we can explore the **official view** which looks upon rural industry specifically in the context of pre-specified socio-economic objectives. Then, we may visualize an **analytical view** which can differentiate one group of rural industries from another, on the basis of certain objective criteria (e.g. scale of production, technology-in-use, market coverage, etc.). Luckily, some of the nation-wide surveys on industries, upon which most research effort is based in India, provide adequate scope for operationalizing the analytical view that we have in mind. It would be in the fitness of things to dwell a bit more on the two views.

3.3.1 Official View

In official parlance, rural industry is covered, under the composite expression 'Village and Small Industry' - VSI sector. The VSI sector is divided into eight sub-sectors, namely Khadi, Village Industries, Handlooms, Sericulture, Handicrafts, Coir, Small-scale Industries and Powerlooms. While the last two represent the modern small industries, the other six sub-sectors constitute traditional industries. Modern small-scale industries and powerlooms, widely dispersed between rural and urban areas, use modern technologies, usually generating full-time employment and register comparatively faster growth whereas the traditional industries are fairly largely rural in character which sustain and create employment opportunities for rural households (both part- and full-time), increase income generation and, many among them, preserve craftsmanship and art heritage of the country (Govt. of India, 10/1985: 98).

The first two sub-sectors (namely khadi and village industries) of the traditional segment of the VSI sector are the most typical examples of household village enterprises which have been institutionally supported by a strong semi-government organization (Khadi and Village Industries Commission) and which are currently at the most threatening stage of their existence. Khadi is a cloth woven on handlooms from cotton, silk or woollen yarn, usually handspun. Nurtured in the Gandhian tradition of 'self-reliance of the village economy', such enterprises usually intend to provide supplementary part-time employment to the weaker sections among the rural populace. With the same objective of providing some additional employment and earnings, rural households are encouraged and financially supported to mount a wide range of self-employing industrial ventures such as cottage pottery, handmade paper, cane and bamboo products, bee-keeping, oil extraction, cottage soap and leather, brass and copper metal, and so on. Apart from many other weaknesses that such industries suffer from, obsolete technology is their real Achilles' heel.

The VSI sector constitutes an important segment of the economy. It provides maximum employment next only to agriculture. It is estimated to contribute about 50.0 per cent of value-added in the manufacturing sector and accounts for nearly 55.0 per cent of the total exports of the country. The growth in the VSI sector, besides resulting in preponderance of self-employment and wider dispersal of industrial and economic activities, ensures maximum utilization of local resources, both human and material.

The eight sub-sectors of the VSI sector have been devised for facilitating the dispensing of official assistance under various development programmes. Specialized institutions have been created to look after the promotion of each sub-sector at the national-level, in conjunction with parallel agencies operating at the state-level. For reasons outlined later, the sub-sector 'small scale industry' has been the more favourite choice of official attention and support and accordingly, the most dynamic performance under the whole VSI sector belongs to this group of industries. This sub-sector is now manufacturing a wide range of over 7400 products and accounts for more than three-fourth of VSI output.

3.3.2 Analytical View

Analytically, rural industry consists of three sub-sets. At the bottom is a conglomerate of *traditional village industries* including *crafts* and *artisan* industries. *Cottage* and *household industrial activities* are clearly a part and parcel of such industries. These are deeply routed in village life, are carried on mostly as household enterprises, usually with family's own labour, using primitive technology generally based on local resources and family skills, catering mostly to local village or nearby demand (with some exceptions such as, for example, handlooms and 'bidi' industry which have markets much beyond the locale of production), operating at low levels of productivity and earnings, and so on. Most of these industries produce goods meant to cater to final demand and hence, within the inter-industry exchange vortex, they throw up negligible forward linkages. The only noticeable exception is the handloom sub-sector which gets its main input (yarn) from the modern industrial sector. By and large, their products are consumed by low income groups and hence chronic deficiency of demand is a problem peculiar to this group alone (Kurien, 1978: 460). In the opinion of some analysts, productivity in these industries "is mainly dependent upon the skill and devotion of the worker and not on supplementary factors like tools and implements, and they are less dependent on the social overheads" (Vyas-Mathai, 1978: 343).

These household-level traditional village industries have persisted on in India's rural economy for centuries, and in many cases, provide supplementary sources of employment and income to many a rural household. Examples of such industries are: leather tanning and leather products, pottery, rope-making, handlooms, blacksmithy, carpentry, making of jewellery and other wearing apparels, oil extraction, bidi- and sweetmeat-making, dairy products, and so on. For analytical convenience, we call them household village industries (hvi). A very substantial proportion of VSI's traditional segment (comprising the six sub-sectors) closely correspond to the hvi sector; certain varieties of handicrafts may be an exception. It is pertinent to point out, perhaps in an effort to strike some concord between the official view and the hvi sector visualized under our analytical view, that a preponderant majority of village industries under VSI, operating under the KVIC umbrella, would automatically qualify to be a part of the hvi sector.

The next group up on the ladder is the *tiny sector* that accounts for a preponderant majority of units in the small-scale sector. The tiny sector is also a conglomerate of a wide variety of industrial activities, dominated by agro-industries, light-engineering and consumer goods industries. In comparison to the set of traditional, household-level village industries (hvi), the production technology used in the *tiny sector* is usually superior, productivity levels higher, market-coverage much wider, and so on. Examples under this group are: manufacture of wheat flour and rice milling, raw sugar, beverages and tobacco products, dairy products (e.g. butter, cheese, 'ghee' etc.), cotton/ wool/silk textiles, leather, paper and wood products, and so on. We designate such industries as tiny rural industries (tri).

Finally, the group of other small-scale units makes the third subset of rural industry. Relative to hvi and tri, this subset is truly modern in its organizational outfit, technology-in-use, marketing orientation, and so on. The productivity and earning levels here are still higher compared with the bunch of traditional village industries. These industries have the proven potential for dynamic growth, technological upgradation and ability to compete, with their urban counterparts. The product range is also fairly wide, encompassing a wide variety of agro-processing, agricultural inputs, light engineering products and mechanical equipment, consumer goods, and so on. Let us call them small rural industries (sri).

It is very important to point out that location-wise all the three components are not the exclusive preserve of rural areas alone. While the first constituent, viz. *village industries* is, definition-wise, a part and parcel of village economy, the other two sub-sectors have their locale both in the rural and urban areas. It is certain that many of those which are located in the rural areas are the beneficiaries of government's conscious policy of boosting the process of economic diversification of backward areas or to reduce the incidence of urban-congestion and related problems. Quite often, units under the latter two categories are located on the fringe of urban-industrial centres and go as rural industries only in a definitional sense.

It is thus obvious that for grasping the nuance as also for a critical appraisal of India's official approach to rural industry, the analytical differences among the three sub-sets, namely hvi, tri and sri, must be kept in mind. To remind ourselves, the whole lump of hvi is definition-wise located in the rural areas, a fairly big proportion of tri subset is operating in rural India while the third subset sri is gradually expanding its base in the rural areas. In other words, for meaningful rural-urban comparisons, say, for growth and efficiency, we must bring tri and sri sub-sectors face to face with their respective urban counterparts. This is attempted by us to the extent that the available data permit.

Two other considerations need to be kept in mind. First, the three sub-sectors are not (and cannot be) free of their respective internal heterogeneities, whether in terms of technology-in-use or market coverage or productivity/earning levels. Nevertheless, the three sub-groups stand quite apart from one another. The technological, market and productivity dualism between hvi and sri sectors (for that matter, even between tri and sri sectors) is unmistakable, and in most cases, has tended to widen. For these reasons, the hvi sector has languished over time in spite of tremendous official support. It is extremely important to note that highly differentiated technical linkages operate between these three sub-sectors and the rest of the industrial economy. While the sri and, to a slightly lower extent, tri sub-sectors could be made technically and economically viable, and consequently, connected with the large-scale sector, most of the hvi generally stays aloof (Kurien, 1978: 459). This distinction has great bearing on the prospects, motivation and driving impulses for growth and vertical integration of sri sector with the upper echelons of industry.

Secondly, the three sub-sets, especially the tri and sri sectors, do not operate as completely independent compartments. They have a lot of overlap between them (as also with their urban counterparts), e.g. in production lines and market sharing. The rising levels of rural incomes, more expressly with the middle and upper-middle peasantry, coupled with urban-impact on rural life, have been responsible for shifting rural demand for goods and services to urban areas (Vaidyanathan, 1986: A139-A141). Moreover, by their very organizational and technological superiority, the urban industrial and the sri sectors render the position of hvi sector extremely vulnerable. In spite of official attempts at product-line demarcations, the production and demand overlaps have persisted to the detriment of hvi and, to some extent, tri sub-sectors.

As explained earlier under the Location-Linkage discussion, a fairly noticeable proportion of the organized manufacturing units is located in the rural areas. Perhaps, many among them are rural by definition being located just on the fringe of industrial cities and towns, yet, their proliferating march away from the centre of the cities cannot negate the fact that rural areas do command a fairly respectable share of such industrial activities as well. In concrete terms, rural India has the same heterogeneous mix of industrial size categories that punctuate its urban industrial sector. That significant differences do exist, for each comparable category, say, between tiny-rural and tiny-urban units, or, between small-rural and small-urban units, practically for each aspect of their functioning, is, however, a different matter.

Luckily, the nation-wide official surveys on unorganized (rural and urban) industry in India, usually carried out by the National Sample Survey Organisation are so organized that they permit us to devise industrial categories broadly along the lines set out under our analytical view. Let us first familiarize ourselves with a few concepts and definitions of such official surveys carried out by the NSSO.

Industrial surveys in India are conducted under two arrangements. The first is the survey of unorganized manufacturing, conducted every five years, covering three categories of units, separately for rural and urban areas, and the second one relates to organized manufacturing for which data are published on annual basis; since 1987-88, some information on organized manufacturing is given separately for the rural and urban areas. Under the unorganized manufacturing segment, an enterprise owned and operated without the help of any hired worker, employed on a fairly regular basis, is described as an **own-account manufacturing enterprise** (OAME). An enterprise run with the assistance of *at least* one hired worker, employed on a fairly regular basis, is called an **establishment**. An establishment which employs a total of not more than 5 workers is known as **non-directory manufacturing establishment** (NDME). Further, an establishment which employs a total of 6-10 workers is categorized as a **directory manufacturing establishment** (DME). The unorganized sector thus consist of OAMEs, NDMEs and DMEs. Industrial establishments which employ 10 or more workers and use power and those which employ 20 or more workers without using power, are required by law to register themselves under sections 2m(i) and 2m(ii) of the Factories Act, 1948, respectively. Such industrial establishments are factories proper and fall under the purview of the organized (Annual Survey of Industries: ASI) sector.

It is obvious from the above that industrial categories such as OAMEs and NDMEs are more germane to our requirement both because a preponderant majority of rural industrial enterprises are self-employing ventures and employ a very small number of working hands, mostly not beyond the limit of 5, set by NDMEs. Accordingly, when we analyze the problems of OAMEs, we are closely approximating ourselves to the tiny rural industry (tri). The small rural industry (sri) visualized under our analytical view would then broadly correspond with the NSS unorganized manufacturing categories of NDMEs and DMEs put together. This leaves out the traditional, household village industry (hvi), the third component visualized under our analytical view. This, in our opinion, closely corresponds with the traditional component of the officially designated VSI sector, comprising as many as six industrial categories (khadi, village industries, handloom, handicrafts, sericulture and coir). Finally, the organized segment of the rural industrial sector is a category by itself for which rural-urban break-up is now available, on a continuous basis since 1987-88.

In sum, like in the urban areas, in rural areas too, we have a wide hierarchical structure of industries. Beginning with the traditional cottage and village industries at the bottom, we have the large sized organized manufacturing enterprises at the top. In between, we have tiny rural industries which roughly correspond with OAMEs under the unorganized manufacturing segment, followed upwards by small rural industries, roughly corresponding with NDMEs and DMEs of the unorganized manufacturing segment put together. For an in-depth, and analytically acceptable, study of the rural industry in India, each of the segments sketched out above need to be covered. In what follows, we marshal information from many different sources and look through the working of rural industry, in all of its incarnations sketched out above.

4

Performance of Rural Industry

4.1 V.S.I. Sector

The time-series data on the VSI sector is difficult to deal with. First, the series begins only from 1973-74 onwards. Then, there are many information gaps: no data either on production or employment for the years 1974-75 to 1978-79; no information on employment for the years 1980-81, 1981-82, 1982-83. Such gaps do undermine the quality of data. Second, production figures at current prices are oddly mixed up with those at constant prices, sometimes even for the same year; a uniform series either at current or constant prices is not available. The best that one can do is to construct three production series, at 1979-80, 1984- 85 and 1993-94 prices, respectively. Towards this end, certain adjustments/assumptions have to be made which may not be the best to go by. To quote a few examples, for some years, production data for a specific sector available only in physical terms were converted into monetary terms, using the 'implicit unit price' prevailing in the base year. Obviously, no regard is paid to the changing composition of output within that sector. Again, the available data for the post 1990-91 years are largely available at current prices only, and one could put them at constant prices using price index with 1993-94 as the base. The resultant production figures (at 1993-94 prices) are not completely free of price deflator bias, especially for the years 1990-91, 1991-92 and 1992-93 when the deflator works in the opposite direction. Value of output in the handicrafts sub-sector is available only up to 1996-97; for 1997-98 and 1998-99, we go by extrapolated figures.

Third, for a number of reasons, there is really no way of arriving at comparable per worker productivity figures for individual segments of the VSI sector. First, except for the group of small scale industries, part-time employment is reported, in varying form and degree, practically by all other constituents of the VSI sector, and there is no way of arriving at the standard full-time equivalent labour units, without indulging in 'blind guesses'. Second, the ratio between part- and full-time workers varies fairly substantially among individual segments of the khadi sector itself (Chadha, 2000a: 8). Third, again for the khadi workers themselves, although the part- and full-time workers' division is available, yet the daily work duration of part-time workers/artisans is not known. Moreover, part- and full-time workers' division is not given for other industries, as is given for khadi workers. Fourth, for some sectors (e.g. sericulture), employment for some years includes the connected-work in agriculture while for others, no such mention is made. In total terms, we can neither ignore the reality of part-time employment nor can we convert part-time workers into full-time workers, for seven of the eight VSI segments. Accordingly, estimating figures of per worker productivity, without getting involved into the intractable problems set out above, may perhaps be misleading, especially if the intention is to compare the productivity levels among the eight sub-sectors. The advisable course, at this stage of our analysis, is to look at the performance profile of the individual VSI sub-sectors with reference to output and employment only, without getting into the fragile estimates of productivity.

Building a temporal profile for employment too is not free of blemishes, for reasons which are partially set out in the preceding paragraph. Nonetheless, since the division between part- and full-time workers in the khadi sector does not seem to have changed much over time, most markedly during the recent decade, growth rates for employment in this sector built on the given series of khadi workers, would not distort the reality by a big margin. Employment growth rates for the other VSI sub-sectors would suffer much less distortions since the proportion of part-time workers is possibly much lower and, like khadi sub-sectors, has not changed much over time (Chadha, 1996: 60).

Lastly, the (compound) growth rates are computed on point-to-point basis for the sub-periods 1973-74 to 1984-85 (Series I) and 1984-85 to 1989-90 (Series II) and through estimation of the standard semi-log functions for the period 1990-91 to 1998-99 (Series III); in the case of Series I and II, the number of available observations is too small to justify a semi-log function. We know that our growth rates under Series I and II are highly sensitive to base- or end-year variations and are not, therefore, completely reliable yet they do capture the uneven pace of output and employment expansion, across the sectors and across the three sub-periods devised by us. Most surely, the declining or slumbering 'spots' stand out as contrasts to their expanding counterparts. In brief, the time-series data for VSI Sector do have their serious limitations, yet for fixing ideas on temporal changes, these are the only sources to go by.

The VSI sector consists of eight sub-sectors (Table 1). Location-wise, five sub-sectors (i.e. Khadi, Village Industries, Handloom, Sericulture and Coir) are preponderantly rural, handicrafts are largely divided between rural and semi-urban locales while small-scale and powerloom sub-sectors are spread over rural, semi-urban and urban locations. In other words, looking across the six industrial groups under the traditional sector, one is really comparing one industry group with the other largely within the rural areas while the modern sector delivers ideas on a mix of rural- and urban-located industries. Moreover, the intra-group heterogeneity in terms of the size of operation, persons employed, technology-use, market coverage, etc., are bound to be far greater among the group of small-scale industries which are indeed a heterogeneous mix of enterprises ranging from tiny, cottage, household-based activities, on one end, and modern factory-based enterprises, on the other. These observations may be kept in mind while inter-group or rural-urban comparisons are made from Table 1.

Table 1 (split into two parts: Sub-Table 1A gives production expansion while Sub-Table 1B takes care of employment) throws up a few disturbing features for the traditional sub-sector in general and khadi and handloom in particular. First, all along, output in real terms has shown impressive expansion in the modern sector compared with the traditional sector. A growth rate of 10.9 per cent per annum among the small scale industries, during 1973-74/1984-85, compared with 4.2 per cent among the traditional industries, testifies to the relative dynamism of the former, partly facilitated by comparative size and location advantages and partly by more buoyant demand conditions; the Khadi Sector also grew rather impressively (@ 7.8 per cent per annum) during this period. During the subsequent period 1984-85/1989-90, output growth rate improved among many traditional groups but the modern sector fared much better so that the gaps between the two got widened. For example, the growth rate in the small-scale sector climbed up to a high of 12.8 per cent compared with 3.6 per cent only for the Khadi. In fact, khadi/handloom output growth rate was the lowest among the traditional set of industries, let alone in relation to small-scale modern industries and the power-loom. In plain terms, a big decline in output growth was faced by khadi, and a moderate decline in village industries during the post-1984 years while for most other sub-groups, it improved by varying margins.

The first three years or so beginning 1990-91 showed a slack, in real output expansion, in most of the traditional sectors, most visibly in the Khadi and Handloom segments, compared with the Power-loom Sector. Even the group of small-scale industries could not insulate itself from the contractionary trend that plagued the industrial sector as a whole since the closing part of the 1980s. In particular, the poor performance in the small scale sector during those early years of the 1990s could possibly be attributed to import compression measures, credit squeeze, high cost of credit, etc. operating during the two-three years since the introduction of new economic policies in 1991 (Annual Plan,

1993-94:276). Happily, the situation was redeemed since 1993-94; output expanded significantly from 1993-94 onwards in small-scale industries, and a few of the traditional sub-sectors. For the whole period 1990-91/98-99, output grew fairly impressively at a rate of 9.5 per cent in the modern small-scale industries. In contrast, in the traditional sector as a whole, the corresponding increase in output growth was only 6.0 per cent, although in some of the traditional sub-sectors (e.g. village industries, sericulture, handicrafts, etc.), the rate of growth of output fell by sizeable margins during sub-period III compared with sub-period II. Khadi fared the worst; the growth rate of output was a mere 0.1 per cent during 1990-91/1998-99 compared with 3.6 per cent during 1984-85/1989-90.

Second, throughout the post-1973 years, employment expanded at fairly high rates in many of the VSI sub-sectors (Sub-Table 1B). Of course, the level and pattern of employment growth did vary markedly among individual segments, from one sub-period to the other. In general, employment expansion was relatively sluggish in khadi and coir sub-sectors. On the other hand, powerloom and small-scale industries under the modern segment and handicrafts and village industries under the traditional segment threw up, *almost dutifully*, impressive employment growth rates, in each sub-period. The handloom sector too performed well except during 1984-85/1989-90. On the whole, the picture on employment expansion has not been too bad, except for khadi and coir ever since we stepped into the mid-eighties.

Third, contrary to the usual perception, employment growth in the modern sub-sectors has usually been higher than that in their traditional counterparts. For example, during 1973-74/84-85, it was 8.5 per cent per annum in the modern segment against 4.5 per cent in the traditional segment; 6.1 per cent against 5.6 per cent in the two segments during 1984-85/89-90; and 4.4 per cent against 4.6 per cent during 1990-91/98-99, and so on. The khadi sector in particular stands out as an example of employment reverses in recent years given the fact that an overwhelming proportion of khadi workers are engaged only on a part-time basis; in net terms, the employment profile of the Khadi sector really pales into insignificance, especially in relation to the modern small scale industrial activities, for the post-1984 years. In other words, the most avowed objective of (non-farm) employment generation for the rural masses, through khadi and handloom sub-sectors, seems to have been fulfilled only partially; in an accounting sense, the number of people employed in the khadi sector has certainly been increasing, *albeit very moderately at times*, yet the economic content of this employment has not been much since a preponderant majority of khadi workers have been part-time workers only. For most of such part-time workers, especially the female workers engaged in spinning, the usual work-time does not go beyond 3 hours or so per day and accordingly, their earnings stay at ridiculously low levels (Chadha, 2000a: 13).

Fourth, the uneven output and employment growth performance of individual industry groups readily convinces us that the absolute level of productivity in traditional rural industries should be many times lower than that in the modern sectors. Still more important is the fact that over time, the ratio between the high-productivity sector (small-scale industries) and low-productivity sector (say, khadi) has been expanding, almost on a continuing basis. From this point of view, *modern small-scale industry must be looked upon as a hope for the future.* If mere expansion of numbers is to be taken as an index of employment, most of the VSI segments, except Khadi, have acquitted themselves well. However, if productivity level and its growth are the basic criteria for viability, sustainability and growth of rural industrial units, including their long-run capability to take on more and more of working hands, only small-scale industrial units seem to fill the bill. In most other segments, employment expansion without much regard for productivity and earning levels seem to have guided the course of events. Khadi undoubtedly failed on both fronts; undoubtedly, it is the declining or sagging levels of productivity that must have been responsible for cutting into its employment capabilities since 1984-85. In recent years, employment in the Khadi has indeed been the most distressing spot in the VSI sector.

One more striking contrast between the traditional and modern segments is that, unlike in the earlier two decades, during the 1990s, the gap between the output and employment growth rates has tended to narrow down relatively much more in the case of the former, while it has tended to widen in respect of the modern small scale industries. The close correspondence between growth of output and employment, in the case of some of the traditional sub-sectors, was due presumably to the compulsions of taking on additional working hands from within the family; alternative employment opportunities are not so easy to come by, especially for workers engaged for long spells in the traditional industries, especially khadi, handloom, village industries, sericulture, etc. For them, low level of education and lack of alternative skills are big constraints.

Table 1 also shows the changing relative importance of individual segments of the VSI sector (Cols. 2 to 11 as a percentage of Col.12, both in Sub-Tables 1A and 1B). As is expected, the modern segment accounts for a lion's share of output while the bulk of employment is offered by its traditional counterpart. In the modern segment, both output and employment shares have expanded while the opposite has happened with the traditional segment. It seems the latter segment is being pushed to a corner as far as its share in output is concerned; in 1998-99, it had to contend with a mere 8.00 per cent share in output against as high as a 59.14 per cent share in employment; way back in 1973-74, the two figures were 19.21 per cent and 67.28 per cent, respectively. The implications towards productivity levels should thus be clear. *Over time, the traditional rural industries have steadily lost their ground to modern small-scale industries, whether located in the rural or urban areas.* Interestingly, the power-loom sub-sector seems to have been an absorber of many additional working hands even while losing tremendously in its share in output. Thus, as said earlier, in *de facto* terms, productivity/worker profile in the power-loom sub-sector has put it more in the league of traditional sub-sectors rather than modern small-scale industries.

An especially distressing picture emerges for the handloom sub-sector where in 1998-99, a mere 1.26 per cent share in output was accompanied by as high as a 27.06 per cent share in VSI employment; in 1973-74, the two shares were 7.39 per cent and 34.30 per cent, respectively. This sub-sector seems to serve as a dumping ground for a lot of additional labour force, presumably because alternative employment opportunities are not available to those already engaged in it, especially to those weavers who have been in the craft for a long time and primarily due to lack of education and alternative skills, cannot shift to other jobs. What else can explain the weakening of this sub-sector during the past decade or so?

Khadi has been losing its ground even more precipitously, and that too, both from output and employment angles. For example, in 1973-74, it had as small a share in VSI output as 0.29 per cent, against a 5.79 per cent share in employment; in 1990-91, the output share declined to a negligible level of 0.14 per cent, against 3.33 per cent share in employment; and finally, in 1998-99, the output share was a ridiculously small figure of 0.08 per cent, against a 2.35 per cent share of employment. The decline in Khadi's share of employment may not look terrifying from these figures, yet given the fact that nearly 70.0 per cent of the khadi workers are part-time workers only, the real decline would indeed be steeper still if full-time equivalent of part-time workers could somehow be ascertained.

While the inherent weaknesses of the handloom sector cannot be wished away, the economic tug of wag incessantly going on since the 1960s between the handloom and power-loom sub-sectors has played a decisive role in the secular decline of the former. The history of textile industry points to a number of policy slants, especially those connected with price of yarn and chemical dyes, working against the handloom sector; the mill-sector lobby, working in league with the power-loom lobby, on the one hand, and, the lackadaisical and disinterested administrative responses, on the other hand, have brought about the gradual squeeze of the handloom sector. Its future seems equally grim because, *inter alia*, it suffers from technological and commercial weaknesses of its own and, most importantly, because the handloom weavers themselves are not an organized forum with a significant reckoning (Srinivasulu, 1994: 2332- 33).

In total terms, looking back to the past three decades, it is fairly obvious that, by and large, the traditional rural industries have acquitted themselves well in fulfilling their avowed objective of providing employment to the expanding army of rural labour-force. In the context of wide-spread rural poverty, especially that occasioned by the rising incidence of rural landlessness and marginalization of land holdings, on the one hand, and under- (if not un-) employment of a big mass of rural workforce, on the other, it has not been a trivial development. Yet, for making a decisive dent into rural poverty, a more lucrative employment status, most essentially in terms of high productivity and earning levels, is an inescapable pre-condition. Unluckily, productivity expansion nowhere seems to have been in sight, either during 1973-74/ 1984-85 or during 1990-91/1998-99. This was largely so because employment growth closely chased, and in some sub-sectors (most notably, the Khadi sub-sector) exceeded output growth, most visibly during the 1990s. The periodic up- and down-swings in production has been another noticeable feature of some among the traditional industry groups. The modern sector offers a contrast. In relative terms, the picture about small-scale industries is fairly satisfactory in the sense that production and employment grew at satisfying rates, practically during each of the three sub-periods, a two-year slack during 1991-92 and 1992-93 notwithstanding; improving levels of productivity clearly followed here which, unfortunately, was not the case for most of the traditional segments under the VSI sector.

4.2 Tiny and Small Rural Industry

Before we go over to the unorganized sector, it is in the fitness of things to have a *quick overview of the rural industrial structure.* Four distinguishing characteristics for the rural industrial sector need to be underlined. First, unorganized manufacturing occupies an extremely domineering position in India's rural industrial sector. Around mid-1990s, nearly 90.0 per cent of rural manufacturing employment was in the unorganized segment alone (Govt. of India, Annual Survey of Industries: 1994-95, 11/1997: 116). Second, within the rural unorganized manufacturing, tiny or household-type enterprises (OAMEs) hold the central stage. Again, around mid-1990s, OAMEs alone accounted for as much as 81.0 per cent of the unorganized manufacturing employment; even in terms of total manufacturing employment, the OAMEs' share was as high as 72.0 per cent (Govt. of India, 1998: A1-A36). Third, between rural and urban areas, nearly three-fourth of the total unorganized manufacturing units in India were located in the rural areas, with a two-third share of employment. Among the tiniest of the unorganized manufacturing units (OAMEs), the rural areas had, again around mid-1990s, a 78.0 per cent share in the number of enterprises and 79.0 per cent in employment. Finally, the preponderance of OAMEs in the unorganized manufacturing units, and of the unorganized segment in the manufacturing sector as a whole, stand out far more stoutly in the rural compared with the urban areas. In total terms, any study on rural manufacturing must, therefore, begin with the unorganized sector, must throw bare the strengths and weaknesses of its most dominant household-based segment (OAMEs) and should then go over to the organized component. To remind ourselves, we take OAMEs under the unorganized sector as the same as tri enterprises as per our analytical view; accordingly, the sri segment of our perception is expected to cover the total of NDMEs and DMEs under the unorganized sector.

4.2.1 Performance of Tiny/Small Rural Industry

We can measure the performance of the unorganized manufacturing units (UMUs) in more ways than one. Output elasticity with respect to inputs, total factor productivity, net value added per worker, etc. are the commonly used indicators. On the basis of the available data, we prefer to compare productivity (gross value added per worker) in different product lines (classified at two-digit level), between rural and urban areas. Before we do that, let us have a look at an important structural parameter, namely capital:labour ratio, which typifies, in a fairly workable manner, the nature of technology at work, as also the changes in labour absorbing capability of rural against urban units. Table 2 gives us capital:labour ratio for 1984-85, 1994-95 and 2000-01, for the three categories of UMUs, in each of the sixteen branches of manufacturing.

4.2.1.1 Capital Intensity

Capital:labour ratio and value added per worker are computed in real terms (at 19981-82 prices). A separate Weighted Index of Wholesale Prices in India was used for each manufacturing sub-sector (Govt. of India, Statistical Abstracts of India: 2001, 2002: 316-18)). Table 2 throws up many points.

First, among the unorganized manufacturing as a whole (Cols.12-14), the urban units had, during 1994-95, higher capital:labour ratio in as many as 15 out of the 16 branches of production; basic metal was the only exception. This was not so a decade back; in 1984-85, in as many as 7 branches of manufacturing, the rural units worked with higher capital:labour ratio. It is thus noteworthy that during 1984-85/1994-95, rural units have moved relatively much more towards labour intensive processes of manufacturing. This has been happening through an absolute decline in capital:labour ratio in as many as 13 out of the 16 branches of production in rural, against only 7 in the urban areas. In some branches, e.g. textile products, wood and wood products, leather and leather products, non-metal products, (non-electrical) machine tools, repair of capital goods, etc., capital:labour ratio declined fairly sizeably among rural unorganized manufacturing units, between 1984-85/ 1994-95; the decline among the urban units was relatively milder, in most such branches. Consequently, the urban-rural gaps in capital:labour ratio have tended to widen during 1994-95, compared with 1984- 85, in a wide range of unorganized manufacturing activities. In normal course, this should lead to a relatively greater expansion of employment among the rural compared with the urban units. This indeed did happen in ten product lines in rural, compared with only seven in the urban areas, where a negative growth rate of capital:labour ratio is accompanied by a positive growth rate of employment, or a positive growth rate of the former has led to a negative growth rate of the latter. A one-to-one correspondence between changes in capital:labour ratio and in employment cannot, however, be insisted, since other structural parameters (e.g. growth rate of capital and capital:output ratio) do matter as well.

During the post-1994 years, the situation tilted further in favour of the urban unorganized manufacturing units. In 2000-01, capital:labour ratio was higher among urban units, compared with their rural counterparts, in all the sixteen branches of production. Except for basic metal industries, and, very marginally for beverages, rural units too witnessed a varying degree of increase in their capital:labour ratio in no fewer than 14 of the 16 branches of manufacturing. But then, the increase among urban units, occurring as it did among all the 16 branches of manufacturing, was of a much higher magnitude, so that the rural:urban gaps in capital:labour ratio became wider still in 2000-01, compared with those in 1994-95. The gaps became quite glaring in certain branches, e.g. wood, leather and chemicals and their respective products, machine tools, transport equipment, and repair of capital goods. In plain terms, the rural:urban dichotomy in terms of capital needed to create an additional workplace has widened in recent years so that the urban unorganized manufacturing units have become still more capital intensive, in comparison with their rural counterparts. To interpret it in a somewhat different manner, the rural manufacturing units, in spite of an unambiguous increase in their own capital:labour ratios, are still demanding much lower level of capital for every additional workplace created; in terms of conventional wisdom, the rural units, in relation to their urban counterparts, are thus continuing to discharge their responsibility of providing additional employment, in conformity with domestic resource endowment.

Second, the picture revealed by the whole group of the unorganized manufacturing holds true, in varying form and content, when we look at the three sub-groups, namely OAMEs, NDMEs and DMEs. To recapitulate, OAMEs are the 'tiniest' units, owned and managed by members of the household, while DMEs are the 'biggest' among the unorganized units, employing six or more persons, with at least one worker engaged from outside; NDMEs roughly stand between the two. The rural-urban gap in the direction and magnitude of change in capital:labour ratio are milder in respect of the tiniest units (OAMEs) and it becomes most manifest among the biggest of the three categories (DMEs). For example, during 1984-85/1994-95, among the OAMEs, the rural units witnessed a decline in capital:labour ratio in as many as 13 out of 16 (against 8 only in urban areas) product lines, while among the DMEs, the decline was witnessed by 3 among rural and none among the urban units. But then, as witnessed above in the case of the total of the unorganized manufacturing units, during 1994-95/2000-01, among the OAMEs, the rural units witnessed a decline in capital:labour ratio only in two product lines (wood and wood products, and, chemicals and chemical products), while it happened only in one branch (chemicals and chemical products) among urban units. Further, while among the urban DMEs, capital:labour ratio declined in none of the manufacturing segments, among the rural DMEs, the decline occurred in no fewer than five branches. In other words, the tiniest units (OAMEs) have one important characteristic common between rural and urban areas. It is the inescapable need for economizing on the use of fixed capital, in relation to labour, that makes many of them, relatively more commonly in the rural areas, to expand labour-use against their limited stock of capital. All OAMEs in rural (as also in urban) areas are not alike, most critically in terms of their access to commercial capital on the one hand, and in maintaining the labour cost advantage, on the other. Moreover, the intra-group variations in respect of other aspects of production organization, most ostensibly the availability and pricing of inputs, and product marketing, are likely to be far more sharper among OAMEs than among DMEs.

Third, Table 2A confirm the contrast between 1994-95/2000-01 and 1984-85/1994-95, in a much more telling manner. Going by growth rate of capital:labour ratios, for the pre- and post-1994 periods, it is abundantly clear that, for the tiniest of the rural manufacturing units, the period 1984-85/1994-95 was one of shedding capital intensity of employment. Not only that capital:labour ratio grew negatively in as many as 13 of the 16 manufacturing lines but the magnitude of decline was as high as 11.2 per cent in beverages, 17.7 per cent in textile products, 19.8 per cent in wood and wood products, 13.7 per cent in leather and leather products, 13.5 per cent in non-metallic mineral products, 20.6 per cent in metal products, 22.1 per cent in machine tools, 19.6 per cent in other manufacturing, and 13.7 per cent in repair of capital goods. The post-1994 years showed a diametrically opposite scenario; for these very production sectors, the growth rate of capital:labour ratio flipped over from negative values during 1984-85/1994-95 to 9.8 per cent, 25.3 per cent, -0.1 per cent, 5.4 per cent, 8.4 per cent, 11.3 per cent, 14.5 per cent, 26.4 per cent and 23.1 per cent, respectively, during 1994-95/2000-01. In plain terms, the period 1984-85/1994-95 clearly showed an attempt to provide greater employment for every unit of capital invested, practically among the whole lot of the tiny rural enterprises (rural-OAMEs). During 1994-95/2000-01, this tendency got considerably diluted, practically among all varieties of rural OAMEs. The same type of contrast occurred, *mutatis mutandis*, during 1984-85/1994-95 and 1994-95/2000-01, in respect of rural NDMEs and rural-DMEs. Perhaps, after the onset of economic reforms in 1991-92, and strong competitive propensities relegating every other market parameter to a subservient station, the increase in capital intensity of production was natural to follow. That it did happen, perhaps thunderously even among the tiniest of the rural manufacturing enterprises, clearly signals the supremacy of capital as an agent of production in the coming years of increasing liberalization, globalization and privatization.

Finally, as we move from OAMEs to NDMEs and finally to DMEs, capital:labour ratio, goes on rising, practically in each product line. For a given amount of capital, the most crucial social resource, especially in the rural economy, OAMEs offer employment many times more than DMEs. But then, productivity levels do not seem to move in favour of OAMEs. As we saw earlier in the VSI sector, it is the group of (modern) small scale industries that enjoy productivity levels many times higher than the traditional village/rural industries. In the present case, a fairly big majority of DMEs correspond with the (modern) small scale industries while a preponderant proportion of OAMEs would fall under the category of traditional village/rural industries. Substantial productivity differentials, therefore, exit as we move up on the size ladder of the unorganized manufacturing units. As we see in a while, the differentials are more pronounced in the rural areas.

4.2.1.2 Labour Productivity

Table 3 gives us the level and growth of labour productivity in the unorganized manufacturing units, in rural and urban India, for and between 1984-95 and 1994-95, and 1994-95 and 2000-01. A variety of contrasts come up at once. However, before we start counting those contrasts, it is essential to point out that productivity figures, especially those for OAMEs, both among the rural and urban units, are only indicative of the relative position of say, OAMEs against NDMEs, or, of NDMEs against DMEs. As we see later in Section

4.2.1.3 (Employment Scenario), a fairly sizeable proportion of labour involved in such categories, most noticeably OAMEs, are part-time workers. Since we have no information to convert part-time into full-time workers, we have to rest content with labour productivity figures, as rough and approximate indicators of the performance reality.

First, between 1984-85 and 1994-95, real *labour productivity* increased, in varying proportion, in a majority of sectors, both in rural and urban areas; nonetheless, it can hardly escape our notice that it declined in five branches in rural and nine in urban areas. It is particularly heartening to see that labour productivity in rural areas improved in all the nine non-agro based manufacturing (Codes 30-39) sub-sectors; in some of them, e.g. rubber, plastic and petroleum products, basic metal and alloys, non-metallic mineral products, machine and equipment, repair of capital goods, it improved quite sizably. At the same time, it is no less disturbing to see a decline in 5 out of 7 agro-based (Codes 20+21 to 29) sub-sectors; again, in some segments, e.g. paper and paper products, and, wood and wood products, it was a sizeable decline. A similar story of productivity increases mixed with decreases is discernible for the urban units as well, although in their case, the increases are relatively more weighty and the decreases relatively milder, compared with their rural counterparts.

It is equally interesting to see that a varying degree of productivity increase occurred commonly in rural and urban areas, in the same sub-sectors (e.g. cotton textiles-wool-silk- man-made fibre textiles, jute and other vegetable fibre textiles among the agro-based manufacturing, and rubber-plastic-petroleum products, non-metallic mineral products, basic metal and alloys, machine tools and equipment, and other manufacturing, among the non-agro based manufacturing). Common declines in productivity levels are also discernible in food products, beverages-tobacco, wood and wood products, paper and paper products and leather and leather products, all confined to agro-based manufacturing. In other sub-sectors, it was either a situation of productivity increase for rural and its decline in urban areas, or vice versa. In total terms, the rural areas offer a mix of productivity gains and losses, much as is the case with their urban counterparts. For unorganized manufacturing as a whole, rural areas showed a productivity gain of 2.1 per cent per annum against only 1.2 per cent among the urban units. But then, it is extremely vital to keep in mind that the productivity levels have been much lower among the rural compared with urban units, both in 1984-85 and 1994-95, in most of the manufacturing sectors.

The post-1994 years demonstrate a productivity scenario vastly different from the one that prevailed during 1984-85/1994-95. For example, during 1994-95/2000-01, productivity levels in rural areas witnessed a varying degree of increase in all the seven segments of agro-based manufacturing and all the nine segments of non-agro based manufacturing, compared with five and eight segments, respectively, in the urban areas. To some extent, the productivity estimates may be over- or under-estimates because of the presence of the part-time workers, yet in overall terms, the rural unorganized manufacturing enterprises seem to have put up a better performance in the post-1994 years, compared with their urban counterparts. That this should have been happening during the post-reform years may cause a pleasant surprise to public analysts. Perhaps, the pressure of outside competition, during the first 5-6 years of the post-reform regime, fell more directly on the urban unorganized manufacturing enterprises, especially those exposed to import onslaughts; rural enterprises might have enjoyed an interim reprieve.

Second, largely consistent with the rural-urban differences in capital:labour ratio, the rural-urban productivity gaps for the total of the unorganized manufacturing units as also for each of the three segments (i.e. OAMEs, NDMEs and DMEs) are discernible practically in each branch of manufacturing, in 1984-85, 1994-95 and 2000-01. Let us first look at the total of all unorganized manufacturing enterprises. In 1984-85, productivity was higher among the urban, compared with the rural, units in each of the sixteen branches of manufacturing. In some branches (e.g. food products, cotton textiles, chemicals and chemical products, metal products, and machine tools and equipment), productivity in urban units was three or four times as much high as among their rural counterparts; in many other branches (e.g., textile products, wood and wood products, paper and paper products, leather and leather products, non-metallic mineral products, basic metal goods, transport equipment, other manufacturing and repair of capital goods), the productivity differential was no less than 2:1. For the aggregate of the unorganized sector, the productivity of urban units was three times higher than that of the rural units. Such productivity differentials persisted in 1994-95 although, in a number of branches, the rural:urban gaps declined while in others, they increased. At the aggregate level, it was a decline. The scenario really changed substantially during 1994-95/2000-01 when productivity levels witnessed sizeable improvements, both among the rural and urban enterprises. Here again, as we notice below in Section 4.2.1.3., some element of over-estimation may be present ostensibly because the number of partptime workers increased far more sizably, especially among OAMEs, during 1994-95/2000-01. Be that as it may, in relative terms, productivity gains among the rural enterprises were more authentic so that, between 1994-95 and 2000-01, the rural:urban productivity gaps tended to decline, by varying degree, in as many as thirteen of the sixteen branches of manufacturing. The relatively better performance of the rural unorganized manufacturing units, in recent years, cannot obliterate the fact that productivity levels among the rural units are still way behind those among the urban units; in some branches, the differentials continue to be 3:1 or 2:1. This is indeed a cause of concern.

Such productivity differentials have been in existence way back in the sixties and the seventies. Clearly then, it is a reflection of the one-sided attention fixed on employment expansion in rural industry that explains the persistence of lower levels of productivity among the rural industrial units (Chadha, 1986: 164-66). It seems, in spite of the numerous policy initiatives undertaken to promote industrialization in rural India, the basic pre-requisites such as the needed degree of skill formation, technological exposures, organizational improvements, market linkages, and above all, infrastructural backup, all intended to boost productivity levels, have been favouring urban units far more than the rural units (*ibid*: 164).

Third, the types of rural:urban productivity differentials observed earlier for the total of unorganized manufacturing, are also discernible, in varying form and content, for each of the three layers, namely OAMEs, NDMEs and DMEs; with stray exceptions, productivity is higher among the urban, compared with the rural units, in each of the three segments. It is nonetheless true that over time, especially during the post-1994 years, the rural:urban gaps have tended to decline, in a wide range of manufacturing areas, among OAMEs, NDMEs and DMEs. For example, for the total of OAMEs, the ratio of urban to rural productivity fell from 2.33 in 1994-95 to 1.66 in 2000-01; among individual production lines, it declined in as many as fourteen of the sixteen lines. In spite of the narrowing of the productivity gaps, the relative disadvantage of the rural-OAMEs continued to be quite sharp, even in 2000-01, in certain areas of manufacturing; the conspicuous examples are food products, wood and wood products and leather and leather products, among the agro-based manufacturing, and rubber-plastic products, basic metal and alloy products, metal products and parts, machine tools and equipment, transport equipment and parts, other manufacturing, and repair of capital goods, among the non-agro based manufacturing. But then, such rural: urban productivity differentials among DMEs, declined as they did, between 1994-95 and 2000-01, in as many as ten of the sixteen production lines, continue to be fairly high in 2000-01, in a number of manufacturing branches; the most noticeable examples are food products, beverages, cotton textiles-wool synthetic-textile products, textile products, and leather and leather products, under the agro-based segment of manufacturing, and chemicals and chemical products, other manufacturing and repair of capital goods, in the non-agro based manufacturing. An overview of the OAMEs, in contrast to the DMEs, clearly shows that the locational disadvantage of rural units is relatively milder in respect of agro-based OAMEs, compared with their non-agro based counterparts. In a broad sense, this is a reflection of higher levels of technology- and skill-intensive production pre-requisites in the case of non-agro based manufacturing which the urban OAMEs are able to organize somewhat better than their rural counterparts; on the other hand, the technology and skill gaps between rural-DMEs and urban-DMEs are not as sharp, as in the case of OAMEs, so that the productivity gaps between urban-DMEs and rural-DMEs in a number of non-agro based manufacturing lines are milder, most noticeably in 2000-01.

Finally, thanks to the low levels of their productivity in 1984-85, the rural units registered a higher productivity growth during the next decade (1984-85/1994-95) in a large number of product lines under each of the three categories. Nevertheless, the reverse too holds in many branches. In any case, it looks a little pleasing that, for example, productivity growth for the total of all unorganized manufacturing units grew annually, during 1984-85/1994-95, by 2.1 per cent in rural compared with 1.2 per cent in urban areas; for rural-DMEs, it was as high as 4.6 per cent against just 0.6 per cent for urban-DMEs, and for NDMEs, it was 2.1 per cent in rural against -0.9 per cent in urban areas. But then, an equally non-pleasing fact is that the growth of productivity among the tiniest rural manufacturing enterprises (OAMEs), that constitute the bulwark of the rural non-farm economy, could not go beyond 1.3 per cent per annum against a fairly impressive high of 2.8 per cent per annum for their urban counterparts. Happily, the situation improved dramatically during 1994-95/2000-01. For the total of all manufacturing units, productivity grew in the rural areas at as high a rate as 6.4 per cent against 2.5 per cent in the urban areas. Among rural-DMEs, it grew by 6.1 per cent against 2.9 per cent among urban-DMEs; among rural-NDMEs, it grew by 5.7 per cent against 4.6 per cent among urban-NDMEs; and most happily, it grew by 6.4 per cent among rural-OAMEs against a meager 0.5 per cent among urban-OAMEs. Going into individual production sectors, at each of the three layers of the unorganized manufacturing, the rural areas put up a more creditable performance; for example, among the total of all manufacturing branches, growth rate of labour productivity increased, by varying degree, in fourteen of the sixteen production lines among the rural enterprises against eleven among their urban counterparts. In spite of this pleasing scenario, it must again be underlined that rural-urban productivity gaps, although narrowing down in many product lines under each of the three categories of enterprises, still remain a big challenge to rural unorganized industry. Given the extreme preponderance of OAMEs in the rural industrial sector, the productivity gaps in this segment continue to be a cause for worry, in particular.

4.2.1.3 Employment Scenario

As was the case with productivity growth (Table 3), employment too shows a mixture of positive and negative growth rates (Table 4). In overall terms, urban units have been doing better, first during 1984-85/1994-95, and then during 1994-95/2000-01. A few significant features need to be underlined.

First, during 1984-85/1994-95, employment in rural unorganized manufacturing as a whole witnessed an annual decline of 1.7 per cent . The decline was not uniform among the three layers of the unorganized manufacturing sector. For the total of the tiniest enterprises (OAMEs), it was 2.0 per cent followed by 2.5 per cent for the middle-level units (NDMEs); only for the 'bigger' sized units (DMEs which roughly correspond to 'modern' small scale industries under the VSI sector; see Table 1), employment witnessed a positive growth of 2.1 per cent per annum. In plain terms, the process of mushrooming of self-employing tiny manufacturing enterprises seems to have come under arrest; to a slightly lower extent, this seems to be happening in urban areas as well. A more convincing proof of this trend comes from a combination of positive growth rate of productivity (last row, Table 3) and a negative growth rate of employment (last row, Table 4), both for rural and urban areas. On the basis of the employment experience during 1984-85/1994-95, it was probably pre-mature, and somewhat risky, for some analysts, to declare that the tiniest of the unorganized manufacturing enterprises (OAMEs) had started losing their ground, much more in rural than in the urban areas, as a source of non-farm self-employment; the subsequent developments disproved such apprehensions. Yet, it is all too clear that, during 1984-85/1994-95, all good and dynamic features (e.g. a 7.2 per cent increase in capital:labour ratio, a 4.3 per cent growth of real labour productivity, and a 2.1 per cent growth rate of employment, etc; see last row of Tables 2,3 and 4) seemed to be getting concentrated in rural-DMEs, in contrast to what was going on with rural-OAMEs (e.g. a –12.1 per cent increase in capital:labour ratio, a 1.3 per cent growth of real labour productivity, and a –2.0 per cent growth rate of employment). All these developments threw strong signals that scale economies had started coming in, that proliferation of self-employing numbers (typical of OAMEs) was not a sustainable proposition, that employment expansion independent of productivity growth could not go for long, that technology upgrading was the life vein for production units to survive in an open market economy, and so on.

The post-1994 developments gave a kind of new lease of life to rural-OAMEs although the onward march earlier registered by rural-DMEs during the pre-1994 years, continued as well. For example, among rural-OAMEs, the growth rate of capital:labour ratio improved dramatically from –12.1 per cent during 1984-85/1994-95 to as high as 9.4 per cent during 1994-95/2000-01, the growth rate of real labour productivity improved from 1.3 per cent to 6.4 per cent, and the rate of growth of employment too improved sizably from – 2.0 to 1.2 per cent. But then, varying degree of improvement, in each of these development indicators, had occurred among the two upper layers (NDMEs and DMEs) of the rural unorganized manufacturing as well; For example, for rural-DMEs, improvement in the rate of growth of capital:labour ratio from 7.2 per cent during 1984-85/1994-95 to 9.9 per cent during 1994-95/2000-01, of labour productivity from 4.3 per cent to 6.1 per cent, and of employment from 2.1 per cent to 2.9 per cent, clearly point towards further strengthening of their position in the rural industrial sector.

Second, during 1984-85/1994-95, at the level of the unorganized manufacturing as a whole, both rural and urban units commonly suffered employment setbacks in food products, cotton textiles-woolen synthetic, textile products, rubber-plastic-petroleum-coal products, basic metal and alloys, and transport equipment and parts. The common setback is very clearly discernible for all these sectors, in respect of OAMEs also. And it is visible for four sectors of NDMEs and five of DMEs as well. In plain words, there are a number of unorganized manufacturing branches where employment had been shrinking, by varying degree, during 1984-85/1994-95, both in rural and urban units, irrespective of the scale of their operation or the nature and degree of technological upgradation effected by them. To put it differently, a fairly big proportion of the unorganized manufacturing sector, irrespective of its locale, was throwing many of their workers out of job; the axe seemed to have fallen far too heavily on self-employing workers (*a la* much higher negative employment growth rates in the declining OAME segments). In short, during 1984-85/1994-95, *a big part of the unorganized sector was thus bleeding under rising dis-employment*.

But then, the situation seemed to have improved during 1994-95/2000-01, compared with 1984-85/1994-95, if we do not take cognizance of the rising proportion of part-time workers during the post-1994 years. For rural unorganized manufacturing as a whole (Cols. 8-9, Table 4), the growth rate of employment improved dramatically in a majority of production sectors. The most striking improvement was from –5.54 per cent to 11.87 per cent in textile products, from –4.98 per cent to 11.98 per cent in chemicals and chemical products, from –4.25 per cent to 17.48 per cent in basic metal and alloys, from –3.42 per cent to 5.03 per cent in metal products, from –2.95 per cent to 9.67 per cent in machine tools and parts, and from –6.62 per cent to 1.08 per cent in transport equipment and parts; on the other hand, the two most disappointing sectors were other manufacturing and repair of capital goods, both of which suffered huge setbacks in growth rate of their employment. In any case, on the whole, the post-1994 gains in the growth rate of employment were far more substantial than the losses so that at the aggregate level, employment growth rate for the total of rural unorganized manufacturing improved from –1.70 per cent during 1984-85/1994-95 to 1.35 per cent during 1994-95/2000-01.

Third, the employment setbacks during 1984-85/1994-95, were far too widely spread among rural compared with urban units. For example, among the sixteen production branches, employment declined, in varying degree, in as many as nine of rural-OAME branches against only seven in their urban counterparts, in ten groups of rural against only six of urban-NDME branches, and in nine in rural against seven in urban unorganized manufacturing as a whole. As pointed out earlier, only for DMEs, the rural and urban enterprises are doing equally unwell; in either locale, nearly one-half of production branches showed a decline in employment. But then, going plainly by the number of workers, things improved substantially, during the post-1994 phase, from the bottom to the top of the unorganized sector, both in the rural as well as urban areas. Consequently, the relatively severer sufferance of the rural areas, carried over from the pre-1994 phase, appeared to have got mitigated, in varying degree, in a number of production lines. For example, during 1994-95/2000-01, among rural-OAMEs, a negative employment growth rate was registered by six branches against five among urban-OAMEs; during 1984-95/1994-95, it was nine branches among rural-OAMEs against seven among urban-OAMEs. Similar improvements are clearly discernible for rural-NDMEs, rural-DMEs, and the total of rural unorganized manufacturing enterprises against their urban counterparts. Going by the sheer number of workers, we may be tempted to declare that employment scenario improved, during the post-reform period, in many branches of the rural unorganized manufacturing sector, in tandem with its urban counterpart. Nonetheless, it is pretty much clear that in terms of the rate of growth of employment, the rural unorganized manufacturing sector is still suffering a relative disadvantage, both in terms of the number of sectors involved, and the relative gaps in the growth rates of employment. And most importantly, the vastly changing composition of workers between full- and part-time workers, during 1994-95/2000-01, brings in new dimensions on the employment front.

Finally, it is advisable also to look at employment situation in terms of absolute numbers and in terms of part- and full-time workers (Table 4A); as we shall see in a while, absolute numbers do convey the sufferance of rural-OAMEs in a more telling manner. It is at once clear that, in terms of the sheer magnitude of job losses, during 1984-85/1994-95, the bleeding was more profuse in rural against urban enterprises. For example, at the aggregate level, between 1984-85 and 1994-95, as many as 4.15 million of the rural unorganized manufacturing units were closed and 4.14 million rural workers lost their jobs while 0.40 million additional jobs became available to their urban brethren in spite of the closure of 1.07 million units. It is especially disconcerting that 90.6 per cent of the rural workers losing their jobs were full-time workers while in the urban areas, the job loss was confined exclusively to part-time workers. Understandably, because of their numerical preponderance, rural-OAMEs bore an overwhelmingly big share of the job losses; as high as 92.0 per cent of the unorganized manufacturing units facing closure in the rural areas came from the OAME segment alone and 88.4 per cent of rural workers facing dis-employment belonged to this segment alone; the remaining job losses went to the share of rural-NDMEs since no job loss was reported by rural-DMEs. Inasmuch as the job losses in the rural areas were very largely because of closure of units, nearly 91.0 per cent of the job losers in the rural-OAME segment were full-time workers while their percentage in the urban areas was around 50.0 per cent only. Yet again, the proportion of part-time workers engaged in rural-OAMEs increasing from 14.8 per cent in 1984-85 to 16.2 per cent in 1994-95 (contrasted to its decline from 10.3 per cent to 6.2 per cent in urban areas) against a 20.0 per cent decline in the number of full-time workers, unambiguously testifies to the distress of the self-employing rural tiny sector against a 'market-savvy' wage-employment restructuring that had been the main-stay of the urban labour market.

As observed earlier in respect of capital:labour ratio, productivity levels and employment growth, things appeared to be improving during the post-1994 years. It is evident now that for rural-OAMEs, this was rather a myopic illusion. Perhaps, looking at the numbers, in a detailed manner, would show how this is so. During 1994-95/2000-01, the number of rural-OAMEs increased by 1.52 million units (a net increase of 16.0 per cent) while the number of rural-NDMEs and rural-DMEs declined by 0.04 million (a net decline of 5.82 per cent) and 0.05 million units (a net decline of 16.12 per cent), respectively. Employment in rural-OAMEs increased as well, by 1.3 million workers (5.62 per cent); it increased by 0.10 million and 0.45 million in rural-NDMEs and rural-DMEs also. But then, the real caveat comes in. The whole lot of 1.3 million incremental workers, coming up in the rural-OAME segment, during 1994-95/2000-01, were part-time workers; more than one-third of the incremental workers coming up in rural-NDME segment but none in the rural-DME segment were on part-time basis. In other words, what was lost by the most domineering segment of the rural unorganized manufacturing sector (rural-OAMEs) during 1984-85/1994-95 was 3.7 million of full-time jobs, and what was later recouped during 1994-95/2000-01 was 1.39 million of part-time jobs; in fact, rural-OAMEs lost another 0.09 million full-time jobs even during 1994-95/2000-01.

The statistical delusion is thus broken. It is clear that the most domineering segment of the rural unorganized manufacturing sector (rural-OAMEs), consisting of self-employing household enterprises, did not come off so well during the post-reform years, as did another segment (rural-DMEs), especially from the point of the composition and level of employment. We are thus persuaded to say that, in the case of rural-OAMEs, it is largely a case of expansion under duress. After losing a total of 3.9 million rural-OAME units during 1984-85/1994-95, only 1.5 million rural-OAME units were recouped during 1994-95/2000-01. In other words, in 2000-01, compared with 1984-85, the number of rural-OAME units were nearly 18.0 per cent lower. Again, after losing as many as 4.07 million (3.71 million full-time and 0.36 million part-time) jobs during 1984-85, the rural-OAMEs could recoup 1.3 million (-0.09 million full-time and 1.39 million part-time) jobs during 1994-95/2000-01. In plain terms, in 2000-01, compared with 1984-85, the number of self-employed workers in rural-OAMEs was 12.63 per cent lower. Further, the number of full-time workers, engaged in rural-OAMEs, declined from 18.66 millions in 1984-85 to 14.96 millions in 1994-95 and further down to 14.87 millions in 2000-01 while the number of those engaged on part-time basis declined from 3.25 millions in 1984-85 to 2.89 millions in 1994-95 but recouped to 4.28 millions in 2000-01. In other words, in 2000-01, compared with 1984-85, the number of full-time workers employed in rural-OAMEs was more than 20.0 per cent lower, while the number of their part-time counterparts was 31.7 per cent higher. Still more pointedly, the whole lot of additional rural-OAMEs coming up during 1994-95/2000-01 was manned by part-time workers only. The distress is obvious.

What led to the massive closure of rural-OAMEs and the associated steep decline in employment, during 1984-85/1994-95, and the subsequent revival of some of them, and a sizeable tilt in favour of part-time work, during 1994-95/2000-01? It seems, when agricultural growth picked up well during the 1980s, especially in the lagging eastern states, non-farm activities including a host of rural industries too grew fast. The initial spurt was in the nature of *ad hoc* response to rising demands from agriculture, partly for production and partly for consumption purposes. The hard yardsticks of price efficiency, product quality, rural-urban competitiveness, etc. did not immediately intervene. But then, after a while, market considerations seemed to start overtaking the *ad hoc* adjustments. This tendency gained strength when the early phase of limited economic reforms and marketization ensued in the late eighties, and got more intensified after full-fledged economic reforms came in July 1991. What came up as an *ad hoc* source of additional household income, could not be interpreted as a market creature. When the economy started maturing, and markets started expanding, non-market creatures naturally faced a varying degree of squeeze, if not outright extinction. A part of the rural-OAME story is indeed of the kind caricaturized above.

But then, the recent story of nearly the whole lot of the additional rural-OAMEs coming up during 1994-95/2000-01, being manned by part-time family workers only, must essentially be seen, *inter alia*, in terms of employment setbacks suffered by other sectors of the rural economy, most pointedly, by agriculture and its allied sectors. It needs hardly to be emphasized that if employment in other sectors was not growing, or was growing at a much slacker pace during the post-1994, compared with the pre-1994 years, rural job aspirants would have started self-employing themselves, in a variety of ways. For those additional job seekers not getting self-employed in agriculture, or not wishing to be absorbed in agriculture, the next best choice to get self-absorbed is to go to the other commodity sectors. Rural industry is the most obvious choice; incidentally, the proportion of self-employed rural male workers declined from 61.0 per cent in 1993-94 to 58.0 per cent in 1999-2000, and of rural female workers, from 59.0 per cent to 57.0 percent (Chadha, 2003: Table 5). Admittedly, for a majority of rural job aspirants, self-employment is not as much negotiable in the services/tertiary sector as it is in the commodity sectors of agriculture or industry. On the contrary, if services/tertiary sector employment too is suffering serious setbacks, and wage-paid employment is not easy to come by, people would flock back either to agriculture or the other commodity sector, i.e. industry. It is the sum total of many-sided employment setbacks that seems to have ushered rural work seekers into the self-employing segment of the rural industrial sector (OAMEs) without, at the same time, severing their connection with agriculture. That is how, nearly the whole lot of incremental workforce joining rural-OAMEs during 1994-95/2000-01 consists of part-time workers.

To buttress our argument of many-sided employment setbacks leading to the increased incidence of part-time employment among rural-OAMEs, let us look at the recent rates of growth of employment in the major economic sectors. Most noticeably, the rate of growth of employment in agriculture fell from 1.38 per cent during 1983/1993-94 to 0.18 per cent only during 1993-94/1999-2000 (Chadha-Sahu, 2002: 2014); it fell more depressingly among non-crop segments, e.g. from 1.89 per cent to –1.12 per cent in forestry-logging, from 4.09 per cent to –6.37 per cent in fishing, and from 3.84 per cent to –2.28 per cent in mining-quarrying. It fell in many other, non-agricultural, sectors as well, e.g. from 3.72 per cent to 1.81 per cent in trade, from 5.99 per cent to 2.51 per cent in finance-insurance-real estate, from 3.13 per cent to 0.32 per cent in community-social-personal services, and so on. In fact, the employment squeeze in community-social-personal services encompassed nearly each one of its constituents; for example, the rate of growth of employment fell from 4.92 per cent during 1983/1993-94 to –15.60 per cent during 1993-94 in sanitary services, from 2.27 per cent to 0.73 per cent among medical and health functionaries, from 3.74 per cent to –4.62 per cent in community services, from 7.72 per cent to –10.07 per cent in recreational and cultural services, and from 3.75 per cent to –0.63 per cent in respect of personal services (*ibid*: 2014). Most certainly, the extraordinary squeeze in employment in a wide range of community-social-personal services owes itself to curtailed public expenditure after the onset of economic reforms, and for a number of workers relieved from these services, as also from other sectors in the rural economy. Venturing into some self-employing rural industrial activity, *albeit* on a part-time basis, was a more acceptable choice, both because agriculture could not absorb them as full-time workers and because the other option of remaining unemployed could never be acceptable. But then, the most convincing part of our argument about their absorption into the rural industrial sector, as part-time entrepreneurs, in addition to being part-time helpers in family-based agriculture, comes from noting that the rate of growth of employment in the agro-based segment indeed improved from 1.45 per cent during 1983/1993-94 to 2.16 per cent during 1993-94/1999-2000 while in the more difficult, technology-savvy, education-and skill-intensive non-agro based segment, it declined from 3.58 per cent to as low as 1.03 per cent (*ibid*, 2014). We are thus led to a depressing scenario. Rural-OAMEs are acting as a sponge; they are holding on a sizeable proportion of their workers on part-time basis primarily as an adjunct to agriculture, independent of what the market for industrial goods would brook in the days to come. This poses some policy dilemma.

The foregoing analysis unambiguously shows that the operational disadvantages among the tiniest of the rural manufacturing units (OAMEs) could not be overcome, all these years, through the package of protective state support; such rural units have to stand on their own, in competition with their urban counterparts, and for that, improvement in productivity is the most inescapable pre-requisite. In recent years, productivity improvement did occur among rural-OAMEs, just as it did among rural-NDMEs and rural-DMEs (Table 3A). Nonetheless, a high growth rate of productivity among rural-OAMEs could not hide the extremely low levels at which their productivity was operating even in 2000-01, most ostensibly, in comparison with rural-DMEs. It can thus be concluded that *relatively bigger-sized rural manufacturing units, unorganized though they may be, are likely to fare well in competition with their urban counterparts, in sharp contrast to the tiniest of the rural units which continue to reel under numerous technology, marketing and quality infirmities.* Perhaps, in the same product line, the tiniest units (OAMEs) are more deeply embedded into local rural life and economy, and face a dwindling demand prospect while their bigger-sized counterparts (say, DMEs), many amongst them being located in the 'rural areas' out of a different set of considerations, are more easily linked with the nearby and/or distant urban economy, and sometimes with external market. While, in most cases, it is the economic distress which causes a local proliferation of (self-employment in) rural OAMEs, as it was indeed the case during the post-1994 years, it is a well-calculated economic choice to locate some DMEs out of the urban-municipal limits, in numerous cases, not far from the economic heartland of towns and cities. The two groups of rural manufacturing are thus totally different entities. That it is indeed so is also proved through the differential behaviour of employment during recent years. In brief, *the rural OAME segment is in trouble, most visibly on the employment front, and the policy administrators can no more take for granted its so-called 'vast employment potential'.* Such illusions must go.

4.2.2 Inter- and Intra-Group Productivity Variations

In section 4.2.1.2, we developed a clear view of the lower level of productivity per worker in all categories of rural industries, compared with their urban counterparts. The rural-urban gaps were manifest even in respect of the lowliest of the industrial ventures (i.e. OAMEs) although, as we climb higher on the industrial ladder, the differences tend to become larger in some cases, and narrow down in others. In any case, the inferior performance of the rural units stands out unquestioned and, in most cases, for reasons of institutional, infrastructural and technological backwardness.

We have a few interesting facts to take note of from our own April-June 2000 field survey. Table 5 confirms, once again, the lower level of productivity/worker in rural units, compared with their urban counterparts in the corresponding employment size category. What is really important to underline is the much higher level of the coefficient of variation among the smaller rural units employing 2, 3-4 and 5-6 persons, while it works the other way round when we are confronted with units employing 7-8 and more than 8 persons. The production bottlenecks are thus more glaring among some of the tinier units located in the rural areas while for the bigger ones among them, such handicaps get mollified. This point gets adequately corroborated if we look at the minimum and the maximum productivity levels achieved by rural against urban units, in each employment size category. For example, among the rural units employing 3 or 4 persons, the minimum level of productivity/worker is Rs. 5000 only against a maximum of Rs. 16,50,000; in urban areas, the minimum and the maximum for this category stand at Rs. 5975 and Rs. 8,55,000. Still more telling is the appalling gap between the minimum productivity level of the rural and that of the urban units, for each employment size category. In other words, the 'most inefficient urban unit' is still way ahead of its rural counterpart. *The inherent weaknesses of the rural enterprises are thus adequately encapsulated in the low and highly uneven levels of their productivity/worker.* There are studies to show that productivity and earnings per worker in some of these enterprises are lower than what is available even in agriculture. The rural industrial enterprises of this description are thus only an excuse for non-farm ventures; in concrete economic terms, their situation is no better than 'all is fish that comes to his net'.

The depressing working conditions in the rural industrial sector, as sketched out in the preceding analysis, are directly responsible for depressing *productivity levels*. Table 6 bears adequate testimony to this effect. For each industrial segment, per worker productivity is significantly lower in the rural compared with that in its urban counterpart. For example, it is only 60.2 per cent as high in the rural-OAMEs compared with that in the urban-OAMEs; only 61.0 per cent in the rural-NDMEs against that in their urban counterparts. Rather interestingly, per worker productivity in the organized segment is a little higher in the rural areas. As is borne out by empirical studies, the presence of technically-trained personnel, management experts, technology-in-use, market linkages, etc. are all at par in the rural against urban organized industrial units (Chadha, 1999b: 894-99). Most importantly, in the organized industrial segment, the working environment and economic benefits accruing to rural workers do not vary as significantly from their urban counterparts, as they do in the unorganized segment. The productivity setbacks to the rural unorganized units is, therefore, a foregone conclusion.

It is equally interesting to see productivity setbacks as we move down on the firm-size hierarchy, both in the rural and urban areas. For example, within the rural areas, productivity in OAMEs is just about 3.6 per cent, in NDMEs about 7.7 per cent, and in DMEs nearly 8.6 per cent, of that in the organized industrial segment. Such differences are discernible in the urban areas as well but are of considerably lower magnitude Since the tiny segment (i.e. OAMEs) constitutes an extremely preponderant proportion of the rural industrial sector with all its productivity and associated infirmities, it is directly responsible for keeping the overall productivity level in the rural industrial sector just about 42.0 per cent of what it is in the urban sector.

4.3 Small-Scale Rural Industry

Through an extensive nationwide survey of small-scale industries, which stood registered as on March 31, 1988, extremely useful insights came up on their operation, separately for rural and urban areas. A similar survey of small-scale industries, although based on a much smaller sample size, was undertaken during 1994-95 also. In this section, we bring out some important insights emanating out of these two surveys; for fixed investment at the two-digit level of industrial grouping, the rural-urban break-up is not available for the 1994-95 survey. To remind ourselves, the small-scale industrial sector consists of a highly disparate group of units, varying markedly in terms of capital employed, technology used, number of persons employed, the range of market operation, linkages with higher echelons of industrial enterprises, and so on. All these details are not available separately for units in rural and urban areas. All the same, rural-urban contrasts can be captured in a variety of ways.

Tables 7 and 8 set out rural-urban and backward:non-backward area differences in respect of a few important indicators. As expected, for rural areas, the share of each of the total fixed investment, investment in plant and machinery, and employment is much lower than their share in the number of units while the reverse is true for metropolitan cities; for urban areas, all the shares generally move in tandem. Consequently, per unit levels are the lowest for rural areas, next higher for urban areas, and much higher for metropolitan cities, practically for all indicators. We are thus introduced to a different complexion of small-scale industry operating in rural India contrasted with that in the urban and metropolitan cities. *On an average, during 1987-88, for a small-scale unit in urban areas, investment in fixed assets or in plant and machinery was 50-60 per cent higher while the number of persons employed was only about 25-30 per cent more than with its rural counterpart. The rural-urban gaps have tended to widen, most markedly in respect of employment per unit, during 1987-88/1994-95.* It implies that the employment content of every unit of capital invested is relatively higher with rural units compared with urban units, and still higher compared with metropolitan units. In recent years, the employment content of capital invested in rural units has gone up still further.

Table 9 gives distribution of small-scale industrial units and their production in terms of 4-5 major (semi-aggregated) industrial categories, separately for rural and urban and backward and non-backward areas. It is interesting to see that during 1987-88/1994-95, on an average, as many as 44-46 per cent of the units in rural areas were engaged in manufacturing/assembling activities and they commanded a tidy share of 71-76 per cent of rural industrial output in this sector. This pattern held true for urban and metropolitan areas too, as also for backward and non-backward areas. It follows that among different industrial activities, manufacturing/assembling is relatively more productive, irrespective of their locale. In particular, repairing/servicing and job-work activities contribute an extremely small proportion to output in relation to the numerical strength of workers employed. Such units have very small turnover although they have a tendency to proliferate in response to locale-specific demand.

Table 10 looks at the share of rural areas as also of the backward areas, for the same set of industrial activities as in Table 9. The small size and inferior position of the rural units is evident from the fact that under each type of industrial activity, their share of production is smaller than their share in the number of units. In metropolitan cities, it is the reverse while in respect of urban units, there is a nodding balance between the two shares. The backward area units share the fate of rural units.

Table 11 gives a more detailed picture, for 1987-88 and 1994-95, on rural areas' share in the number of small-scale units, employment, fixed investment (for 1987-88 only) and production, for 18 two-digit level major industry groups. It is pertinent to point out that the two-digit classification on which Table 11 is based cannot give a highly satisfactory rural-urban comparisons; for any industry group, the detailed composition at 3- or 4-digit level may strikingly differ between rural and urban areas. In particular, industrial activities based on raw materials originating in rural areas (e.g. food processing, beverages and tobacco products, cotton textiles, wool and silk textiles, wood, paper and leather products, etc.) would have an entirely different competitive complexion compared with those which draw upon materials, skills, markets, etc. from the urban areas. The picture at 3- or 4-digit level is not available, and accordingly, the rural-urban comparisons at 2-digit level would be reflective of broad contrasts only.

Although the relative placement of the four types of shares differ from one industry group to the other, in rural and in urban (inclusive of metropolitan) areas, yet, on a broad plane, it is fairly obvious that for most of the agro-processing industries (industry division 20-21 to 29) in the rural areas, the employment, investment and production shares do not deviate much from one another. It is equally noticeable, however, that the share of rural units in all these categories is much higher than the other three shares. It follows that rural units in all these branches are of relatively smaller size, most notably in terms of per unit level of output. Such rural-urban differentials were discernible earlier also when we looked at the employment and production structure of the unorganized manufacturing sector.

Many among the other set of industries (industry division 30 to 38) portray a sharp contrast. For example, for rural units engaged in the manufacture of rubber and plastic products, chemicals and chemical products, non-metallic mineral products, basic metal products, electrical machinery, etc., there is a remarkable balance among the four types of shares. These are the modern small-scale industries located in rural areas perhaps under the special development programmes and possibly due to the well-measured economic calculus of urban entrepreneurs, and so on. The tendency of proliferation, discernible on a subdued scale, under the agro-based group of industries, is ruled out in their case; their location and operation are selective and hopefully governed by a pre-calculated economic rationale of the entrepreneurs engaged in such enterprises. The outcome is thus reassuring; the case of rural industrialization need not necessarily be prompted by employment consideration alone; in the matter of fixed investment and production shares too, such industries in rural areas compare well with their urban counterparts.

4.4 Organized Manufacturing

Contrary to the conventional thinking, rural India has a fairly noticeable presence of organized manufacturing also. For example, in 1997-98, rural areas' share was 33.7 per cent in organized manufacturing units, 40.6 per cent in fixed capital, 32.3 per cent in employment and 33.5 percent in net value added, and so on (see bottom of Table 13). *It is essential to emphasize in particular that the share of rural areas in all these aspects has witnessed a steady increase all through the nineties.* It is no less important to emphasize that the presence of organized manufacturing in rural India is discernible, in varying degree, in each major area of manufacturing. For example, again in 1997-98, 50.0 per cent of the organized manufacturing units engaged in the manufacture of food products, 24.0 per cent of those engaged in beverages, tobacco, etc., 41.0 per cent of those in cotton textiles, 62.2 per cent in jute, mesta and other fibre textiles, 45.0 per cent in wood and wood products, 29.0 per cent in leather and its products, 59.0 per cent in non-metallic mineral product units, and 43 per cent of those in storage and warehousing service units, were located in rural areas (Govt. of India, Annual Survey of Industries 1997-98, 1999: 98-106). Clearly, therefore, organized manufacturing is an important, and an expanding, component of the rural industrial economy.

It needs, however, to be reiterated that unlike the unorganized manufacturing activities, especially those carried on in the tiny sector (OAMEs) in an *ad hoc* or semi-commercial milieu, organized manufacturing units in the rural areas are largely the outcome of well thought out locational strategies. For example, these may reflect a deliberate choice of the state in respect of public sector units, or an attempt of the private sector to avoid urban congestion (and its associated 'labour problems') on the one hand, and to avail of the numerous facilities/concessions expressly offered by the state, under different programmes aimed at fostering rural industrialization, on the other. In that case, *many among the organized manufacturing units, especially those in the private sector, would tend to be located around or fairly close to the outer limits of towns and cities.* The Indian experience of organized manufacturing expansion is replete with numerous examples of such location choices; in recent decades, many towns and cities have witnessed a phenomenal expansion of industrial activity, practically along each of the roads that lead into such towns/cities. Definition-wise, these industries are rural but operationally, these are urban. In any case, rural workers do also chip off a share of employment in such 'on-the-border-of the-town' industries. In *de facto* terms, we should not expect the rural (in contrast to the urban) segment of the organized manufacturing to be faring as poorly as we saw earlier in the case of rural unorganized units (widely spread into the countryside) in contrast to their urban unorganized counterpart. The available data uphold our faith, in more ways than one.

4.4.1 Performance of Organized Manufacturing

Under the auspices of the Annual Survey of Industries (ASI), separate information on rural and urban organized manufacturing (factory sector) started coming in from 1987-88 onwards; until recent months the latest available ASI survey data were for 1997-98. Our analysis of rural (and urban) organized manufacturing is thus confined to the period 1987-88/1997-98. Incidentally, these are the years that witnessed the most formidable changes in the industrial policy regime ever effected in the history of India's planned economic development. With the available data, we should, therefore, be able to develop ideas on how the rural organized industry (in relation to its urban counterpart) is faring, most importantly, around the time that Indian industry is tending to become a part of the global production and trading systems.

4.4.1.1 Employment Expansion:

We begin with growth rates for a few important variables. Table 12 clearly suggests that the organized manufacturing is a sharp contrast to its unorganized counterpart. For example, in most sectors, employment of workers expanded, in some sub-sectors fairly sizeably, during 1987-88/1997-98, both in rural and urban areas (Col. 3). The most remarkable feature is that in each of the ten non-agro based sectors, and in six out of the nine agro-based segments, the growth rate of employment of workers has been strikingly higher in rural manufacturing units compared with their urban counterparts. An equally striking rural-urban contrast is that, during 1987-88/1997-98, only in two of the nineteen manufacturing sectors (viz. jute-hemp-mesta textiles and repair services), employment of rural workers declined while for their urban brethren, a negative growth of employment was discernible in three of the nine agro-based sectors and in four of the ten non-agro based segments. As a matter of fact, negative employment growth rates for the whole period 1987-88/1997-98 in the two rural sectors were primarily due to excessive shrinkages in investment, output, employment, etc. in the years upto 1992-93; beyond 1992-93, both jute-hemp-mesta textiles and repair services staged a fast recovery and a splendid expansion in each aspect of their existence. A similar story of recovery followed by fast expansion is discernible for the urban units as well.

From an overall point of view, the organized rural manufacturing throws up an extremely pleasing employment scenario during the nineties. Employment expansion in rural factories was fairly high (say, 5.0 per cent or more per annum) in as many as 10 of the 19 manufacturing sectors (against only five in the urban areas); for the total of organized manufacturing, employment grew every year, during 1987-88/1997-98, by 4.7 per cent in rural, against just 1.7 per cent in urban areas.

In respect of utilities, however, the position for rural areas is not as pleasing. For example, the number of workers engaged in rural electricity declined steeply by as much as 5.8 per cent per annum, during 1987-88/1997-98. It seems, the formidable shrinkage of public sector employment in rural electricity was consciously effected, possibly under the dictates of the new economic compulsions, a concerted drive towards higher capacity utilization and higher production efficiency; as was to be expected, increase in productivity ensued (Col.6) and that more than compensated for the loss of jobs.

As discussed earlier (Section 4.2.1.3), between 1984-85 and 1994-95, the unorganized manufacturing lost as many as 4.14 million jobs/work places while its urban counterpart gained 0.40 million additional jobs. On the contrary, in the organized sector, there was a net accrual of additional jobs during 1987-88/1997-98, both in the rural and urban areas, 0.99 million in the former and 0.55 million in the latter. In a limited sense, this lends credence to the oft-repeated assertion that, in a developing economy, the informal sector steadily graduates itself to the formal sector. But then, the transition witnessed in the Indian case is more a cause of worry than satisfaction. The expanding employment frontiers in the organized (*alias formal*) sector could not take on even one-fourth of the people being relieved by the unorganized (*alias informal*) sector. This could not be otherwise, in a short span of a decade or so, primarily because of the gigantic size of the dwindling rural unorganized sector, on the one hand, and as yet, a fairly small size of its expanding organized counterpart, on the other; obviously, the tail could not wag the dog. It is the big loss of jobs in the unorganized segment, more expressly in the rural-OAMEs, during 1984-85/1994-95, that might have contributed its share to the slow-down of rural poverty reduction beyond 1987-88, in sharp contrast to the steady decline registered prior to 1987-88.

Besides persons engaged in the actual process of manufacturing or in work incidental to or connected with it, the ASI data also gives information on persons engaged in supervisory, managerial, sale-purchase activities, etc. (Govt. of India, 1997: 78). These are usually the people with a fairly strong academic background, skilled and trained in diverse managerial, marketing and promotional activities. For analytical convenience, we call them 'technical personnel'. It is heartening to see that the organized industrial network is sustained by a growing number of technical personnel, in rural as in the urban areas; between 1987-88 and 1997-98, the number of technical personnel grew by 5.5 per cent per annum in rural and only 2.6 per cent in urban areas. It is, however, a different matter that the growth rate of such employees differed sharply between rural and urban areas, in respect of individual sectors. The rural units showed a remarkably faster absorption of such technical personnel in eight of the nine production sectors under agro-based manufacturing, and in eight out of the ten production sectors under non-agro based industries. As noted earlier, a sizeable presence of a wide variety of organized manufacturing units in rural areas, typically marked by increasing capital:labour ratio, an expanding capital base, a fairly high and increasing presence of technical personnel, etc. all testify to the dispersal, relocation and proliferation of modern industrial activity in rural India. To cap all these developments, during the nineties, the rate of absorption of production workers too has been of a fairly high order in the rural areas.

4.4.1.2 Capital Intensity and Productivity Growth:

It is redeeming to see a fairly high growth rate of employment simultaneously with a high growth rate of productivity, in a preponderant majority of production sectors in rural (as also in urban) areas. This is largely because capital:labour ratio has also tended to increase in a preponderant majority of sectors, both in rural and urban areas. But then, increase in capital:labour ratio, depending as it does on the balance between growth rate of capital against that of labour, could not have tilted in favour of rural areas, not because growth of capital was lacking but because growth rate of workers was substantially higher in rural than in urban areas, practically in each branch of organized manufacturing. Naturally, therefore, in respect of their technological outfit, as encapsulated here by the growth rate of capital:labour ratio, the rural areas lag behind their urban counterparts, in some of the production sectors. These are textile products, wood and leather and their respective products, under agro-processing manufacturing, and non-metallic mineral products, machine tools and equipment, transport equipment and other manufacturing, under non-agrobased manufacturing. But then, in a few sectors (e.g. food products, beverages and tobacco, cotton textiles, wool-silk-man-made fibre textiles, and jute-hemp-mesta textiles under agro-based processing, and, basic metal and alloys, chemicals and chemical products, rubber-plastic-coal products, metal products and parts, and repair of capital goods under non-agrobased manufacturing), capital:labour ratio grew faster in the rural than in the urban areas.

The sector-wise picture on the growth of capital:labour ratio is, therefore, a mixture of advantages and disadvantages for the rural against urban areas. Nonetheless, in aggregate terms, the rural organized manufacturing stands pretty well in comparison to its urban counterpart. For example, real capital:labour ratio grew, during 1987-88/1997-98, by nearly 13.4 per cent per annum in rural agro-processing manufacturing compared with about 5.8 per cent in urban areas, by 10.3 per cent per annum against 8.8 per cent in urban non-agro based manufacturing, and, by 10.5 per cent per annum in rural against 5.3 per cent in urban manufacturing as a whole. In sum, from the point of view of technology-in-use, organized manufacturing activities in rural areas compare very well with their counterparts in the urban areas; this is a striking deviation from the kind of decisive urban technological edge witnessed earlier, in Table 2, in respect of the unorganized manufacturing segment.

The varying degree of technological improvement, as signified by growth of capital:labour ratio, recorded by the rural organized manufacturing sectors during the nineties, brought them a fairly sizeable expansion in productivity levels. In a number of sectors, productivity growth has been higher among the rural units compared with their urban counterparts, while the reverse holds true for the rest (Col.6, Table 10). The total picture on productivity growth does not at all reflect an all-round disadvantage to the rural units. For example, for the sub-group of agro-based manufacturing, productivity grew by 6.7 per cent per annum in rural against 4.2 per cent in urban units, by about 12.0 per cent per annum in rural against 7.9 per cent in urban units in respect of non-agro processing manufacturing, and by 10.4 per cent per annum in rural against 7.0 per cent in urban manufacturing as a whole. It needs especially to be underlined that the rural units have been catching up with or superseding their urban counterparts *even* in respect of more capital-intensive non-agro processing branches of manufacturing, most discernibly chemicals and chemical products, rubber, plastic and petroleum products, and metal products and parts.

Two connected, and still more impressive, off-shoots of the performance of the rural organized manufacturing are growth of net value added and real wages (Cols. 7 and 8, Table 12). First, a negative growth of net value added occurred, during the nineties, in only one sector (jute-hemp-mesta textiles) of the rural agro-processing manufacturing against two in urban areas, and, in none of the rural non-agrobased manufacturing against one (repair services) in the urban areas. As explained earlier, the negative growth rate of net value added (-16.4 per cent) in jute-hemp-mesta textiles operated only between 1987-88 and 1992-93; during 1992-93/1997-98, it achieved a remarkably fast (+ 17.8 per cent) growth rate. Second, in six of the nine agro-based manufacturing sectors, and in nine of the ten non-agrobased sectors, growth rate of (real) net value added was higher in the rural compared with the urban units. Third, a more or less identical picture emerges in respect of growth rate of real wages.

In total terms, it speaks remarkably well for the rural organized manufacturing that a number of production sectors, both in the agro-processing and non-agrobased segments, could register a substantial increase in capital:labour ratio along side a sizeable expansion of employment. This was possible since the rate of growth of investment (here proxied by the changing stock of fixed capital) was also of a substantial order, practically in each branch of rural organized manufacturing. The most striking fact is that in none of the rural organized manufacturing sectors, the real investment faced a decline during 1987-88/1997-98. On the contrary, in fourteen out of the total of nineteen manufacturing sectors, real investment grew at a faster (in some sectors, much faster) rate in rural against urban units. It would thus seem that during the nineties, the house of rural organized manufacturing has maintained a pleasing balance between employment, investment and productivity expansion. The most pleasing, and somewhat unexpected of the typical rural labour markets, final outcome is the high growth rate of employment side by side with an equally high growth rate of real wages, in most of the product lines.

4.4.1.3 Productivity Levels

The pleasing picture on rural organized manufacturing gets further corroborated when we look at productivity levels in combination with the changing levels of capital:labour ratio (Table 13). In many branches of organized manufacturing, capital:labour ratio has consistently been higher among rural compared with urban units. In other words, during the nineties, a wide range of rural organized manufacturing activities have been upgrading their technological outfits either better than or at par with their urban counterparts; the consistently higher or matching levels of capital:labour ratio among rural against that in the urban manufacturing units, clearly testifies to this fact. Because of this edge, the rural agro-based, non-agrobased and total manufacturing, all operated at higher levels of capital:labour ratio in 1987- 88, compared with their urban counterparts, and their edge was duly carried forward to 1997-98. Naturally, therefore, productivity levels too showed an edge of the rural manufacturing, in a wide range of production groups.

An overview of the organized manufacturing sector, therefore, clearly shows that rural manufacturing does not, in any way, reflect the distress of the kind that was discernible in the unorganized sector in general, and the tiny unorganized enterprises (OAMEs) in particular. Their technology base, market linkages, quality of work-force, level and growth of labour productivity, output growth, increase in real wages, etc. all put them comfortably in the league of their urban counterparts.

However, as we saw earlier, in the unorganized segment of rural manufacturing, directory manufacturing establishments (DMEs) gave a fairly satisfactory account of themselves while tiny enterprises such as own-account manufacturing enterprises (OAMEs) revealed an umpteen variety of structural, technological and other weaknesses; in fact, rural OAMEs seem to be losing their ground, most ostensibly in terms of productivity and earning levels, compared with their urban counterparts, and their employment base too has been shrinking. In general, household industrial enterprises (which, in our case, constitute an overwhelming majority of rural OAMEs) have been a declining house. It has been so even during the earlier decades (Chadha, 1986: 153); their relative decline seems to have become faster in recent years. In plain terms, therefore, the process of labour going into the informal, household type enterprises continues simultaneously with that of labour moving out of such enterprises, into non-household type industrial activities (such as DMEs in the unorganized segment of manufacturing) or, as yet, to a limited extent, into the organized segment of rural manufacturing. On the face of it, this kind of labour shift looks pleasing which indeed it is. Yet, there are reasons for a policy concern behind this facade. The labour absorbing capacity of such capital- and technology-intensive enterprises is limited, and the process of moving-into-and-out-of specified categories may soon get exhausted. More importantly, entry for rural job aspirants into education-, skill- and training-oriented industrial enterprises (e.g. most of the product lines under the organized segment, and to a lesser extent, DMEs in the unorganized segment) is likely to become more difficult. From the demand side of the labour market, under ever increasing pressure of domestic as well as international competition, new jobs, including the viability aspect of self-employment, are bound to become more knowledge-, information- and technology-intensive, and are likely to get fewer in every future phase of industrial expansion. From the supply side, the future cadres of rural job seekers, do not seem to be getting prepared for meeting the rising educational, technical and managerial job requirements. The emerging demand-supply hiatus in the rural labour market thus poses a formidable challenge to India's educational system in general, and to rural labour market in particular (Chadha, 2000b: 740-41).

4.5 An Overview of Employment Scenario

Employment promotion has to be the central issue in all policy interventions. As we suggested at the very outset, the developing economies, especially those where land frontiers have already reached their plateau, most of the future employment expansion for the rural households has to be explored, and worked for, outside agriculture. Rural industry holds considerable promise in this regard. The recent experience of industrial employment for the rural households is not a source of happiness to policy makers and other public analysts. Let us take a hurried look at what the official sources tell us.

4.5.1 Share of Rural Employment through Small-Scale and Organized Manufacturing Surveys

Table 14 gives a broad idea of the share of rural people in employment in the two 'modern industrial sectors', namely small-scale and organized manufacturing. For reasons outlined earlier, the 1994-95 figures for the small scale sector are not strictly comparable with those for 1987-88, yet, the table gives a fairly clear idea that till 1994-95, there has been no serious diminution in the rural people's share in employment, under this sector; in fact, in some of the production sectors, e.g. beverages, textiles, chemicals and chemical products, basic metal products, etc., their share has registered an increase.

It is no less pleasing to see that even in the organized manufacturing, there has been no substantial change in the rural people's share of employment, except in jute and other vegetable fibre textiles and textile products. It may not be out of place to reiterate that a large part of the organized manufacturing activities, reported under the rural areas, owes itself to a definitional subterfuge. Nonetheless, it does show that rural people too chip off some share of employment in such modern industrial activities. It is, however, important to emphasize that rural workers are engaged in unskilled or semi-skilled jobs, broadly consistent with their low educational and training background while most of the supervisory and technical jobs go over to their urban brethren. This kind of job segregation goes on magnifying itself as we move out of the village to the semi-urban settlements and further on to full-fledged urban centres. The worst sufferers are the rural females. Unluckily, the published data on organized manufacturing do not give any break-up between semi-urban and urban locales, nor between male and female workers.

5

Regional Pattern of Rural Industrial Development

One of the major aims of planned economic and industrial development is to achieve balanced regional development. Reduction of regional disparities in the medium term, and their elimination in the long run, is always conceived as an ideal goal of socio-economic development. Some public analysts believe that rural industrialization can contribute to the process of evening out regional disparities in general, and inequalities in rural development in particular. The actual experiences, however, have not been so much supportive of this hypothesis, more certainly the first part of it. Saith looks through a variety of Asian experiences of rural industrial development (e.g. China, Korea, Malaysia, the Philippines, Taiwan, etc.) and discovers that, except for Taiwan, in none of the other economies, rural industrial development has played a decisive role in reducing unevenness in regional economic development (Saith, 2000: 88-91). In India's case, no imposing evidence is forthcoming either way, because of conceptual problems and data constraints. To quote him:

> The evidence is scattered, based on a disparate range of non-comparable sources, censuses, sample surveys, other industrial surveys or other regional, state or district-level data. It applies variously to output, to various categories of employment or to the number of enterprises. Some of these data have been utilized for testing various hypotheses econometrically, though in most such cases, there are severe problems of the coherence of the data set, its interpretation as proxies for appropriate variables and concepts, and also problems of specification. Further, the internal heterogeneity of the rural non-farm sector itself makes it very hazardous to interpret data or findings unambiguously (Saith, 2000: 89-90).

But then, Saith plainly admits that it would be rather a miracle if rural industrialization succeeds in mitigating regional disparities. Again, in his own words:

> rural industry might not be the best policy instrument with which to address this difficult problem. The more appropriate method might be the old-fashioned route to focusing on agriculture and supporting infrastructure, aided by policies of direct human development. Rural industrialization has

generally not served the purpose of reducing regional disparities, nor is it likely that it really could, except under very special circumstances (*ibid*: 91).

We are not as much unsure about the other half of the hypothesis, i.e. about the beneficial effects of rural industrialization on rural development. In any case, it is important, in its own right, to see if regional disparities in the matter of rural industrial development itself have tended to decline in India, whatever its overall income and employment impact may be. This follows now.

The regional pattern of rural industrialization can be gauged through in many different ways primarily because rural industry itself has many faces and connotations. The conventional methods are to look through the shares of individual states in the number of enterprises, or rural industrial assets or output or employment, at different points of time, or to work with coefficients of variations for these variables, or to draw inferences through the standard statistical measures of concentration or dispersal, and so on. The analysis can go over various sets of rural industrial classifications, say, organized versus unorganized, or, household versus non-household. In our view, the regional pattern of rural industrialization, in the Indian context, would be adequately captured if we concentrate on its most dominant component, namely, the unorganized manufacturing. Also, without multiplying statistical exercises, major issues of inter-state variations in the rural industrial development would be thrown bare if we look into (1) the change in each state's share in the number of enterprises and employment, for each segment of the unorganized manufacturing sector, during 1984-85/1994-95 and 1994-95/ 2000-01, the two sub-periods broadly characterizing the pre- and post-reform realities, respectively; (2) the state-wise growth of employment and real productivity; (3) the grouping of states on the basis of productivity per worker; and (4) the changing magnitude of Hirschman-Herfindahl Index to see the degree of regional concentration/dispersal. For (1), (2) and (4), we go by each of the three components of the unorganized manufacturing sector, namely OAMEs, NDMEs and DMEs, while for (3), it stays at the aggregate of the unorganized sector.

Before we embark upon our analysis, it is in the fitness of things to point out that there were important changes in the composition of employment between full- and part-time workers when we moved from 1984-85/1994-95 to 1994-95/2000-01 (see Section 4.2.1.3); during the later period, the incidence of part-time employment was much higher, most markedly among OAMEs. This naturally affects our estimates of employment growth, and productivity levels, in respect of individual states. Nonetheless, we believe that it does not seriously affect the relative rankings of individual states. In any case, a more detailed analysis is needed to confirm our conjecture.

5.1 States' Share in Enterprises and Employment

Tables 15-A and 15-B inform us about the changing share of each state in terms of the number of enterprises and employment, respectively, for each of the three layers of the rural unorganized manufacturing enterprises. To ensure empirical firmness about the change in either type of share, first between 1984-85 and 1994-95, and then between 1994-95/2000-01, Chi-Square test (with one degree of freedom) is applied, for each state, for each of the OAMEs, NDMEs and DMEs, under the null hypothesis that the share of the state changes neither during 1984-85/1994-95 nor during 1994-95/2000-01. For capturing the changes simultaneously occurring in both types of shares, an Inter-State Concentration Index (ISCI), constructed as a ratio of each state's share in employment to its share in the number of enterprises ($ISCI_i = Emp_i/Ent_i$ where Emp_i is the share of the ith state in employment and Ent_i is its share in the number of enterprises), is put to Chi-Square test, as is done separately for the two types of shares (Table 15-C).

It is interesting to see that out of seventeen states, only in two states, the share in the number of rural-OAMEs changed significantly between 1984-85 and 1994-95 (Table 15-A); in Orissa, it increased from 5.26 per cent to 13.79 per cent while in Uttar Pradesh, it declined from 33.79 per cent to 17.63 per cent. On the whole, it is fairly clear that no noticeable inter-state reshuffling, in terms of each state's relative effort to launch new tiny rural enterprises or prevent liquidation of the existing ones, occurred during 1984-85/1994-95. For the post-reform years (1994-95/2000-01), the changes are all the more conspicuous by their absence; even in Orissa and Uttar Pradesh, the pre-reform changes in Ent_i have completely vanished. As a matter of fact, major changes in Ent_i in respect of rural-OAMEs is not to be expected for two strong reasons. First, each state is under a kind of perpetual pressure to expand non-farm employment in rural areas and the easiest way of such a pressure getting neutralized, inter alia, is through expansion of self-employing OAME type of tiny rural enterprises. It seems, this tendency has been operating equally pervasively practically in each state. Second, it seems, the filter-down and multiplier effects of the changing structure of industrialization that ensued since the early 1990s, could not reach the rural-OAME segment till the close of the 1990s; perhaps, it was a bit early to expect such effects to have travelled over to the rural areas in general, and the lowest echelon of the rural industrial sector in particular, within a brief span of 5-6 years. India's rural economy has its own logic of slumber.

The situation is only a shade different in respect of rural-DMEs. During 1984-85/1994-95, in the two southern states, namely Andhra Pradesh and Karnataka, the share of rural-DMEs increased sizeably while in another three states (viz. Kerala, Madhya Pradesh and West Bengal), it declined, by varying margins. The increased share of Andhra Pradesh and Karnataka is a clear signal of the relatively faster proliferation of small-scale modern industrial activity, during the pre-1994 decade, most markedly in the area of information technology, in rural (as well as urban) areas of Karnataka. The post-1994 scenario, however, shows reversal of the pre-1994 trend in these two states while two other states, namely Kerala and West Bengal gained substantially in their respective shares of the number of rural-DMEs. For most of the other states, the relative shares changed but little. On the whole, neither during 1984-85/1994-95 nor during 1994-95/2000-01, a major reshuffling was in evidence in respect of rural-DMEs.

At the level of total unorganized rural enterprises (Cols. 5, 9 and 13, Table 15A), the trend of changes in their inter-state shares gets fairly straightened out, when we move from the pre-1994 to the post-1994 years. For example, during 1984-85/1994-95, it is only Orissa that increased its share from 5.16 per cent to 12.82 per cent and Uttar Pradesh that witnessed a decline from 33.01 per cent to 17.81 per cent; all other states witnessed a small or negligible degree of change. During 1994-95/2000-01, Orissa's share fell from 12.82 per cent to 7.79 per cent while that of Uttar Pradesh from 17.81 per cent to 14.67 per cent. While the two major changes during the pre-1994 years were statistically significant (based on Chi-Square Test with one degree of freedom), none of those during the post-1994 years were significant. In a way, this lends further credence to our contention that the unorganized industrial enterprises, at each of the three layers of their structured hierarchy (OAME, NDME and DME), located in most parts of rural India have not witnessed big inter-regional locational shifts, in spite of the vast structural changes overtaking all segments of the Indian economy; the most conspicuous segment that has witnessed, until now, negligible inter-regional shifts, consists of the tiniest enterprises (OAMEs).

No major inter-state reshuffling in terms of the share of employment seems to have occurred either (Table 15-B); in fact, the trends are smoother in the case of employment, compared with the number of enterprises. Nonetheless, a few significant differences between the two types of shares need to be underlined. Consistent with what was observed in Table 15-A, in respect of the share of rural-OAMEs, during 1984-85/1994-95, the share of employment in rural-OAMEs increased in Orissa and declined in Uttar Pradesh. But then, the sizeable increase in the share of rural-DMEs for Karnataka and Andhra Pradesh was not accompanied by a sizeable increase in employment. In fact, Gujarat is the only state whose relative share of employment in the rural-DME segment increased. The post-1994 years, however, leveled off these changes. Except for a stray exception of Jammu- Kashmir, and that too presumably because the 2000-01 field survey here was carried out under disturbed and less-than-fully-satisfying circumstances, none of the other states shows any significant increase or decrease in its share of employment, for any of the three layers of the unorganized manufacturing enterprises. This is, yet again, a confirmation of our contention that, at every stage of its development, each state faces a built-in compulsion of augmenting rural non-farm employment of which industrial employment is a precious constituent. As we argued earlier in Chapter 3, employment in a large part of the unorganized manufacturing sector, most certainly in the tiniest segment (OAMEs), is based on local economic dynamics. Since it is hard to believe that rural economic base of some states has witnessed a remarkably fast restructuring under the impact of economic reforms, and of others, it has remained completely unchanged, it is only logical to expect that some states would show a little accretion or decretion, in relation to others. This is precisely the typical scenario of the post-reform years. Perhaps, 'greater upheavals' have yet to come off.

Looking at each state's share of rural enterprises simultaneously with its share in employment, for 1984-85,1994-95 and 2000-01 (Table 15-C), it is more than evident that no significant change occurred in any of the seventeen states, either during 1984-85/1994-95 or during 1994-95/2000-01, either in respect of rural-OAMEs or rural-NDMEs; in other words, the process of increase/decrease in the number of the bottom two categories of rural enterprises seems to have been accompanied by a proportionate increase/decrease in the number of workers employed so that the ISCI remained unchanged, first between 1984-85 and 1994-95, and then between 1994-95 and 2000-01. The situation of no-change was not, however, so pervasive in the case of rural-DMEs, the top of the three unorganized manufacturing segments. For such enterprises, the two green revolution states of Haryana and Punjab seem to have effected an interesting mingle of expansion/contraction of enterprises and employment, between rural–DMEs and rural-NDMEs; rural-OAMEs, however, declined both ways. The decline in Punjab's share of rural-DMEs (from 0.75 in 1984-85 to 0.38 in 1994-95) can possibly be attributed to the rising terrorist activities; without doubt, in the fear-stricken rural Punjab, DMEs were likely to attract the attention of ransom-seekers much more than OAMEs and NDMEs. In Haryana's case, it was probably under the impulse of the steadily expanding technological hook-up between the organized and the unorganized manufacturing, triggered off by the state's accelerated pace of industrial growth during this period, that prompted scaling-up in some areas and scaling-down in others; the changing values of Enti and Empi in respect of rural-OAMEs, on the one hand, and rural-DMEs, on the other, lend some credence to this conjecture. But then, during the post-1994 years, when terrorism subsided in rural Punjab, the state's share both in respect of the number of rural-DMEs as also in employment increased so that the value of ISCI remained unchanged between 1994-95 and 2000-01. This was typically true of all other states as well.

In total terms, barring a few exceptions, neither the pre-reform (1984-85/ 1994-95) nor the post-reform (1994-95/2000-01) period reveals major inter-state re-shuffling either in terms of each state's share of rural-OAMEs, rural-NDMEs or rural-DMEs or in terms of its share of employment in each of these segments; in any case, whatever change occurred in the number of enterprises was, more or less, accompanied by a proportionate change in employment, in each of the three segments, without causing a major shift in the relative ranking of the seventeen states. The regional spread of rural unorganized industrial sector has thus remained nearly the same till 2000-01. That no major re-shuffling has been in evidence during the post-1994 years brings a kind of relief to policy makers and other observers of rural economic change. That it would remain so in the coming decade or so is difficult to conjecture. Perhaps, in the coming years, under pressure from the domestic urban industrial sector, and through the changing composition of India's foreign trade, strong impulses may be unleashed, inter alia, for augmenting rural industrialization processes in some states more than in others. That may put some states way ahead of others. Finally, the regional scenario in respect of the organized industrial sector in rural India (which we have not gone into in this chapter) may throw up widening inter-state variations; in that event, rural industrial development may well become a cause of varying level of general economic development. Already, some meek hints are available on the regional shifts of capital in the organized manufacturing sector, say from some states in the north to some in the south.

5.2 Spatial Pattern of Employment and Productivity Growth

Table 16 (split into 16-A and 16-B) gives state-wise growth rates of employment and productivity per worker, during 1984-85/1994-95 and 1994-95/2000-01, for each of the three segments of the unorganised manufacturing. Let us first look at the employment growth scenario during the pre-reform (1984-85/1994-95) decade. It is only in five of the seventeen states, namely Assam, Gujarat, Himachal Pradesh, Karnataka and Orissa that employment among rural-OAMEs registered positive growth of any consequence during 1984-85/1994-95; as many as ten states witnessed a varying degree of negative employment growth during these years. Somewhat surprisingly, even in the green revolution states of Punjab, Haryana and Uttar Pradesh, employment growth in rural-OAMEs was negative. It really seems that OAMEs were losing their appeal as an important source of non-farm employment in rural India. The situation is not much different with the NDMEs either. Except for Madhya Pradesh and Karnataka, all other states witnessed a negative growth rate of employment that varied from −14.21 per cent for Jammu-Kashmir to −1.04 for Kerala; in as many as nine states, the per year loss of employment was 5.0 per cent and more. Happily, the house of directory establishments (DMEs) performed markedly better in terms of employment growth; the negative, and substantially heavy, growth rate of employment was confined to five states only (Assam, Jammu-Kashmir, Kerala, Madhya Pradesh and Rajasthan); for the remaining twelve states, employment grew positively in varying proportions that ranged from 1.00 per cent in West Bengal to as high as 10.01 per cent in Gujarat. Interestingly, the three green revolution states registered fairly substantial employment growth rates among DMEs against negative rates among their NDMEs and OAMEs. The employment scenario, for each of the three segments, was much less frightening in the urban areas. While a negative growth of employment was discernible for many states, among each segment, yet the overall situation was a shade better than in rural areas.

Looking at OAMEs, NDMEs and DMEs together, it is clear that the negative growth rate of employment in rural areas, among each of the three segments, occurred only in three states, namely Jammu-Kashmir, Rajasthan and Kerala; for Andhra Pradesh, it was more a situation of non-growth rather than negative growth. In other words, DMEs were proving to be the saviour of employment in rural India. But then, the sheer size of the rural-OAME segment that witnessed wide-spread squeeze in employment growth rate, robbed away the pleasing scenario of wide-spread expansion of employment growth in the small-sized rural-DME segment. Nonetheless, it signalled the beginning of a significant development in the rural industrial sector; the process of industrial restructuring in favour of non-household type enterprises (here typified by DMEs) seemed to have set in well before the arrival of economic reforms during the early 1990s. It was not a trivial development that against a negative growth of employment in OAMEs in as many as ten of the seventeen states, the employment grew not only positively but at fairly high rates among DMEs, in as many as eleven of the sixteen states. Perhaps, the rural industrial sector had started coming of age, partly because of the onslaught of the urban competition facing the rural industry as a whole and partly because of the scale economies that had probably started asserting themselves in favour of DMEs compared with NDMEs/ OAMEs. In one word, scale upgradation was ostensibly at work in respect of the unorganised segment of the manufacturing sector, both in the rural and urban areas, more demonstrably in the latter.

The post-1994 scenario did witness some setbacks; the pre-1994 roles were now inter-changed between rural-OAMEs and rural-DMEs. During 1994-95/ 2000-01, employment among the rural-OAMEs grew negatively only in three states (Assam, Orissa and Uttar Pradesh; we leave aside Bihar and Himachal Pradesh which witnessed virtually no employment growth) while it did so among rural-DMEs in as many as seven states (Bihar, Gujarat, Haryana, Karnataka, Orissa, Tamil Nadu and West Bengal). But then, it cannot be denied that employment growth among rural-DMEs was positive and of a very high order among many states (e.g. Assam, Himachal Pradesh, Jammu-Kashmi8r, Kerala, Madhya Pradesh, Punjab, Rajasthan, Uttar Pradesh and Maharashtra). For India as a whole, the process of scale upgradation continued with its forward march inasmuch, during the post-1994 years, the rate of growth of employment among rural-DMEs was as high as 2.87 per cent against 1.18 per only among rural-OAMEs.

The above tendency is likely to magnify itself in the times ahead, firstly because the rural industry can no more operate in isolation, under the changing export-import regime, and secondly because, some 'weeding' is a natural corollary of a maturing economy. It is time to realise that rural industry too is carving out some moorings outside agriculture; the agriculture-industry linkage is still the best source of employment multiplier, yet, in recent years, the character of rural industry itself has been undergoing a drastic change, thanks to the policy of industrial re-location away from the congested urban centres and special emphasis on the development of industrially backward regions, on the one hand, and the reality of steadily expanding rural tertiary sector with its own forward and backward linkages with industry, on the other. If this were not so, the green revolution states of Punjab and Haryana would not have flipped over from negative growth rate of employment during 1984-85/ 1994-95 to positive and very impressive rates during 1994-95/2000-01; in Punjab, it was from –4.28 per cent during the pre- to 6.53 per cent during the post-reform years among rural-OAMEs, from –1.99 per cent to 6.21 per cent among rural-NDMEs and from 6.84 per cent to as high as 15.06 per cent among rural-DMEs, and in Haryana, it was from –6.86 per cent to 1.65 per cent among rural-OAMEs, and from –1.50 per cent to 6.05 per cent among rural-NDMEs, and so on.

For the unorganised rural manufacturing as a whole, employment growth rate witnessed a varying degree of improvement during the post-, compared with the pre-reform period, in as many as fourteen of the seventeen states. In many states, the improvement was rather marked; a change-over from –0.54 per cent during 1984-85/1994-95 to 4.03 per cent during 1994-95/2000-01 in Andhra Pradesh, from –4.73 per cent to 1.09 per cent in Haryana, from –11.38 per cent to 34.47 per cent in Jammu-Kashmir, from –4.77 per cent to 7.87 per cent in Kerala, from -0.06 per cent to 7.94 per cent in Madhya Pradesh, from –3.45 per cent to 4.65 per cent in Maharashtra, from -3.11 per cent to 7.71 per cent in Punjab, from -4.57 per cent to 3.80 per cent in Rajasthan, from -.3.25 per cent to 2.30 per cent in Tamil Nadu, from –7.46 per cent to –1.25 per cent in Uttar Pradesh and from 0.43 per cent to 3.28 per cent in West Bengal, bears adequate testimony to the process of an all-round bettering of employment growth rate in the rural unorganised manufacturing sector.

Table16-B looks at growth of productivity per worker, during the pre- as well as post-reform periods, among the three segments of the unorganised manufacturing, in rural and urban areas. A highly disparate pattern of productivity growth is discernible among the seventeen states, for both the periods. For example, during the pre-reform decade, productivity grew positively in each of the three segments in six states (Karnataka, Kerala, Punjab, Rajasthan, Tamil Nadu and West Bengal); it grew negatively among OAMEs and/or NDMEs but positively among DMEs in four states (Andhra Pradesh, Gujarat, Jammu-Kashmir and Uttar Pradesh); it grew negatively among DMEs but positively among OAMEs and/or NDMEs in four states (Bihar, Haryana, Maharashtra and Orissa); it grew negatively among all the three segments in one state (Madhya Pradesh), and so on. Nonetheless, the overall picture for the country clearly conforms to the growth pattern of employment analysed in Table 16–A above; productivity per worker increased annually by 1.6 per cent among the OAMEs, by 2.4 per cent among NDMEs and by as high as 4.6 per cent among DMEs. Our earlier conjecture that employment among the tiny and household-type rural manufacturing enterprises cannot grow unless productivity also grows, gets duly validated. Admittedly, this causation is not neatly discernible among each of the seventeen states; for example, there are states where employment growth has been positive but productivity grew negatively, and, there are others where the reverse is true. Perhaps, the transitory problems of effecting scale up-gradation operating variously in different states, during 1984-85/1994-95, were responsible for such deviations. In any case, an in-depth analysis is called for to clearly delineate the relationship between the growth of productivity and employment.

The post-1994 performance was markedly better. At the national level, the rate of growth of productivity was a respectable figure of 6.35 per cent during 1994-95/2000-01, compared with 1.26 per cent only during 1984-85/1994-95, among rural-OAMEs, at 5.70 per cent against 2.11 per cent among rural-NDMEs, at 6.12 per cent compared with 4.27 per cent among rural-DMEs, and at 6.38 per cent against 2.14 per cent among the total of all manufacturing establishments. Most happily, among the tiniest of the rural manufacturing units (OAMEs), none of the seventeen states registered a negative growth of per worker productivity during the post-1994 years, contrasted to as many as seven states (Andhra Pradesh, Assam, Bihar, Gujarat, Jammu-Kashmir, Madhya Pradesh and Orissa) showing varying levels of negative growth rates during the pre-reform years. Still more pleasing is to see that, for this segment of manufacturing enterprises, there was a marked improvement in the level of productivity growth rate in as many as twelve of the seventeen states; a switch-over from –0.49 per cent during 1984-85/1994-95 to as high as 8.81 per cent during 1994-95/2000-01 in Andhra Pradesh, from –1.75 per cent to 13.19 per cent in Assam, from –2.83 per cent to 7.88 per cent in Bihar, from –6.70 per cent to 4.25 per cent in Gujarat, from –5.71 per cent to 19.86 per cent in Jammu-Kashmir, and from –2.61 per cent to 8.54 per cent in Orissa are examples of outstanding improvements. A similar story, although with differing magnitude, unfolds itself for other segments of the unorganised manufacturing sector, most notably rural-DMEs.

The foregoing analysis reveals three distinct characteristics of rural industrial development in India, during the eighties and the nineties. First, during 1984-85/1994-95, the tiny and household-based manufacturing enterprises could not escape contraction of jobs, in some states fairly sizeably. The overall picture on employment during these years has been fairly disappointing. Second, there is a clear tendency for relatively bigger-sized units, say, DMEs among the unorganised manufacturing enterprises to take over, both on the strength of productivity and employment growth. This is another way of confirming that small-scale non-household type enterprises hold the key to the future of rural industrialisation. Third, even in the midst of the overall gloom caused by the common tragedy of employment losses, most widely among the OAME segment, there took place a significant reshuffling of rankings of individual states, in terms of productivity levels. Happily, in the post-1994 years, things improved. Most noticeably, the productivity and employment setbacks, suffered by many states during 1984-85/1994-95, among the three layers of the unorganised manufacturing enterprises, were reversed. Consequently, considerable reshuffling of rankings followed. Table 17 lends sufficient empirical firmness to such reshufflings.

Rank correlation coefficients have been computed, first, between productivity levels of 1984-85 and 1994-95, and 1994-95 and 2000-01, separately for rural and urban areas, and second, between productivity levels of rural and those of urban areas, separately for 1984-85, 1994-95 and 2000-01, for each of the three layers of the unorganised manufacturing enterprises. In the context of the changing regional pattern of rural industrial development, the null hypothesis that we test for the first set of rank correlation coefficients is that the computed coefficients are not significantly different from unity, both for 1984-85/1994-95 and for 1994-95/2000-01; in other words, it maintains that there is no change, whatsoever, in the rankings of individual states between 1984-85 and 1994-95, or between 1994-95 and 2000-01, implying a correlation coefficient of unity. Fisher's Z Transformation Test is handy for this purpose (Kapur-Saxena, 1967: 354). The null hypothesis for the second set of rank correlation coefficients is that each state commands the same rank for rural as for urban productivity, in respect of each of OAMEs, NDMEs and DMEs, for

1984-85, 1994-95 and 2000-01. Here too, an appeal to Fisher's Z Transformation works well. Table 17 clearly warrants that the null hypothesis be rejected for both sets of correlation coefficients. In other words, the level and growth of per worker productivity have moved unevenly among the seventeen states, both in the rural and urban areas, as also between the two. Section 5.3 below lends further confirmation to this process of reshuffling.

5.3 Spatial Pattern of Productivity/Worker

Table 18 shows significant regional shifts in the level of real productivity per worker, first between 1984-85 and 1994-95, and then between 1994-95 and 2000-01, for major states of India; productivity is split into three notional levels: low, medium and high. In 1984-85, as many as six states were languishing at low levels of productivity, eight of them were in the medium range while only two had reached a high level of productivity per worker. After ten years, in 1994-95, only one state (Orissa) stayed back in the low productivity trap while four of their erstwhile companions climbed up to medium and one to the high level of productivity. Similarly, out of the nine states that stood at the medium level of productivity in 1984-85, as many as five climbed up to the high level in 1994-95. It is only Jammu-Kashmir that marched a downward movement of productivity, from a high to a medium level; perhaps the spate of political disturbances in rural areas were directly responsible for worsening the productivity performance in the state. On the whole, it is fairly evident that, between 1984-85 and 1994-95, different states tended to achieve a varying degree of improvement in the level of productivity per worker in their rural unorganized manufacturing.

Productivity improvement continued to occur during 1994-95/2000-01 as well. Barring Orissa, which continued to languish at the low level of productivity even in 2000-01, out of nine states that stood at the middle-level of productivity in 1994-95, in 2000-01, as many as five (Karnataka, West Bengal, Bihar, Himachal Pradesh and Jammu-Kashmir) had climbed up to join the group of high productivity states. Seven other states (Gujarat, Haryana, Kerala, Punjab, Rajasthan, Tamil Nadu and Maharashtra) continued to stay in the group of high productivity states. In total terms, productivity improvement among the rural unorganized manufacturing enterprises has been occurring continuously since the eighties; it reinforced itself during the nineties.

The changing regional scenario manifests itself also in terms of the share of employment, value added, fixed assets, etc. enjoyed by low, medium and high productivity regions, in 1994-95 contrasted to 1984-85, and in 2000-01 contrasted to 1994-95. It is indeed heartening to see that against 67.0 per cent of the enterprises, 71.2 per cent of employment, 59.3 per cent of the value added and

22.5 per cent of fixed assets in the unorganized manufacturing, located in the cluster of low-productivity states in 1984-85, stood drastically reduced to 13.0, 14.0, 5.3 and 5.1 per cent, respectively, in 1994-95. This drastic all-round reduction was ostensibly because of the ascendancy of five of the six states from low productivity level in 1984-85 to medium productivity level in 1994-95; most of the erstwhile low-productivity states climbed up to join the medium productivity states. As a consequence, the share of the medium productivity group of states in enterprises, employment, and value added improved, respectively, from 30.7 to 67.3 per cent, from 27.2 to 66.2 per cent, and from 36.8 to 61.8 per cent, between 1984-85 to 1994-95; only for fixed assets, the group's share declined from 76.0 to 57.2 per cent. The most noticeable has been the shift of a number of states from low to the high level of productivity. The group of high productivity states, therefore, commanded a very impressive improvement of its share in the number of enterprises, employment, value added and fixed assets in the unorganized rural manufacturing from 2.4 to 19.1 per cent, 1.6 to 20.3 per cent, 3.9 to 32.9 per cent, and, from 1.5 to 37.8 per cent, respectively, between 1984-85 to 1994-95. In brief, the decade 1984-85/1994-95 did witness a shift of many states from low to medium, and, of others from medium to high levels of per worker productivity, in the unorganized manufacturing segment of their rural economies. In fact, only one state (Orissa) continued to languish at low level of per worker productivity. In other words, during the decade following 1984-85, there was a clear tilt in the share of enterprises, employment, value added and fixed assets away from low to medium, and still more happily, from medium to high productivity cluster of states. Regional disparities in rural industrialization, looked at from this perspective, seem to have declined since mid-1980s.

More changes in states' shares in employment, value added, fixed assets, etc. occurred during the post-1994 years. For example, during 1994-95/2000-01, the share of the group of low productivity states in the number of the rural unorganized manufacturing enterprises, employment, value added and fixed assets declined, respectively, from 12.8 per cent to 7.8 per cent, from 13.6 per cent to 8.7 per cent, from 5.3 per cent to 3.8 per cent and from 5.1 per cent to 2.6 per cent. These shares for the group of medium productivity states declined from 67.3 per cent to 33.0 per cent, from 66.2 per cent to 35.1 per cent, from 61.8 per cent to 29.5 per cent, and from 57.2 per cent to 31.1 per cent, respectively. To cap all, the four shares for the group of high productivity states improved remarkably, during 1994-95/2000-01, from 19.9 per cent to 59.3 per cent, from 20.3 per cent to 56.2 per cent, from 32.9 per cent to 66.1 per cent, and from 37.8 per cent to 66.3 per cent, respectively.

The improvement in productivity levels, and the rising share of enterprises, employment, value added and fixed assets have occurred in urban areas as well, but the scenario here is markedly different compared with the rural areas. While the ascendancy from low to medium level of productivity is quite unambiguous, from medium to high levels, it is not comparable with that in the rural areas. Consequently, during 1984-85/1994-95, medium level of productivity seems to have strengthened its hold in the unorganized manufacturing in urban India. In this sense, rural India seems to have acquitted itself better in terms of leveling off the sharp regional disparities in its industrialization chart, compared with urban India.

Crossing over from low to medium, and from medium to high level of productivity by states does not necessarily connote a steep upward jump in their productivity level. A mingle of growth trends is involved. Table 18 clearly shows this mingle of positive and negative productivity growth rates, varying from state to state, even though all of them show the same trend of ascendancy. For example, during 1984-85/1994-95, for Uttar Pradesh, West Bengal, Andhra Pradesh, and Karnataka, it was a positive growth in their per worker productivity, ranging from 1.11 per cent to 5.72 per cent, that pushed them up from low to medium level of productivity; most happily, it was a very high (8.30 per cent) growth rate of per worker productivity that brought Tamil Nadu out of the group of low productivity states to the league of high productivity states. Similarly, it was an extremely satisfying growth of per worker productivity, ranging from 5.72 to 7.11 per cent, that pushed Haryana, Rajasthan, Punjab and Kerala from the group of medium productivity states in 1984-85 to the one of high productivity states in 1994-95. The most authentic proof of the high growth of productivity pushing up states from medium to high levels of productivity comes during 1994-95/2000-01, in respect of Jammu-Kashmir, Himachal Pradesh, Karnataka, West Bengal and Bihar, where productivity grew impressively at rates varying from a minimum of 8.2 per cent in Karnataka to as high as 19.7 per cent in Jammu-Kashmir.

But then, what do we say about the states which stayed on in the same cluster. Table 18 lends them no cheers. Practically, each of these states witnessed a negative growth in their productivity levels; Jammu-Kashmir witnessed a decline in its productivity status most convincingly because of a big (-4.95 per cent) decline in its productivity level. The cheers that we gather because of the ascendancy hypothesis set out above need to be mollified because many states stayed on, in 1994-95 compared with 1984-95, and in 2000-01 compared with 1994-95, within the same range of productivity, where they were in 1984-85 and/or 1994-95; a negative growth in their productivity level did remain a distressing fact.

The distress of the kind pointed out above is manifest far more acutely in the case of employment; many states which remain either in the same productivity range or jump over to the higher productivity range, suffer from a high degree of employment contraction. It really seems that, in the case of a majority of states, productivity growth is accompanied by a decisive squeeze in employment. For 1984-85/1994-95, the cheers that we associated with the declining regional disparities in terms of productivity levels are now mixed with the disturbing element of negative growth of employment, witnessed in varying degree, for a number of states. In plain terms, what the right hand was giving, the left hand seemed to be taking back. But then, the post-1994 scenario is not as fuzzy. Here, employment growth rate also improved, along with the improvement in productivity levels, in respect of many states that climbed from medium to high levels of productivity during these years. We have thus some proxy reason to assure ourselves of a decline in regional disparities in rural industrialization in recent years.

5.4 Regional Concentration Index

Inter-state disparity in rural industrialization can be looked at through numerous statistical measures such as Weighted Coefficient of Variation, Gini Concentration Ratio, Kuznets TDM, Theil's Enthrophy, Atkinson's Index, Hirschman-Herfindahl Index, and so on (Mathur, 1983: 215; Awasthi,1981:101). We do not intend to multiply statistical measures for paucity of time and space; Hirschman-Herfindahl Index is good enough to testify whether rural industrial development is getting more diversified over space. Table 19 suggests an interesting mingle of adjustments, as we climb up from OAMEs to NDMEs and further on to DMEs. The Index is computed for four major variables: number of enterprises, employment, fixed assets and value added. There was an unmistakable tendency for the Index to decline between 1984-85 and 1994-95, for each of the variables, in respect of the tiny rural enterprises (viz. rural-OAMEs) and slightly bigger establishments (viz. rural-NDMEs), in contrast to a slight increase in respect of rural-DMEs; the decline is far more sharp in respect of rural-OAMEs. This clearly suggests that, during 1984/85/1994-95, tiny enterprises proliferated throughout the length and breadth of rural India, often under conditions of duress and devoid of hard commercial considerations, whereas the bigger-sized manufacturing units in the unorganized sector (viz. DMEs), perhaps better described as small scale industries, followed a selective and commercially well articulated calculus. In a way, the Hirschman-Herfindahl Index reinforces the conclusions of Section 5.1, namely the segment consisting of the tiny rural industrial enterprises (OAMEs), facing employment setbacks, showed a clear tendency towards regional dispersal

The period 1994-95/2000-01 carried forward the trends of the preceding decade but on a very modest scale. For example, the Hirschman-Herfindahl Index did register a decline for each of the four variables, for each of the three layers of the rural unorganized manufacturing enterprises but on a scale that would prompt any keen observer to declare it a situation of no-change. In other words, regional concentration or dispersal of rural unorganized manufacturing (see particularly Col. 5, Table 19) had got only marginally affected since the arrival of economic reforms in the early 1990s. Perhaps, it was too much, and too early, to expect that in the matter of rural unorganized manufacturing, most markedly its tiniest segment (OAMEs), certain regions would have gone much ahead of others, because, the new economic policies offered them special advantages or opportunities. The nearly static situation, for the post-1994 behaviour of the Hirschman-Herfindahl Index, say, in respect of the number of enterprises and fixed assets, lends adequate weight to our contention. In brief, the post-reform phase of rural industrialization, here caricaturized by a brief spell of 5-6 years, does not reflect a tendency of divergence or convergence; a status quo seemed to have prevailed.

6
Major Problems

In Chapter IV, we have looked through the strengths and weaknesses of all types of industries that can possibly be put under the rubric of "rural industry". This included village industries and a substantial part of small-scale industries under the VSI sector, rural-located own-account enterprises, non-directory and directory establishments under unorganized manufacturing, and rural-based organised manufacturing. It comes up clearly that in spite of a wide penetration of modern industrial activity into the country-side, including a sizeable presence of the organised manufacturing in certain product lines, the rural industrial sector is still dominated by tiny enterprises, variously described as household or cottage or own-account manufacturing enterprises (OAMEs); we have chosen to call them tiny rural industries (tri). The weaknesses of such a lopsided industrial structure should be fairly obvious, especially because the economy is now open to all varieties of international trade and investment flows. Our analysis has thrown up many inherent weaknesses of the rural tiny sector, most visibly in terms of its incapability of sustaining a low-productivity industrial regime during the times that the rural industry has started facing tough competition from its urban counterpart on the one hand, and the more liberal import regime, on the other. That the tiny rural sector lost as many as 4.14 million jobs during the decade 1984-85/1994-95, is believed to have contributed to a widely reported near-halt or a marginal decline in rural non-farm growth, during recent years. This, in turn, may convincingly explain the recent slowdown that rural India witnessed on the front of poverty reduction. The Indian experience shows that rural industry, employment and earnings are inextricably linked with rural poverty. The future of rural industry is thus as much an issue of rural welfare as of market efficiency, growth and sustainability.

It is patently wrong to predict that under the new dispensations, every section of rural industry would suffer growth reverses, or, equally serious job losses. As noted above, the *rural organised manufacturing*, in no major aspect of its functioning, lags behind its urban counterpart. The higher segments of the *rural unorganised manufacturing* too, most noticeably the rural-DMEs, are doing fairly well in relation to their urban counterparts. The real worry is in respect of most segments of the traditional industries under the VSI sector or, looked at from a different perspective, for many of the product lines under the tiny rural manufacturing sector, officially known as OAMEs, and to a slightly lower extent, NDMEs. Their weaknesses on technology, productivity and marketing fronts are becoming all too obvious, and many of them have staged a closure primarily because they cannot sustain themselves any more in the open market system. Apart from the above problems, rural industries are reported to be facing many other infirmities, especially when competition with higher echelons of industry at home, and the freer flow of imported goods, are kept in mind. Inadequate and irregular supply of raw materials, unappreciative rules and regulations, lack of organised marketing channels, imperfect knowledge of market conditions, inadequate availability of credit, constraint of infrastructural facilities (most notoriously, the erratic supply of electricity), deficient managerial and technical skills, and so on, are the handicaps commonly attributed to such industries (Chadha, 1992: 202).

To develop an uptodate, *albeit* broad, idea of the difficulties being faced by tiny industrial units, especially in rural India, the 1999-2000 NSSO survey of the informal manufacturing enterprises is the best to draw upon. Table 20 gives an adequate hint about a very big proportion of tiny enterprises and small manufacturing establishments suffering from one or more problems, in their day-to-day operations. For example, more than 40.0 per cent of rural manufacturing establishments and 37.0 per cent of rural tiny enterprises complain of capital shortage; lack of infrastructure, 'local problems' which in most cases means harassment at the hands of local officials, competition from larger units, and non-recovery of service charges, are other problems commonly reported by such enterprises.

In this chapter, we concentrate on some of the emerging major problems of rural industry which, in our opinion, is adding to their vulnerability under the open trade regime and is becoming a cause of great national concern, most ostensibly because of the huge job losses witnessed in recent years.

6.1 Thin Institutional Support

In spite of many claims, and financial allocations, in the name of institutional support to rural industrialization, what has been actually falling to the share of the tiny rural enterprises is anything but pleasing. The institutional support can be visualized in many different ways. For example, formal institutions can help prospective entrepreneurs in setting up, and sustaining, tiny or household rural enterprises through imparting of training (in ITI, polytechnic, engineering college, etc.), providing initial investment funds (through cooperative, commercial and regional rural banks or Small Industrial Development Bank of India), imparting market intelligence, assisting in technology up-gradation, helping in input procurement and product sales, and so on. A recent survey of tiny and small rural industries, conducted by us during April-June 2000, in three states of India (namely West Bengal, Mahararashtra and Haryana) clearly reveals that public support is rather thin, in many aspects of institutional help. Table 21 lends adequate support to the view that a very high proportion of these industries, irrespective of their rural or urban locales, have either to fall back upon informal institutions (such as, for example, friends and relatives, fellow entrepreneurs) or struggle on their own. This is true for most aspects of their existence and operation (e.g. market intelligence, product sale, procurement of raw material, training for launching the enterprise, getting institutional finance, etc.). The slightly better position of the urban units is not a matter of great satisfaction because the absolute levels in their case are also very low; in any case, the rural units suffer these infirmities in a more telling manner (Chadha, 2001b).

Another recent (1999-2000) NSSO nationwide survey of the informal manufacturing enterprises, in rural and urban India, clearly points to a negligible role played by public institutions either in arranging basic input supplies or in helping sale of the final product (Govt. of India, 2000b: 94-99). For example, less than 2.0 per cent of the tiny rural enterprises (OAMEs) get their input supplies through government agencies and cooperative/marketing societies; likewise, less than 2.0 per cent of such enterprises are helped by such agencies in the sale of their product. As a consequence, such enterprises have to fall back upon private trade channels that result in pecuniary disadvantages which, at their meagre scale of production, are quite substantial in terms of per unit cost of production or net return. Quite often, such tiny enterprises are tied with specific sources for input supplies or for product sale or both. The 1999-2000 NSSO survey clearly shows that nearly 80.0 per cent of the rural OAMEs are tied to a single agency for input purchase, and there is only one destination agency for more than 90.0 per cent of them. Interestingly, there is not much difference between the rural and urban OAMEs in terms of lack of institutional support for input supplies or product sales; perhaps, it is the tiny-ness of their size and all its attendant production and marketing infirmities that puts them together rather than the rural or urban locale of their operation.

Similarly, as our analysis under Section 5.3 shows, public institutions were of limited avail to the tiny and small rural enterprises in effecting technological improvements, howsoever limited, whether connected with improved machinery or new products or product designs. The only silver lining has been that the nationalized commercial banks could provide loans to some of the tiny and small entrepreneurs, especially for installation of improved machinery; technology upgradation in the form of introduction of new products or new raw materials or new designs did not attract the attention of the banking sector. In total terms, a very big percentage of the tiny and small enterprises who dared to innovate in any of these areas had to do it at their own risk.

The neglect of the tiny sector owes itself, *inter alia*, to a faulty policy perception that has somehow continued to persist. To say the least, lumping of 'tiny rural industry' with 'small industry' under a single official umbrella called 'VSI' sector, especially with no clear locale perspective for the latter, was bound to generate wrong perceptions on the total needs of the 'VSI' sector on the one hand, and its internal constituents, on the other. The composite 'VSI' sector has traditional tiny rural industries as one part, important as it were in providing a lion's share of employment irrespective of the level of productivity, and modern small industries as the other which accounts for a lion's share in output against a small share in employment. The teaming up of un-matching entities was thus bound to create a weak partnership, and a relative sufferance of the former.

In effective terms, for every aspect of official support, the two constituents received 'unequal' treatment most ostensibly because of an understandable tilt in favour of the 'modern constituent' since 'impressive' outcomes of official dispensations could be shown only that way. For example, "the 'protection' offered to some of the cottage and village industries has been without a firm commitment. Organized industry was *often* allowed to violate the restrictions and employment in the cottage sector" (Jain, 1980:1748). Again, "even in government purchases, the small sector has had price preference and organizational backup but not the cottage sector. The small sector also gets technical and organizational support through Small Industries Service Institutes, but there is no matching technical service for the village industries whose need is even greater" (*ibid*: 1748). An evaluation study on the working of the Rural Industries Projects revealed

> that there had been some deviations in the implementation of the programme to the extent that some part of the assistance was provided to relatively larger amongst the small scale units and also in towns which were excluded from the purview of the scheme. On the other hand, rural artisans did not receive adequate assistance, particularly in respect of technical advice, credit, training and marketing (Thakur, 1985: 39).

In some sense, the tiny rural enterprises are themselves to blame for the thin institutional support that has fallen to their share. A preponderant majority of them are not registered with any official agency. The 1999-2000 NSSO survey reveals that not more than 4.0 per cent of rural OAMEs are registered with one or the other type of official agency; the most popular agency for registration is the local body while a multiple of other agencies such as state directorate of industries, KVIC/KVIB, handicraft/handloom boards, etc. draw big blanks (Govt. of India, 2000b: 58). Clearly, there is a lack of rapport between the number of official, semi-official and autonomous development agencies floated for rural industrialisation and the vast army of tiny industrial entrepreneurs.

6.2 Weak State, Unfriendly Rules

The state has to play diverse roles to ensure a smooth functioning of the economy. Broadly, its functions fall under two categories: regulatory and promotional. Under the former, the state has to ensure that the production units conform to the prescribed environmental discipline, that the physical working conditions conform to the prescribed standards, that workers are protected against occupational hazards and diseases, that economic benefits prescribed under the law are duly dispensed, that exploitation of child and women workers does not take place, and so on. That bureaucratic procedures, law and order machinery including protection of the right to property, and public institutions concerned with day-to-day functioning of economic enterprises (e.g. electricity authorities, labour officer, district industries centres, etc.) work to promote such enterprises, are also a part of the state's regulatory responsibilities. On the other hand, the promotional roles have a wide canvas that encompasses provision of infrastructural facilities, technology upgradation, investment in human capital formation, and so on. We have already spelt out the weaknesses and strengths of public authorities and institutions in India as far as their promotional roles are concerned. In this brief note, we make some observations on how effectively the state has been performing its regulatory role, and to what extent, the normal entrepreneurial responsibilities have been discharged or dodged by the class of rural entrepreneurs.

The public perception about the standard of economic governance is not very pleasing. One comes across grumblings of a wide variety, practically from all parts of the country. It is widely believed, and often openly voiced, that the government machinery, rules and regulations, and lax law and order, work in an unfriendly manner, especially when tiny and micro rural industrial enterprises are at stake. A sizeable proportion of such enterprises would not touch their promising expansion plan just because, at every turn of their existence, they have to rub shoulder with corrupt field officials. Excessive interference by state functionaries, most dreadfully the chain of inspectors, under one pretext or the other, is another formidable bottleneck that India has not been able to tide over in spite of claims to the contrary. A heavy tax burden, especially in terms of its weight in per unit cost of production among the tiny and micro enterprises, is another deterrent that keeps many of these enterprises under threat of liquidation. Lax law and order machinery also creates its own adverse impact. Finally, the prevalence of pro-labour laws, under which firing of an errant worker is an extremely difficult proposition, is also quoted as a reason against executing an expansion plan; most of the existing rural enterprises are of the OAME type that employ family workers only and stay outside the jurisdiction of labour laws, and the moment they expand, *inter alia*, through a larger number of workers, they attract all types of labour laws, and bureaucratic hassles attached to them.

How is the wage-paid labour faring? Our own April-June 2000 survey of tiny and small rural enterprises shows that a very big proportion of workers engaged in rural industrial enterprises generally lack any kind of formal social protection or access to social security (Chadha, 2001b). Of particular concern is the non-compliance with *labour legislation and core labour standards*. To a large extent, such a non-compliance is due to the fact that a majority of the workers in such enterprises are self-employed or unpaid family workers; these enterprises are not subject to many legal obligations. In the case of those enterprises which do hire labour, compliance with the full range of labour regulations, including those governing hours of work, weekly rest, holidays with pay, minimum wages and social security contributions would more than fully absorb the very low profits made by such enterprises and may in fact drive many of them out of business.

Yet another interesting fact that needs to be underlined comes through the manner in which such enterprises operate. Labour relations are not subject to explicit and enforceable contracts; no job security is enjoyed or expected by wage-workers employed in tiny and micro rural enterprises. In the absence of trade unions in such micro-enterprises, labour relations tend to be paternalistic, with the owner of the enterprise working alongside his employees and apprentices. Moreover, the incorporation of such units into contributory social security systems scarcely seems feasible in view of the instability of the employment relationship (Oberoi-Chadha, 2001:49).

Much has been talked about labour policy reforms during the post-reform years. Unluckily, not much seems to have been done for the workers engaged in the unorganised industrial enterprises that nearly completely dominate the rural industrial sector. Issues such as minimum wages, insurance and provident fund, fixation of working hours, application of workmen compensation act, streamlining of hire and fire policy, etc. have hardly been pursued with the needed degree of seriousness. In short, labour conditions continue to be as bad today as they were before the arrival of economic reforms, if not worsened. The status quoist trend on the front of labour policy changes is more than evident in the Indian case, most certainly in the case of rural enterprises. That the state does not seriously view the unwholesome working and economic conditions of people engaged in the tiny and micro rural enterprises and that the public grievance redressal mechanisms are not upto their assigned task, is clearly authenticated by the fact that more than three-fourth of the rural enterprises do not know if labour reforms have been enacted during the past five years or so. In rural Haryana and West Bengal, nearly the whole lot of them express ignorance on this account (Chadha 2001b). It is only among rural enterprises in Maharashtra that some affirmative responses are forthcoming. On the whole, it is difficult to believe that rural entrepreneurs consciously deny the reality of labour reforms when some have indeed been enacted; the reality is that no much has happened on this front.

We must hasten to add that the inability of the rural industrial sector to comply with certain aspects of labour legislation is not necessarily an indication of defects in the legislation itself; it should rather be taken as a reflection of the low productivity conditions under which the sector has to operate. Deregulation of the labour market would do little, if anything, to improve those conditions. The general approach should, therefore, be to regard the basic standards and provisions of labour legislations as non-negotiable goals to be attained progressively in the rural industrial sector, and to establish the needed institutions to promote their attainment rather than to regard the precarious and unregulated nature of work in it as the norm for the rest of the society.

The progressive application of labour standards need not wait until the rural industrial sector starts catching up with the modern sector. There are certain core standards that are so fundamental that their non-observance should not be tolerated, irrespective of the sector involved. For example, fundamental human rights at work (freedom of association, abolition of forced labour and child labour, non-discrimination in occupation and employment) cannot go beyond the purview of any production sector, big or small, urban or rural; they are fundamental to human dignity, and indeed to the success of efforts to integrate the rural industrial sector with the general industrial sector, and into the rest of the economy. It is a pity that effective institutional intervention to remove gender discrimination in the matter of recruitment and wages has not been enforced. Such discriminations have been in existence for long, and legislations to check them have also existed for long; this is perhaps an area of institutional failure which shows weakness of the state many times more than its strength in other areas.

Another area which deserves priority attention is occupational safety and health. While it may not be possible for the rural industrial enterprises to comply with the full range of government safety and health regulations, there is no reason why they should not be able to benefit from information and guidance on the often simple and inexpensive measures that can be taken to reduce risks or from occupational health and safety counselling provided through community-based programmes, perhaps supported by NGOs (Oberoi-Chadha, 2001:54-55).

Finally, there is a case for extending the umbrella of social protection to workers engaged in the rural industrial sector. To begin with, the well-established social security schemes of the formal urban industrial sector could be extended to workers in the rural enterprises, wherever a suitable framework can be found, such as in the case of more developed micro-enterprises. For this reason, the Union Government should strengthen the national social security institutions, and, hopefully, the public's confidence in them. It should also encourage, and where possible, assist the state governments to strengthen locally-based institutions. The involvement of groups from civil society is essential in order to reach out to widely-spread workers in the rural areas. Some states have already extended social protection to workers in the rural areas. A number of NGOs too, most notably Annapoorna Mahila Mandal, Self-Employed Womens' Association, Asian Centre for Organisation, Research and Development, etc., have developed successful schemes providing at least basic social security benefits at the 'grassroots' level (Oberoi-Chadha, 2001:56). Such initiatives and experiences need to be documented and replicated.

6.3 Infrastructural Weaknesses

On the practical side, lack of adequate infrastructure has been a proverbial weakness that has thwarted the process of rural industrialization. Among economic infrastructures, transport and power have been the two most crucial constituents which kept rural development in general and rural industrial development in particular, on a low keel. But then, banking and credit, trading and marketing services, vocational training programmes, research and extension assistance, etc. have never been able to support rural industrial development beyond a point (Vyas-Mathai, 1978: 345-6). To this, one may now add communication and IT network that would govern the future working of the industrial systems in all parts of the world, rural India being no exception. Among the social infrastructure, a weak human capital base has always been a worrisome feature of India's rural society. Political infrastructure too has been an unhappy episode; the manner in which the grass-roots political institutions (e.g. panchayats, cooperative societies, etc.) have been functioning, especially under the local political pressures and caste divides, is too well known.

Going by the express concern of our study, let us confine ourselves to economic infrastructure. Our own April-June 2000 field survey has many eye-opening facts to reveal about the availability of infrastructural support at the grass-roots level. Table 22 informs us about the common availability of infrastructural facilities in and around the local area. More than 63.0 per cent of the rural and 46.0 per cent of urban tiny and small units do not at all have the benefit of an information centre; hardly 11.0 per cent of the rural and about 40.0 per cent of the urban units do have this promotional facility within a distance of 5 kms. More than three-fourth of the rural and about two-third of the urban tiny and small enterprises are without the support of a product-designing centre; such a centre is accessible to just about 7.0 per cent of the rural and nearly 20.0 per cent of the urban units within a distance of 5 kms. The unsatisfactory position about the availability of infrastructural support in the form of a training centre or a repair workshop is nearly the same, especially for the rural enterprises. The only silver lining appears in the case of banking facilities. Not more than 4.0 per cent of the rural and less than 1.0 per cent of the urban units are operating without the banking support; more than three-fourth of the rural and about 88.0 per cent of the urban units do not have to go beyond 5 kms. for availing of the banking facility. The situation is equally comforting as regards the existence of paved road in the vicinity; nearly 80.0 per cent of the rural and 90.0 per cent of the urban units have a paved road within less than one km. of their locale.

Again Table 22 throws up a mixed picture on infrastructural base inside the production units. It cheers us to see that more than 93.0 per cent of the rural and 99.0 per cent of the urban units have electric connection provided to them. This is highly deceptive, most certainly in terms of the adequate and timely availability of electricity. It is widely known that electric connections are provided, but electricity is not available for hours, and sometimes for days, together. This fate is quite apart from the wide-spread corruption that the tiny industrial units have to suffer at the hands of electricity officials whenever something goes wrong. The water availability does not, however, invite any doubt or suspicion. But then, sewerage is really a non-starter for a preponderant majority of the rural units; the urban units are relatively better off.

The rural units are a stark contrast to their urban counterparts in the matter of communication and IT support. For example, as many as 84.0 per cent of the urban units have a telephone connection inside the unit against 55.0 per cent in the rural ones; 20.0 per cent of the urban units have a fax machine against only 7.0 per cent in the rural units; and about one-third of the urban units have a computer against only 15.0 per cent in the rural areas.

In total terms, the infrastructural weaknesses stand out rather glaringly in respect of a number of items, especially the common facilities that are usually considered as the backbone of the growth triggering process. Items that usually figure in the domain of public sector investment, e.g. industrial information centre, product designing centre, industrial training centre, repair workshop, etc. are unambiguously the weak links in the process of rural industrialization in India. The public sector has thus a vital role to play. It might dilute its effort elsewhere but strengthening of rural infrastructures must be a top priority. In other words, now is the time to put together the plethora of *promotional programmes* intermittently introduced in the past and devise (and aggressively implement) a *comprehensive policy* towards modern industrial activity in rural India. The competitive economic regimes emerging fast from within the country and without must be seriously reckoned with.

6.4 Finance as a Major Constraint

Our April-June 2000 survey data throw up many crucial insights about the availability of institutional finance to the wide mass of tiny and small rural industrial enterprises in India (Chadha, 2001b). For example, institutional finance has been playing some role practically in all aspects of rural industries' existence. For example, the formal credit institutions lent help in the setting up of nearly 35 per cent of the survey units (in Maharashtra, their proportion was as high as 62 per cent); more than 40 per cent of the rural industrial units which ventured to invest, during the preceding five years, in improved machinery, were provided loans by commercial banks. The helping hand of public sector financial institutions is visible for many other purposes including provision of working capital. But then, much more needs to be done, especially to accommodate the financial needs of the rural enterprises which are ready with one or the other type of expansion plans but cannot execute them for lack of funds. Our survey data show that 76 per cent of the enterprises in rural India (88 per cent in Haryana, 71 per cent in Maharashtra and 72 per cent in West Bengal) which are keen to expand their business operation do not do so because of inadequate availability of credit; to more than 50 per cent of such enterprises, it is the delay in the actual disbursement of the loan money that stands in the way; complicated banking procedures hold up expansion plans for 43 per cent of the enterprises, and finally, 43 per cent of such entrepreneurs do not go in for their expansion plans because of the fear of encountering high level corruption among bank officials, and so on. Interestingly, the malaise of credit shortage affects the tiny and micro urban enterprises equally, if not more, seriously.

We are thus in a fairly comfortable position to assert that numerous constraints for obtaining institutional finance affect, in varying form and content, micro entrepreneurs in rural as well as urban areas, most ostensibly because they constitute the lower rung of the borrowers to whom neither the banking procedures apply benignly nor do the bankers' mindset is helpful to their specific problems and requirements. Insistence on collateral, small loan amounts involved, and higher transaction cost per rupee of loan advanced, are the major obstacles which stand between the bankers and rural industrial entrepreneurs. But then, it must be recognized that the problem of finance cannot be overcome unless the access of rural industrial enterprises to modern financial institutions is considerably augmented and effectively monitored; they cannot be left to the mercy of the informal credit agencies, especially when cost effectiveness assumes extreme significance.

The real challenge is to develop innovative credit delivery systems. Since, for many years to come, commercial banks will remain singularly ill equipped to deal with small borrowers, alternatives have to be found which combine the flexibility of the trader/money-lender relationship, with access to institutionalised credit. Not only are alternative banking systems/delivery mechanisms needed, but funds must also be steered from the formal banking sector into micro finance, since it is the formal (commercial) banking sector which is presently the custodian of almost all the savings and deposits in the country (Oberoi-Chadha, 2001:50-51).

The most crucial first step in this direction is to assess the credit worthiness of micro-enterprises. By no means, it is an easy task. There are few, if any, tools, techniques and experiences that can be drawn upon for assigning credit ratings to micro-enterprises. The banking/financial sector is simply not conversant with this issue. Perhaps, it is time to make a bold beginning that may trigger the learning process so to say. (Oberoi-Chadha, 2001:49)

A suggestion, forcefully endorsed by the 1998 RBI High Powered Committee (appointed for improving credit delivery system to small and rural industry and simplification of procedures thereof), is to set up small banks for catering to loan needs of small borrowers that would largely include most of the rural micro enterprises (Oberoi-Chadha, 2001:50). Procedures for determining the rating of such banks are not yet evolved; the RBI is still debating on what standards to set for monitoring the proposed small unit banks that are expected to be fairly evenly distributed over vast geographical areas. The high-powered committee has proposed that a self-regulatory mechanism, in which a number of these banks could associate together to decide norms for themselves, be one possible approach. But this idea has its own risks: on what basis can a central bank permit experimentation with people's deposits?

In recent years, many initiatives have been taken to improve the situation. The Small Industries Development Bank of India (SIDBI) provides loans to "modern" small industries which covers a small segment of the rural industry as well. Some commercial banks too have schemes for the modern small-scale sector, and some (very restricted) governmental support too is available to handloom/khadi/village industries. Some initiatives have been launched expressly to obviate the difficulties imposed by the collateral conditionality. For example, an initiative has been launched by some non-governmental organisations (NGOs) engaged in development finance, which has been backed, to an extent, by commercial banks, the National Bank for Agriculture and Rural Development (NABARD) and the Small Industrial Bank of India. The SIDBI is perhaps the most progressive among all agencies; it has created a *Micro Finance Foundation* with a capital base of Rs. one billion which provides loans to rural credit groups through NGOs. It may perhaps be pointed out that the mode of lending nonetheless continues to be *promotional* rather than of mainstreaming the credit requirements (Oberoi-Chadha, 2001: 50-51).

Recent experiments, however, reveal that while small operators may not individually qualify for credit within the stipulated banking norms, their credit worthiness rises if they work in groups. Credit groups composed of small borrowers often begin as savings groups, and while they establish their credibility as savers, they also qualify to apply for group loans - in quantities that banks can administer with reasonable efficiency - and then distribute the amounts among themselves according to each member's needs. The experiments, as yet limited to specified borrowing-groups in specified regions, deserve to be institutionalised at the national level. For this purpose, local governments need to be strengthened to take up the task; perhaps, the 73rd Constitutional Amendment opens up such possibilities.

Among the numerous recommendations made by the 1998 RBI High Powered Committee, delegation of more powers to branch managers for granting *ad hoc* facilities to the extent of 20 percent of sanctioned limit, strengthening of recovery mechanism, opening of more SSI bank branches in localised neighbourhoods in the private sector, are the ones that need to be pursued on urgent basis (Govt. of India, Economic Survey, 1998-99: 110; SIDBI, 1999: 101-02). The major hurdle that the authorities perceive is the difficulty of safe-keeping of money with such "small" unit banks.

6.5 Technology: The Achilles' Heel

The problem of production technology in the rural industrial sector has been handled rather perfunctorily, both at the policy level as well as in implementation, the big institutional structures created for this purpose notwithstanding. The most glaring lacuna is that technology improvement for rural industries has not been viewed as a part of overall technology development. Like other aspects of rural industrial organization, a distinct aloofness has been exercised in this regard too. The respective institutions entrusted with the responsibility of looking after the growth and welfare of rural industrial enterprises generally preferred to plough their own furrow. More often than not, they would rather shun ideas of technological change especially of the type that, in their opinion, would have labour-displacing effects. Numerous other aspects of technological up-gradation, e.g. product-quality improvement to lend further competitiveness, introduction of new working methods, new products, new designs of existing products, etc., at best received routine or subdued attention.

In the matter of effecting technological improvements, especially those involving new production lines, risk of competition, huge financial commitments, etc., the non-resilient attitude of individual production units is too well known. In a competitive market regime, this throws them back more and more over time while consumer preferences tilt in favour of the products of modern industrial units for their edge in product quality and prices. In a sense, the traditional rural industries are themselves to blame for their stagnating or declining demand trends.

In a broad sense, a technological improvement may involve any of the following developments: introduction of new tools/equipment used in production, use of new raw materials, introduction of new products or new designs of existing product varieties, more efficient methods of work, and so on. While the last category of change emanates primarily from individual producer's own initiative, commitment to work, and the degree of skill acquired, the first two types of changes have largely to do with institutional efforts. The introduction of new products or new designs of existing products could come about either through institutional prop or through commercial vision of the individual producer, or through a combination of the two.

We have many studies to show that in spite of the institutional claims to technological up-gradation, a preponderant majority of the rural industrial enterprises have not been able to switch over from traditional technologies, whatever way one looks at them. Unhappily, many branches of the rural industry suffer from this infirmity. For example, a detailed 1990 field survey of pottery units in rural Haryana (Table 23) clearly points to the yawning gap between the potential and the actual switch-over to improved production technology. No fewer than 96.0 per cent of the pottery units knew of a brick kiln for as many as 10 years, but only 21.0 per cent amongst them actually switched over to it; for electrical wheel, the position is far more depressing. Finally, a preponderant majority of the sample pottery units were aware of the existence of new products or new designs of the existing products but not more than a quarter of them actually adopted them. It needs hardly to be emphasized, therefore, that some serious lacunae exist, either at the institutional level or at the level of the producer himself, especially because claims of easy financial support and investment subsidies have been a part of the official policies till the early 1990s.

We have our own recent (April-June 2000) survey to educate us about the slow pace of technological improvement among the rural industry of India. Table 24A clearly shows that, during the preceding five years, not more than 50.0 per cent of the sample rural units knew about the existence of improved machinery specific to their line of production; only half of them reported the actual installation of the improved machinery; in the urban areas, nearly 63.0 per cent of those who knew about the improved machinery did succeed in having it installed. It is highly disappointing that in the present age of a revolution in information technology, not more than 25.0 per cent of rural industries knew of new products in their own specific trade, not more than 12.0 per cent of them knew of the new raw materials commonly used elsewhere, and just about 39.0 per cent of them were aware of new designs in respect of the products being turned out by them.

There cannot be a more firm way of authenticating the resilience on the part of the tiny and small industrial enterprises, especially the rural ones, to effect one or the other type of technological change than the fact that a very big majority of them are not even aware of the changing technological contours in their branch of production. It is a pity that new production tools, changing demand patterns as reflected through new products or new designs of the existing products which have already appeared elsewhere in the market, or even about the new types of raw materials which are already sustaining innovative production processes elsewhere, are not even known, for as many as five years, to a majority of such enterprises, both in the rural and urban areas. The only comforting fact is that more than 90.0 per cent of the whole lot of such rural units which had known about the new products or new raw material or new designs had adopted the same, within the preceding five years. But then, this cannot mollify the harsh reality that a vast majority of the producers continue to operate under the old, cost- and quality-ineffective technologies. In relative terms, the urban units seem to have done much better, practically in each aspect of the technological improvement; perhaps, the handicap of a low level of market intelligence does not operate as severely in the urban as in the rural areas. In any case, information technology has a big role to play in the days ahead, for rural industrial enterprises as also for their urban counterparts.

The total blame for the sluggish technological improvements cannot be put on the tiny and small rural enterprises. Public institutions too were of limited avail to such enterprises in effecting technological improvements, howsoever limited, whether connected with improved machinery or new products or product designs (Table 24C). The only silver lining has been that the nationalized commercial banks could provide loans to some of the tiny and small entrepreneurs, especially for installation of improved machineries; introduction of new products or new raw materials or new designs do not seem to attract the attention of the banking sector. In total terms, an overwhelming percentage of those tiny and small enterprises who dared to introduce new products or new raw material or new designs, had to do it with their own savings, and at their own risk; loans from government agencies and commercial banks were available to just about 10-15 per cent of such 'innovative' units

It is equally educative to see that public institutions have practically nothing to contribute towards the actual acquisition of any component of technological improvements (Table 24B). For example, more than 90.0 per cent of the rural units that effected technological improvement in the form of new machinery, acquired the same in the open market; nearly 80.0 per cent of those which introduced new raw materials had to straddle the open market channels for acquiring the same, and so on. To a fairly big proportion of the rural enterprises, new products and new designs of the existing products, as surrogates of technological improvements became available from their respective parent companies, through the sub-contracting system. Their own innovative endeavours in devising new products or new designs are also discernible amongst a fairly big proportion of rural enterprises; curiously, such endeavours are discernible more frequently among the rural units than their urban counterparts.

Incidentally, the question of technology has never been seen in conjunction with marketing. There are studies to show that whatever little productivity gains are available under improved production technology to some of the rural industries, their benefit is 'usurped' by trade intermediaries or other trader-capitalist combines rather than the tiny producer himself (Chadha, 1992: 230-242, Kurien, 1978:461).

6.6 Quality of Workforce

In our view, *a poor human capital base of India's economy, most markedly for its rural areas, is indeed its Achilles' heel*. Educated workforce in any economy is essentially a byproduct of its educational system. In India's federal democratic system, education and health are the development responsibilities of individual states. Although an overall policy umbrella is set out, from time to time, by the central government, yet priority thrusts on different levels and types of education, per capita expenditure on basic and higher levels of education or on primary and advanced levels of health services, etc. remain within the purview of the state governments. Numerous studies on social infrastructure in India show sharp inter-state variations in education and health services, on the one hand, and the increasing rural-urban gaps, on the other. For paucity of space, we cannot sketch out the state-level picture. Nonetheless, even the national-level position shows a fairly depressing scenario.

In quantitative terms, educational facilities in India have witnessed a tremendous expansion during the past decades, yet millions of children and adolescents, most markedly in the rural areas have had no education, or could not go too far. The situation regarding skill upgradation is particularly weak. For example, only about 5.0 per cent of secondary school level students were found to opt for vocational stream against a target of 25.0 per cent set during the eighth plan (Ninth Plan, Vol. 2, 1999: 122). Training systems suffer from limited flexibility, poor curricula and weak links with industry. The most serious lacuna from the point of rural industry is that training in government training centers is mostly focused on the organized sector which has extremely limited relevance for the economy at large, especially the kind of household, tiny and cottage enterprises that dominate the rural economy.

The weaknesses and lopsidedness of the Indian educational system never revealed themselves as blatantly as in recent years, when the Indian economy opened itself to world outside. The Indian workforce clearly stands divided into three broad compartments in terms of its educational and training capabilities. The top segment comprises a very small number of highly educated and professionally trained persons, hailing nearly exclusively from the urban areas, who are progressively becoming a part of the international labour market or the highly lucrative segment of the domestic market; undoubtedly, they are the product of a few top-class educational institutions (e.g. Indian Institutes of Technology, some engineering colleges, management institutes, etc.) that exist side by side with thousands of India's average or low-quality schools, colleges and other institutes. The bottom consists of those who still remain illiterate or could not go beyond, say, primary schooling, not to speak of their remaining devoid of technical training and professional skills. A fairly high proportion of India's working population falls in this category; by any reckoning, rural workers take a lion's share in this segment of workforce, and acquiesce to stay on in agriculture or in low-paid non-agricultural, including industrial, jobs. Finally, the middle segment, again constituting a fairly sizeable proportion of India's working population, is 'educated' in a formal sense but the quality of their education and training leaves much to be desired. It is this segment of 'educated job aspirants' that has entailed the widening of the mis-match between what the economy can offer and what they are looking for. Rural workers who have a fairly big share in this segment of workforce, are no exception.

For paucity of space, we cannot go into all aspects connected with India's educational system nor can we look through the rural urban differences in their ultimate detail. Nonetheless, it needs to be expressly emphasized that in spite of the progress attained on the educational front, the rot in the rural areas still persists, and is not likely to get mitigated in the near future unless some revolutionary policy steps are undertaken. In what follows, we briefly look at the educational background of the existing lot of workers in the Indian economy as a whole, keeping our more express focus on the rural workforce, and that clearly illustrates that much needs to be done to improve the employability and the quality of their employment, especially in the face of more exacting work standards that have set in during the post-reform phase.

6.6.1 Educational Background of Rural Workers

Table 25 gives the general educational background of rural workers. It is abundantly clear that, with one or two stray exceptions, in all parts of rural India, and, for both categories of rural workers, there has been a gradual decline, first between 1983 and 1993-94, and then between 1993-94 and 1999-2000, in the proportion of illiterate workers and a gradual increase in the proportion of educated ones; following the usual convention, we take secondary or higher secondary level of schooling and other higher qualifications as the dividing line between educated and uneducated workforce. It is as much evident that the proportion of semi-educated rural workers (those with primary and/or middle level schooling) has also witnessed a steady increase over time, practically in all parts of rural India. These are welcome developments, in their own right.

But then, we cannot hide the fact that, at the national level, as late as 1999-2000, only 11.7 per cent of rural male workers and just 5.0 per cent of their female counterparts constituted the 'educated workforce'. For the former group of workers, this percentage ranged from as low as 7.4 per cent in Madhya Pradesh to about 21.0 per cent in Kerala and Himachal Prades; for the latter, it ranged from a ridiculously low level of 2.0-3.0 per cent in Rajasthan, Bihar and Madhya Pradesh to 18.8 per cent in Kerala. Looking at the other extreme, it is rather frightening to see that in spite of the phenomenal expansion of educational facilities during the five decades of India's economic development, India's rural economy has still to contend with no fewer than 41.2 per cent of illiterate male and no fewer than 61.5 per cent of illiterate female workers. The situation is far worse in some of the states. For example, in 1999-2000, the proportion of illiterate male workers was as high as 54.4 in Bihar, 49.1 in Andhra Pradesh, 44.8 each in Madhya Pradesh and Rajasthan, and Uttar Pradesh, and so on. The only soothing pockets are Kerala (15.2 per cent), and to a lesser extent, Himachal Pradesh (26.9 per cent). The situation is rather appalling in respect of rural female workers. For example, again in 1999-2000, the proportion of illiterate female workers was as high as 76.3 in Bihar, 76.0 in Rajasthan, 69.3 in Uttar Pradesh, 68.3 in Madhya Pradesh, 66.5 in Andhra Pradesh, 62.9 in Orissa, 60.7 in Karnataka, and so on. For this category of workers, Kerala is the only pleasing spot (21.3 per cent). Even Himachal Pradesh which has done remarkably well in the matter of rural education, does not seem to have rid itself of the male bias; Table 25 clearly shows that, in the matter of educational standard of its rural female workforce, it is doing no better than many other states.

Table 26 unfolds a few more important facts. First, a fairly high proportion of the educated rural persons are involved in agriculture, primarily because agriculture is the mainstay of the rural economy, and it is not possible for all educated job aspirants to get into one or the other type of non-agricultural jobs. In a sense, it is redeeming to see that the proportion of educated rural persons choosing to stay back in agriculture has been increasing steadily from 44.38 per cent in 1983 to 50.18 in 1993-94 and to 52.26 per cent in 1999-2000; the corresponding figures for rural males have been 45.45, 51.53 and 52.79, and for rural females 26.93, 34.32 and 46.86, respectively (Cols.3 and 4). While for the rural males, the influx of educated persons into agriculture has been much faster during the pre- compared with the post-reform phase, for their female counterparts, it has been the other way round. To the extent that 'new agriculture' too demands higher levels of educational and training pre-requisites, 'modern agriculture', especially that linked with the world outside, is becoming an attractive career to the educated job seekers.

Second, a fairly substantial proportion of the educated incremental workforce, both males and females, has been accommodated by agriculture, during the pre- as well as post-reform years (Cols.5 and 6). It clearly points to the inability of many an educated rural job seeker to gain an entry into the non-agricultural sectors, including rural industry, most ostensibly because the number of such jobs are far too limited and the number of claimants far too large, even if the painful reality of low content of rural education is kept aside. Since the competition for non-agricultural jobs became more intense in the post-reform phase, largely because of the expanding demand-supply hiatus on the labour market, and the rural female job aspirants being the weakest link in the chain of competitors, more than 63 per cent of the incremental educated female workers staying back in agriculture should cause no surprise; during 1993-94/1999-2000, only 36.70 per cent of them could get into non-agricultural jobs while during the pre-reform decade, no fewer than 61.83 per cent of them could go to such jobs.

Third, lest the job entry behaviour of the incremental workforce, (Cols. 5 and 6) should cause any ambiguity or disappointment, it is essential to emphasize that the rate of growth of employment among the educated rural work seekers has been many times higher than that among the job seekers as a whole, irrespective of the sector in which they are ultimately absorbed. It is once again a confirmation of our earlier contention that many among the educated rural female job seekers could not get into the non-agricultural sector, more expressly during the post-reform phase, that the rate of growth of employment in this sector dropped for them from 9.76 per cent during the pre-reform phase to 6.11 per cent during the post-reform years, against its increase from 13.60 per cent to 15.87 per cent, respectively, in agriculture (Chadha, 2000a: 51). For the total of the rural economy, employment growth rates for the educated job claimants declined both for rural males and females, yet these were many times as high as those for the job aspirants in general. The crucial role of education, whether towards creation of additional avenues of self-employment in and outside agriculture, or for getting into wage-paid jobs in non-agricultural activities, is thus more than evident.

Finally, a note of caution is a must. In spite of the high growth rate of employment for the educated persons, inside and outside agriculture, for rural males and females, and, before and after the reform years, the fact still remains that the proportion of such educated persons is very low, and a majority of the rural workers, both in the farm and non-farm sectors, is still devoid of any creditable achievement on the educational front. It is a pity that as late as 1999-2000, not more than 12.17 per cent of rural males, and a ridiculously low of 2.17 per cent of rural females engaged in agriculture constituted the 'educated workforce' (Cols. 13 and 14). With the proportion of educated males and females, engaged in non-agricultural activities during 1999-2000, being 26.69 and 13.06, respectively, the situation is hardly pleasing outside agriculture either. Although these proportions have been increasing steadily over time, yet the low levels in the base year (1983) would not let even an extraordinary expansion improve the situation beyond a point. That is how, the share of educated rural male workers engaged in agriculture, starting from 4.91 per cent in 1983, could not go beyond 8.96 per cent in 1993-94, and to 12.17 per cent in 1999-2000; for their female counterparts, the share could travel from 0.32 per cent to 1.04 per cent, and finally to 2.15 per cent only. The upward journey in the non-agricultural sector commenced from 19.99 per cent in 1983, reached 23.38 per cent in 1993-94, and terminated at 26.69 per cent only, in the case of rural males; for rural females, the three flag points were 5.43, 11.37 and 13.06 per cent only (Chadha, 2000a: 51).

The vulnerability of rural workers in general and rural females in particular surfaces itself most blatantly when we go to technical/professional education, although the expanding network of technical/professional educational facilities is often glibly claimed as a solid achievement of the post-Independence India (Chadha, 1999a: 737). Our own April-June 2000 survey throws up a highly disappointing educational and training background of workers engaged in such industries (Table 27). Hardly 27.0 per cent of rural and 28.0 per cent of urban workers engaged in such enterprises report matriculation or higher level of schooling. On-the job training was reported by as many as 82.0 per cent of the rural and 86.0 per cent of the urban workers; just about 7.0 per cent of them in rural, and 9.0 per cent of them in urban areas, received training through government agencies. The most distressing picture is discernible on the front of technical education. For example, only 8 per cent of rural and 10.5 per cent of urban workers engaged in such industries have had the benefit of technical education; a substantial proportion (65.0 per cent of rural and 48.0 per cent of urban workers) of them nonetheless stopped at the ITI or polytechnic level; workers with management degrees (e.g. MBA) were nearly conspicuous by their absence, both among the rural and urban enterprises.

Substantial differences do, however, exist between family workers employing themselves in such enterprises and those hired from outside on wage-paid basis. In general, the wage-paid hired workers have a slightly better schooling background than their self-employed employers-cum-workers. For example, while about 25.0 per cent of rural family workers self-employed in tiny and small rural enterprises reported matriculation and higher level of schooling, this percentage in the case of wage-paid hired workers was 27.0; the gaps are slightly higher (25.0 per cent against 29.0 per cent) among the urban units. The contrast between family and hired workers is most appalling in respect of training. As many as 94.0 per cent of hired workers against only 52.0 per cent of family workers engaged in the rural enterprises received training about their craft/product line only after taking up the job; the respective percentages for the urban workers are 93.0 per cent and 55.0 per cent, respectively. An equally distressing contrast is discernible in respect of workers' technical education. For example, about 14.0 per cent of self-employed rural family workers reported to have acquired some kind of technical education against just 5.0 per cent of the hired workers; the two figures for their urban counterparts are 26.0 per cent and 7.0 per cent, respectively. Interestingly, among the technically trained workers engaged in the rural tiny and small enterprises, as many as 6.0 per cent of the self-employed family workers had acquired an engineering degree against a negligible number among the hired workers; in the urban areas, these percentages were 15.0 and 7.0, respectively.

It is thus evident, beyond a shade of doubt, that a preponderant majority of the existing workforce engaged in the tiny and small industrial enterprises, most expressly the former located in the rural areas, is hardly qualified to grapple with the challenges of international trade and technology. In the coming years, the rigour of competition that the rural enterprises would face *vis-à-vis* their urban counterparts, on the one hand, and with the unbridled influx of imported goods, on the other, cannot be adequately answered with the educational, training and skill background of the existing lot of workers. In total terms, the picture is fairly gloomy.

6.6.2 Labour-force in the Making

But then, is rural India preparing itself for the impending job market challenges? Will the future cadres of rural labour force be qualitatively superior and technically well equipped to grasp the new job requirements? Unhappily, the answer does not seem to be very encouraging. Let us look at a very simple indicator of human resource development: *current status of attendance in educational institutions by children in different age groups*. Table 28 throws up many depressing features for rural people compared with their urban counterparts, and for females contrasted to males.

Firstly, it is clear that the proportion of children and adolescents not attending any educational institution declined, by varying proportions, between 1993-94 and 1999-2000, yet in each age group, the proportion of rural people not attending any educational institution is much higher than that of their urban counterparts. For example, as late as in 1999-2000, nearly one-third of rural children (age group 5-9 years) do not go to school while for the corresponding urban children, the absenteeism does not touch more than 18 per cent of them. That nearly 28.0 per cent of the rural children (age group 10-14 years) do not go to school is a highly disconcerting feature inasmuch as this is the age at which they should ordinarily be pursuing at least middle level of schooling; a big majority of urban children in this age group is indeed doing so. Again, going by the 1999-2000 data, no less than 64.0 per cent of the rural children in the age group 15-19 years do not attend any educational institution; some of them never ever went to school while others dropped out at one stage or the other. In total terms, the rural people are way behind their urban counterparts in terms of current status on attending educational institutions.

Secondly, rural children, compared with their urban counterparts, in each age-group, are late in reaching a given level of schooling. For example, in the age group 5-9 years, 54.0 per cent of urban children reach primary level of schooling against 48.0 per cent among the rural children; in the age group 10-14 years, 44.0 per cent of urban against 32.0 per cent of rural children reach middle level of schooling; the differences manifest themselves most conspicuously in respect of technical degrees/diplomas, especially when the adolescence is crossed over.

Thirdly, the worst placed are the rural females, in terms of attending school or acquiring varying level of education, in each age group. It is a clear proof of their social handicap that nearly 73.0 per cent of the rural females (against 48.0 per cent of their urban sisters) have done up with education by the time they enter the age-group 15-19 years; the handicap encompasses nearly the whole lot of rural females as soon as they move beyond their teens. The worst for them is in respect of technical degrees such as graduation in agriculture/engineering/technology/medicine and diplomas/certificates in agriculture/engineering/technology/medicine/crafts, etc. Just about 2.3 per cent of rural females (age group 15-19 years) are engaged in such professional studies against as many as 11.0 per cent of the corresponding urban females. In the next age group (20-24 years), their relative position is far worse, for the simple reason that most parents, especially those in rural areas, would like their daughters to be married off, latest in their early twenties. To complete the story, technical qualifications for the rural females, confined as they are to a microscopic minority among them, do not go beyond diploma in (village!) crafts. The rural lasses may better be trained in tailoring, weaving, embroidery, steno-typing, or still better, trained in cooking and 'better child rearing'! (Chadha, 1999a: 162-63).

In brief, the weak educational base of the rural populace that is likely to enter the fiercely competitive labour market after 5, 10 or 15 years, is sure to prove their Achilles' heel. Policy administrators must immediately realise that mass-based education and training policies are inescapable pre-requisites for improving the day-to-day vision of the common people which, in turn, promotes entrepreneurial vision, more durable employment, production efficiency and growth. As a nation, we are proud of our strides in the area of computer expertise and information technology; our experts are already trooping out to some of the most developed economies and many more will follow. But then, this should not obliterate the fact that back home, we have many times more of uneducated and unskilled workers, willing to be absorbed in low-paying menial jobs, and facing grim employment prospects with every new stroke of economic liberalization. This kind of 'uneven playing field' owes itself to the questionable education policy that has generated a 'handful of high-wage jobs' to the neglect of a 'vast pool of low-paid jobs' The future of rural industrialisation is deeply tied with this crucial aspect of social development. While policy analysts the world over are clear that sound education and training policies are more durable in promoting employment when a developing economy opens its frontiers to international trade and investment, it is a pity that such an awakening is not yet discernible, either in policy documents on educational improvements or in the lexicography of trade and development economists in India (Holmstrom, 1999: L3-L5). Can India afford to wait in this vital area of public intervention? Can we allow a vast section of our workforce, especially in the rural areas, to continue to suffer this infirmity *ad infinitum*?

6.7 Incidence of Child Labour

It is gratifying to see that the incidence of child labour has been declining steadily, both in rural and urban economies (Table 29). This accords well with the rising pace of school enrolment taking place in recent years following, *inter alia*, withdrawal of child workers from the rural labour market. In the rural economy, it is mainly the farm sector that absorbs most of the child workers; for example, out of 4.8 per cent of the children who were employed in 1997, as high as 4.2 per cent (i.e. nearly 88.0 per cent) were working in the farm sector alone. As is well known, these are not the usual type of workers; their work is in the nature of occasional help to family farm workers, especially during peak agricultural seasons. In a broad sense, most of these children are 'workers' only in a definitional sense.

It is equally evident from Table 29 that the involvement of children in the age-group 5-9 years, especially in the rural non-farm sector, is a dismissible phenomenon; it is only the senior child workers (aged 10-14 years) whose presence is noticeable in the labour market. But then, their involvement in rural non-farm activities (that include rural industry) too is of an extremely low order.

In aggregate terms, therefore, child labour would not appear to be a serious problem in the Indian economy. Nonetheless, there are specific activities and product lines in which child labour accounts for a noticeable proportion of the total workforce. In particular, a high proportion of hired child workers in many of these product lines is a potent source of their exploitation. For example, according to the 1994-95 survey of the unorganized manufacturing, under the semi-aggregated rural-OAE segment, 32.0 per cent of the total workers hired by food processing units, 28.0 per cent in wool and silk textiles units, 37.5 per cent in those engaged in textile products including garments, 19.0 per cent in non-metallic mineral products, etc. were child workers (Govt. of India, 1998:A1-A3). In more disaggregated terms, *a fairly high incidence of child labour is commonly reported for rural industries such as jewellery-, garment-, carpet-, toy-, lock-, bidi-, match-, brick-, pottery-, and ice-making, glass-, brass- and sports-goods, embroidery works, spinning and weaving, repairs services, etc.* That their exploitation takes place in many different forms, most notoriously through their exposure to unhealthy work conditions, long working hours and low wages, is accepted almost as a truism (Burra, 1989; Khan-Haroon, 2000; Singh, 2000; Roy Chowdhury, 2000). Again, it is equally serious that exploitation of child labour is spread out in different parts of India. For example, sectors particularly notorious for intolerable exploitation of child labour are:

> Power loom industry in Bhiwandi (Maharashtra), the match industry of Sivakasi (Tamil Nadu), gem-polishing in Jaipur (Rajasthan), shellac industry in Bihar and Madhya Pradesh, the carpet industry in Palamau, Varanasi and Mirzapur, the lock Industry in Aligarh, pottery in Khurja and glass factories in Firozabad (all in Uttar Pradesh) and the bidi manufacturers, brick kilns, plantations, tea shops and middle class houses all over the country (Lieten, 2000).

To gauge through the unwholesome working conditions and other types of exploitation of child labour, we draw upon the findings of a few micro studies. Here is an apt description of what is happening to child workers in the silk industry of Karnataka:

> Children work in the units for 10-12 hours, and are paid wages on a daily basis. Wages are not fixed and depend on the discretion of the employer. It ranges from the child not being paid to being paid Rs. 5-10 per day. There are no weekly holidays or leave for the children. When there is no power supply, the children are made to do house work in the employers' houses.

> The units are cramped, dark, wet and poorly ventilated and sometimes have small generators running inside the rooms, which generate carbon monoxide and other noxious fumes. Children suffer from bronchial ailments, cough, cold, persistent back pain, leg pain, lung infection and T.B. Constant exposure to uncleanness of dead worms and the unbearable stench causes dizziness and fever. Children are made to listen to loud music ostensibly to prevent them from hearing the deafening noise of the machines; this often causes deafness. Some children also suffer from silk allergy. Having to stand throughout the day leads to menstrual disorders in girl children and could also cause loss of a child during pregnancy. Many girl children in this sector reach puberty by the time they are 8-9 years. By and large, most children in this sector work under bonded conditions. Parents take an advance from their employers and bond their

children to their employers for several years until the loans are paid back (Maya, 2000: 2-3)

How does the exploitative employment of child labour matters towards a sizeable reduction of cost of production, and becomes a potent source of sustaining profits, is better learnt from the following account of the cotton knitwear industry in Tiruppur in Tamil Nadu:

> Use of child labour has been a feature of knitwear production in Tiruppur right from the beginning...Children would constitute roughly 20 per cent of the work-force in the finishing units. They are employed in 'unskilled' operations and are paid less than half of what adult workers in skilled operations are paid.
>
> It is found that individual direct exports can afford to replace child labour with adult workers without their profit margins being unduly affected ...Sub-contractors to the direct exporters, on the other hand, cannot replace child workers with adults on an individual basis as it would seriously undermine their competitiveness vis-à-vis other sub-contractors in Tiruppur. Moreover, most respondents complained of a shortage of adult manpower in Tiruppur and therefore the unwillingness of adult workers to undertake unskilled and low paying jobs.
>
> At the industry level, it is found that the knitwear sector in Tiruppur competes primarily on the basis of price and hence reduction of wage costs through employment of child labour is seen as essential to the industry's sustainability. Hence, use of child labour is implicated in a competitive strategy based on lowering prices. It therefore becomes imperative for policy measures that address the problems faced by manufacturers to move up the value chain where they can compete on the basis of improved quality and innovation rather than on low wage costs. Further, we also observe that enforcement like ban on use of children, on the contrary, may in fact prove to have a large negative impact by pushing them into sectors where laws governing work are difficult to enforce...
>
> The long work hours make work in the knitting industry completely incompatible with schooling. Vertical mobility within the knitting industry is possible and children after 3 or 4 years of work experience move on to skilled occupations like stitching. This appears to be the only positive aspect of children's work in the knitting industry *although it clearly implies child workers in this industry facing bleak prospects of improving their educational attainments and remaining tied down to this low-paid industrial employment for the rest of their life* (Vijayabaskar, 2000:12-13; italics added).

Yet another woeful story comes from child labour in the glass bangle industry of Firozabad-Uttar Pradesh. A preponderant majority of child workers were school drop-outs, hailing from poor families, and ever willing to get exploited through harsh and unwholesome working conditions in their present employment, with practically no prospect for moving on to better jobs, and so on (Sharma, 2000: 8-10).

It is clear that the incidence of child labour is fairly high in some industrial lines, and that its exploitation, in varying form and content, is a regular feature of the industrial economy in general, and rural industry in particular. It is a pity that till November 23, 2000, India had not yet ratified the *ILO Worst Forms of Child Labour Convention, 1999* (No. 182) under which exploitation in the form of "slavery, debt bondage, prostitution, pornography, forced recruitment of children for use in armed conflict and other illicit activities, and all other work harmful and hazardous to the health, safety or morals of girls and boys under 18 years of age" would be a cognizable offence (ILO, 2000: 6). India's record in respect of the ILO's earlier Core Convention (No. 138) called *Minimum Age Convention*, has not been too good either. As many micro studies vouchsafe, child labour not only continues to abound in certain branches of industrial production but its detection has hardly ever caught public attention, most markedly among the tiny and household-based rural enterprises. Still more depressingly, punishment to the erring enterprises has hardly been heard of. It hardly needs to be emphasized that the problem of child labour can be effectively tackled through a rigorous implementation of the existing laws; no fresh laws are needed.

6.8 Occupational Hazards and Health Conditions

Occupational hazard is an inescapable offshoot of industrial production system. In many industries, workers are exposed to unhealthy substances, dangerous tools, electric shocks, unwholesome place of work, and so on. Chemical agents (e.g. dust, fumes, mist, vapours, gases, lead and solvents, etc), physical agents (e.g. lack of ergonomically correct equipment, vibration, untidy and overcrowded work place, unsatisfactory lighting provision, ultraviolet radiation, exposure to heat and cold, etc.), biological agents (e.g. viruses, rickettsiae, bacteria and parasites of diverse kind), psycho-social factors (e.g. psychosomatic disorders, reduced job satisfaction, over-stretched work routine including night work, etc.) and human factor (most markedly the low level of education, and lack of awareness of health hazards especially those connected with chemicals and industrial fuels and oils, both on the part of the employer and the employee etc.) combine, in varying form and content, to create health hazards for the industrial workers. A wide variety of respiratory diseases, lung diseases, slow poisoning through inhalation, skin irritation producing dermatoses, allergic reactions and cancer are the commonly reported fall-outs of the chemical agents. Physical agents produce injuries of the hands, elbows and shoulders (especially when the semi- or un-skilled workers struggle with drill machines, hammers, user-unfriendly machinery used in, say, saw mills and shoe industry), headache and eye-strain (particularly under inadequate lighting arrangement). Biological agents are responsible for transmitting occupational infectious diseases, such as myotic respiratory diseases or skin infections transmitted through fungi-based organic dusts (e.g. bagasse and raw sugar in rural India). Psychosocial factors affect the nervous system that leads to an increased frequency of fatigue, nervousness, irritation and insomnia, besides peptic ulcer and gastro-intestinal diseases. In many cases, the home-based workers, usually working on piece rate basis, often combining agricultural or household work with industrial employment that necessitates stretching out daily work routine, face a higher level of stress and psychological inferiority. Finally, the weak human factor leads to a poor adaptation to the mechanized and chemicalized industrial environment, a casual attitude to work that often results in accidents, or occupational violence such as verbal abuse, threat and assault (Koren, 1987: 274-288).

While legal provisions for protecting workers against occupational diseases and injuries do exist and are applied, in varying form and content, to workers in organized industries, nothing of consequence exist for, much less applied to, workers engaged in unorganized industry; in India, tiny and small rural industries nearly completely belong to the latter group. Occupational health hazards are even more serious for those employed temporarily on contract basis. It is a pity that acts such as *Workmen's Compensation Act, Employees State Insurance Scheme Act (ESI), Indian Factory Act, Industrial Disputes Act, Dangerous Machines (Regulation) Act, Fatal Accidents Act, Payment of Gratuity Act, and Employers Liability Act do not generally apply to casual and contract workers as well as those engaged in the unorganized sector.* (Anant-Sundaram-Tendulkar, 1999: 36-38). Even for those engaged in the organized sector, relief through these acts does not come that easily (Nihila, 1995:1485). A greater pity is that a few of these acts, e.g. Workmen's Compensation Act, and ESI, which are legally supposed to be applicable to all varieties of industrial workers, are observed more in breach in respect of those working in the unorganized sector (a very big proportion of which consists of rural industry). This is plainly so because, *inter alia*, there is negligible scope for organizing labour engaged in such tiny and geographically scattered enterprises as rural industries are. In a preponderant majority of such rural enterprises, no labour is hired from outside (as in OAMEs); the family workers themselves act as employers as well as employees and in their case, the question of compensation or relief under most of these acts is, at best, a mere academic exercise.

That workers engaged in a wide range of tiny and small rural industries face serious occupational hazards and that their health conditions, including those of the employers themselves, are anything but satisfactory, come out of numerous empirical studies. Leather tanning and footwear, carpet manufacturing, bakery, bidi rolling, stone quarrying, manufacture of detergents, soaps and washing materials, paints and varnishes, matches, explosives and fire-works, clay and lime making, stone crushing units, electroplating, textile mills, asbestos making units etc. are more commonly known examples. For paucity of space, as also for the degree of seriousness that it reflects, we dwell upon the cases of tanning and stone crushing industries only. To capture a graphic account of what is happening to workers in leather tanning industry in Tamil Nadu:

> Leather tanning is a high-risk industry for workers who have to work with wet hides/skins and that too when the machine is in motion. Also, there has been an increase in the number of chemicals used in tanning; it is nearly 225 now ... These chemicals are used frequently and in large quantities in various processes of tanning. Prolonged contact with these chemicals leads to dermatitis, conjunctivitis, nervous disorders, itching of skin, throat, mucous membranes, chest pain, asthma, bronchitis, ulcer, fissures in arms, nose, mouth feet, etc. Some of these chemicals, if inhaled, can be fatal...

> Women tannery workers suffer from specific diseases. Women working in processes related to collecting, cleaning and packing sheep hair are prone to gynaecological problems like menstrual disorders, dysmenorrhoea and leucoma... Premature delivery and still birth, high rate of noe-natal, infant and maternal mortality, prolapse of uterus and miscarriage are some of the other problems reported (Nihila, 1995: 1484-85)

The story of workers in a West Bengal stone-crushing unit (Surendra Khanji in Village Chinchurgeria, Jhargram in Midnapore District) is equally appalling:

> Many workers ... were suffering from silicosis, which is one of the most deadly occupational lung diseases. It is caused by inhalation from silica. The level of risk depends on three factors: concentration of dust in the atmosphere, percentage of free silica in dust and duration of exposure. Cough with sputum, decreasing body weight and general malaise are its symptoms. Chronic bronchitis is frequently associated with advanced silicosis. This may progress to respiratory or cardiac failure... 20 workmen had died due to occupational diseases and another 12 were suffering from them ...All the deceased persons were mostly engaged in jobs like sieving, bag filling with stone dust, loading and handling dust bags in a confined space, ... most of the deceased persons died even after treatment of anti-tuberculosis...(Mukul, 1997: L37-38)

A special characteristic of the rural industrial enterprises in India that adds to the usual problem of health and occupational hazards is that a very high proportion of such enterprises is located in the residential premises themselves. Table 30 clearly shows that nearly 80.0 per cent of own-account enterprises in rural India, and 70.0 per cent in urban areas, are being run inside the residential premises. The vulnerability of household members, especially those involved in such enterprises is particularly high in respect of industries such as paper, leather, chemicals and rubber-, plastic and coal products; the proportion of residence-located OAME units is fairly high in respect of these industries, not only in the rural but also in the urban areas. But then, in many other branches of industrial production, an overwhelming majority of rural-OAMEs are working from inside the residential premises. It is thus clear that in a sizeable proportion of rural industrial enterprises, the workers are exposed to occupational and health hazards practically through every bit of their working and living.

Our own April-June 2000 survey too has some information about occupational and health hazards faced by rural industrial workers. For example, in the matter of health hazards, 23.0 per cent of rural enterprises complained of chest pain, 25.0 per cent of eye straining, and 32.0 per cent of fatigue. The incidence of such complaints was much lower among the urban enterprises. Perhaps, the urban units were relatively better organized or better scrutinized by public health authorities. The rural-urban position was, however, completely different in respect of occupational hazards. For example, only 6.0 per cent of rural, against 14.0 per cent of urban units reported the occurrence of industrial accidents; again, fire accidents were reported by only 6.0 per cent of rural against 10.0 per cent of urban units. The same was true of electric shocks, the rural and urban percentages being 14.0 and 19.0, respectively. The lower rate of occupational hazards among the rural areas is not at all because of greater safety observed by the entrepreneurs or more rigid enforcement of public laws. It is primarily because of a very limited use of accident-prone machines (for that matter, any type of machine per unit of labour), fewer units having power connections, and so on. The moot point that nevertheless needs to be stressed is that rural industrial workers involved in occupational accidents or other health hazards, although fewer in relative terms, face a really hard time in overcoming such contingencies whenever they occur; in India, the rural-urban infrastructural gaps are not as appalling as in the case of medical facilities.

Two implications follow. One, the quality of employment is anything but pleasing, both for the wage-paid as well as the self-employed family workers. It is thus malaise of a different kind that pervades the production regimes of such enterprises that needs to be attacked with different economic and social instruments rather than invoking the formal provisions of Factory Acts and Labour Laws, with all their concomitant abuses. Second, the product quality is the inescapable casualty; we are thus taken back to the issue of human capital base of the lowliest of the workers, which is emerging as the most essential ingredient of efficient and quality production in all product lines. The writing on the wall is clear. Unless such units improve the quality of their products which, in turn, necessitate a drastic restructuring of their working environment and more wholesome working conditions, they are bound to meet their doom in the competitive product market regimes especially through the unbridled flow of imports which has already set in.

6.9 Environment Concerns

It may be naïve to believe that the process of rural industrialization in India is without its environmental cost. The nature and extent of pollution varies from industry to industry, from operation to operation within a given industry, the type and intensity of energy use, the degree of environmental consciousness among the people involved, system followed for waste disposal, and so on. In total terms, industrial pollution in rural areas has more serious adverse consequences. It damages fertility of the soil which, in turn, adversely affect agricultural production and livelihood of a large proportion of the rural population. In the absence of proper health facilities, sanitation and potable water in the rural areas, even a moderate level of industrial pollution can lead to a big loss of human life and cattle population; in fact, this would not leave people living outside rural areas unaffected because products from agriculture and animal husbandry are a part and parcel of their daily life. As we saw earlier in Chapter IV, the house of rural industry in India no more consists of the traditional handicrafts, cottage and household enterprises that used to be typically free of the usual environmental menace. Today, rural India has an assorted mix of all varieties of industries, with their production locales varying from city outskirts to places deep inside the villages. The list includes numerous industries that are plainly susceptible to water pollution or to air pollution or to both. Examples are slaughterhouse, dairy, vegetable oil, distillery, sugar manufacturing, especially of the semi-refined (khandsari) type, bakery, etc. under food processing industries, paper and pulp, tanneries, under agro-based industries, small dye and dye intermediate units, pesticides, etc. under chemicals and pharmaceuticals, electroplating, metallurgical works, lead-based products/activities, battery recycling activities, re-rolling units, foundaries, etc. under metal product manufacturing, ceramic, lime stone, brick-making, cement, etc. under non-metallic mineral products, and so on.

As in other developing economies, in India too, the rising number of rural industrial enterprises has been eroding the natural resource base of the countryside as well as causing pollution through emission of gas, water, solid wastes, industrial dust, and so on. The generation of toxic and hazardous waste, and the release of smoke and other poisonous gases, during the production process, although still on an extraordinarily lower scale compared with what the urban industries are doing, is undoubtedly overtaking the rural industrial locales also, especially in the case of industrial clusters located at varying distances from the major industrial and commercial cities/towns. The example of Tiruppur textiles cluster in Tamil Nadu, a success story of a textile-exporting zone, has its dark side also; the area has no provision for the collection, treatment or disposal of the sewage and other municipal effluents, and the usual practice is that these are deposited into water bodies or on the landmass. Two pollution indicators (namely bio-chemical oxygen demand from sewage, and, electrical conductivity) showed utter neglect on the part all concerned parties (Saith, 2000:81).

The tiny and small industrial units suffer from a number of operational handicaps that make their manufacturing processes more polluting than those of the larger units. There are many studies to show that small-scale units generally use inefficient technologies that lead to loss of raw materials and products in process which, in turn, get mixed with the waste streams.

> In most cases, the maintenance of plant and machinery is poor, and the workers engaged lack skill and training. Poor maintenance leads to leakage of materials, which in turn causes pollution. In many industries, anti-pollution measures are either commercially non-viable or are too expensive to be afforded by small–scale entrepreneurs. Haphazard growth of units in very limited space has also posed a major hindrance in the installation of pollution control equipment in several cases. Inadequate infrastructure and roads in some industrial clusters create difficulties in transporting waste to safe dumping sites, wherever such sites exist. In may locations, proper landfills or dumping sites are non-existent. In the absence of proper waste disposal facilities, many units are found indulging in dangerous dumping practices like off-loading hazardous wastes in open areas or in municipal sewer-system unfit to carry such substances (Bhattacharyya-Bhattacharyya: 2000: 40).

6.10 Industrial Sickness and Closure

It is undoubtedly true that while the number of small scale and tiny manufacturing enterprises has increased manifold over time, practically in each region of the Indian economy, a disturbing feature that has all along accompanied this expanding industrial base has been one of industrial sickness and closure. In common parlance, an industrial unit is described as a sick unit if it incurs a loss in the previous production year and is likely to incur losses in the current accounting year. From a different perspective, an enterprise earns the status of a sick unit if its accumulated losses are equal to or exceed 50.0 per cent of its peak net worth in the immediately preceding 5 years. From yet another perspective, persistent irregularities or faltering in its dealing with a lending financial institution or bank, most expressly a default in paying four consecutive interest payment installments, would also put it in the league of sick industrial units (World Bank, 1992: 43). In general, it is widely reported that the incidence of sickness is relatively larger among the units set up or working with borrowed money, compared with those coming up and sustained with own funds. In their extreme defaulting outfit, many of the sick units either close down their shutters or simply become 'untraceable'. It is not a coincidence that, in report after report on the working of small scale and tiny enterprises, the proportion of 'untraceable' or 'missing' units is reported to be fairly high (Govt. of India, 1992: 20; Govt. of India, 2000: 103).

It is a pity that regular statistics on sick or closed industrial units, most pointedly for the rural industrial enterprises, are not available. At best, ideas about this malaise among the rural enterprises can be framed only by looking at small scale industry as a whole, most ostensibly because an overwhelming majority of sick industrial units belongs to the small scale segment, and that, for all practical purposes, the whole of the rural industrial sector consists of small scale and tiny units; (to remind ourselves, as on 31st March, 1999, nearly 99.0 per cent of the sick/weak units are located in the small scale sector, and during 1994-95, more than 99.0 per cent of rural manufacturing enterprises were in the unorganized segment which nearly exclusively consist of tiny, household and small units).

Table 31 throws up three striking features. First, nearly 35 per cent of rural small scale units get closed down during 1987-88, presumably following varying durations of sickness or undulating financial career, in each product line. Again, in rural areas, one-third or more of the units are closed in as many as thirteen of the nineteen product lines; the worst suffering product lines are rubber-plastic, jute-mesta, chemicals and chemical products, machine tools, etc. where, for one reason or the other, around 40.0 per cent of units are closed in each product line. Second, for most product lines, the percentage of closed units is higher in the urban than in rural areas; the relatively higher incidence of closure is clearly discernible among food products and wool-synthetic, etc. In any case, the slightly better performance of the small scale rural manufacturing units, compared with their urban counterparts, does throw a clear hint about the 'tragedy of the commons'; it is indeed the smallness of the scale of their production, and the associated infrastructural, technological, pecuniary and marketing bottlenecks, that puts rural and urban units in a common league of sickness, finally leading to closure. This is adequately corroborated by a fairly similar pattern revealed by small scale units as a whole (rural + urban) in 1994-95 and 1987-88; the rank correlation coefficient between the proportion of sick units in 1987-88 (column 4) and that in 1994-95 (column 5) is 0.681 which is significant at 0.01 per cent level.

Third, a striking difference is discernible, between rural and urban areas, as regards the distribution of the closed units among various product lines. Within the rural areas, the greater share of the closed units goes to food products, repair and other services, textile products, metal products, wood and wood products and non-metallic mineral products; these product lines together account for nearly three-fourth of the total closed units in rural India. On the other hand, while most of the above product lines together have a major (56.0 per cent) share of the total closed units in urban areas, industrial groups such as chemicals and chemical products, rubber-plastic, machinery and machine parts, paper and paper products, etc. also figure prominently here among the closed units. Once again, the picture for the total of small-scale units (rural + urban) in 1994-95 is strikingly similar to that in 1987-88; the rank correlation coefficient between column Nos. 8 and 9 is as high as 0.96, which is significant at 0.01 level.

In a traditional industrial setting, more expressly when the domestic industry is not so much exposed to competition from abroad, we may generally come across a parabolic pattern of sickness and closure. The rate of mortality is fairly low among the youngest enterprises, possibly because of the untapped enthusiasm of the entrepreneur, relatively lower capital requirement for the initial 2-3 years, limited and manageable market operations, no immediate fear of technological obsolescence, etc. As the enterprise enters into the middle age of its career, many initial advantages evaporate; most essentially, the stress on production technology and market competitiveness goes up, and with that, the need to arrange an enhanced quantum of capital, especially the working capital, increases. Any failure in the financial market, at this stage, puts much higher stakes to jeopardy unlike the limited stakes in the initial stages which can, in most cases, be absorbed even through 'financial help from friends and relatives'. Finally, when the enterprise survives for many years, it develops a determined 'will to expand', acquires sufficient 'experience of the trade', and gains enhanced 'market standing'; accordingly, the prospect for sickness, failure and closure goes down once again (Sandesara, 1993:226).

Things are, however, likely to change when the domestic economy becomes a part of the global economic system, and the domestic industrial sector, including the tiny and small rural industry, has to face fierce competition from abroad. Perhaps, the age of the enterprise ceases to be relevant. Now, the competition from abroad puts tremendous stress on the technological capabilities, product quality and price levels of tiny and small enterprises. Moreover, the technological, product-quality and price gaps between such enterprises and large domestic units also get magnified, primarily because the latter are more readily able to effect all the needed improvements while the former cannot. A gradual withdrawal of the 'protection umbrella' including the phasing out and reduction of input subsidies and other market support, inability to match the higher hygienic, environmental, and product-quality standards entailed by the new trade regimes, add their share to the hastened process of industrial closure among the tiny and small units, most markedly in the rural areas.

In general, one can think of a number of reasons for industrial sickness and closure. Until recently, lack of adequate working capital has been quoted as the most restrictive bottleneck for a fairly big percentage of the closed units. For example, the 1988 census of small scale industrial units found the following major reasons (in the order indicated) for industrial closure: (1) lack of adequate finance, (2) low and fluctuating levels of demand, (3) non-availability or irregular and inadequate availability of raw materials, and (4) infrastructural constraints, most markedly the erratic and expensive availability of power and transport facilities. In terms of our own April-June 2000 field survey, all these factors continue to be responsible for industrial closure but the ordering has significantly altered. It is now the scarcity of raw material that is primarily contributing to closure of small scale and tiny industrial units, followed by power shortage, demand slump, labour and capital shortages, in that order (Chadha, 2001b).

In many product lines, under-utilization of the installed capacity leads to significantly higher per unit production cost which, in turn, entails price disadvantage and a squeeze in demand; the 1994-95 survey of the small scale industrial units clearly shows that, in rural India, nearly two-third of the installed capacity was under-utilized among units engaged in job works, and nearly one-third for those engaged in manufacturing/assembly or processing (Govt. of India, 2000: 79). Poor educational and training background of entrepreneurs as well as workers, leading to inadequate technical expertise and obsolete production methods, are another set of causes generating a high level of sickness among the rural enterprises (Chattopadhyay, 1995: 87-92). Under the sub-contracting arrangement, many tiny and small rural units, most strikingly those feeding urban parent companies, undergo intermittent bouts of closures partly because they receive irregular orders from the parent company or payment for the works executed are inordinately delayed or the production contract is abruptly terminated. At the institutional level, lack of adequate coordination among the various financial institutions and banks has often contributed to sickness and poor performance for new units, sometimes even before the actual production commences (World Bank, 1992: 42-51). Finally, cumbersome regulations and bureaucratic hassles, especially the high-handed and corrupt attitude of local officials, throw many a tiny and small unit out of gear.

Many suggestions are put afloat to tide over the serious problem of industrial sickness, especially among the rural units. First, reliable information about the extent and nature of sickness/failure must be generated through special surveys; perhaps, a special NSS round could be earmarked for this purpose. Second, emphasis must necessarily be more on prevention rather than rehabilitation; ironically, some studies do show that 'sickness is artificially created and prolonged' primarily to grab the benefits of rehabilitation. Third, the quality of lending to the prospective rural industrial entrepreneurs must improve; under the new dispensation, the financial institutions and commercial banks have an added responsibility of scientifically assessing the economic viability of the projects, monitoring their performance, and if need be, acting as catalyst intermediaries vis-à-vis the post-production or marketing channels that their loanees have to contend with. Finally, the orientation of public support must now shift from 'protection' to 'promotion'. Undoubtedly, public agencies must now focus more attention on targeting extension, training and advisory services at the pre-investment stage, rather than extending financial support, input subsidies and other concessions in a blanket manner. To say the least, the human capital base of the prospective entrepreneurs must take precedence over physical capital, and public agencies must play a big role in this regard.

6.11 Marketing Weaknesses

In marketing too, the traditional village industries face diverse problems, both on input and output sides. Most of these industries produce goods meant to cater to final demand and hence have very thin forward linkages, if at all, with the modern industrial sector. The production-market nexus can be divided into two broad categories: small-scale production with small-scale markets and small-scale production with large scale markets (Kurien, 1978: 460). There is no doubt that a preponderant majority of village industries and crafts belong to the former category and their major problems arise out of extremely limited technological and market links with the rest of the economy, apart from the low, and usually fluctuating, levels of local purchasing power. More baffling questions are posed by the other type of production-market nexus. Handloom, 'beedi-making', machine-part manufacturing, and embroidering, are good examples of small-scale production with large scale markets. Here, the exploitation of the tiny producer assumes two major forms. In the first form, a big lot of producers are advanced working capital, generally in the form of material inputs, by a private trader usually with a forward 'contract' for the purchase of the final product, at pre-assigned prices. In effective terms, the benefit of value-adding accrues to trade intermediary rather than to the producer himself (Kurien, 1978: 460; Chadha, 1990). Table 32 exemplifies the point with respect to a typical rural household manufacturing activity: rope making. Three technological levels are at work. It is absolutely clear that operating through a trade intermediary deprives the craftsmen of much of the benefit of value-adding. It bears emphasis, in particular, that the degree of deprivation increases significantly as we move from 'traditional' (hand-operated) to an 'intermediate' (pedal-operated) and further on to a 'modern' (power-operated) technology. Production under such contrived trade regimes is a common feature of rural India, and is clearly a hot-bed of exploitation (Kurien, 1978: 460; Chadha, 2001b).

The second form of exploitation, quite common in certain regions and crafts, is through the medium of non-genuine cooperatives. There are numerous instances of cooperative organizations which *de jure* are producers' cooperatives but *de facto* are traders' cooperatives. A cooperative for the tiny producers under small-scale production with large scale market scenario must assume a more comprehensive role of combining production, financing and marketing responsibilities. For example, "handloom cooperatives are effective and successful where they perform all these functions and where the actual producers are actively involved in the working of the cooperative" (Kurien, 1978: 460-61).

Orderly marketing is no doubt important in its own right. In the case of tiny village industrial units, the fundamental problem, however, is that, by and large, their products are consumed by low-income groups, mostly in the local village itself and/or areas around, with whom deficiency of demand is a chronic problem. The paradox so far has been that the demand for their products has been shrinking with rising (rural) incomes, most convincingly because of consumers' choices tilting in favour of goods produced by modern industrial units, with an urban locational bias. In a sense, the rising rural incomes have been a drain on rural industry and a support to urban industrial expansion. The rural industry must, therefore, expand its market. A growing market for the rural industry will come if only product quality improves, prices become competitive, and consumers' orientation gets diverted, and so on. The fundamental question of production technology thus comes up once again.

A number of institutional measures have been put through, from time to time, to help producers in the tiny and small-scale sector in the marketing of their products. Unluckily, the support measures do not make a distinction between rural and urban producers. Moreover, under the common rubric of 'marketing problems of small scale industries', the specific problems of rural industry in general, and its most dominant component of tiny and household-based own-account enterprises, do not get the needed attention. Nonetheless, looking at the marketing support extended to small scale industry as a whole would apprise us, *albeit partially and sketchily*, of the inadequacies in policy perceptions as far as the bulk of rural industrial enterprises are concerned.

The major interventions have been to (1) accord price and purchase preference; (2) extend fiscal incentives; (3) facilitate participation in trade fairs; and (4) promote ancillarization. Under the *Price Preference* component of (1), a price preference upto 15 per cent is accorded to SSIs over the lowest price quoted by the large units. Under the *Purchase Preference*, nearly 360 items are reserved for exclusive purchase from the small-scale sector. In addition, some more items are specified for partial/graded purchase, to the extent of 50 to 75 per cent, from the SSIs. The actual purchases are effected through the Directorate General of Supply and Disposal, Railways, Defence, and various other central and state government departments and public sector undertakings (Govt. of India, 2001: 154).

An objective assessment of the *Price and Purchase Preference Policy* would reveal that diverse conditionalities are often attached, at state more than at the central level, and at district more than at the state level, by the procuring agencies so that *de facto* purchases never conform to *de jure* obligations. In some cases, the policy simply gets abused by a few vested interests. "Some of the small-scale units have managed to create a monopoly like situation within the price preference scheme and managed to corner huge contracts which at times they are not able to honour" (*ibid*:154). Undoubtedly, the tiny rural industries would stand last in the queue when such conditionalities are imposed or purchase contracts are manipulated. To overcome such lacunae, and to make the scheme really effective, the Gupta Committee recommends assigning it a statutory backing. Further, it recommends that the marketing efforts may be supplemented by State Industrial Corporations or the marketing bodies set up at the regional level, especially because of the limited spread of NSIC including the absence of its wide network (*ibid*:154-55).

Under *fiscal incentives*, the excise benefits are (partially) extended to items produced by the SSI units, using third party brand names. On paper, this facility is extended to SSI units located in rural areas alone. But then, 'rural areas' are not rigorously defined. Consequently, much of the benefit actually accrues to urban units. It is essential that the criterion of 'rural locale' should be rigorously defined and adhered to. Moreover, to overcome the handicap of limited production capability of most of the rural units, a cluster approach should be encouraged to enable SSI produce under a common brand name; individual units should stand exempted from excise duty (*ibid*: 155).

Owing to their poor financial position, small-scale rural enterprises by themselves can ill afford to *participate in trade fairs*; for a vast majority of product lines, a big void thus exist between production capabilities and potential market expansion, especially for units whose products can go much beyond the frontiers of local markets. Although, institutions such as KVIC and SIDBI, give subsidies to encourage participation of small entrepreneurs in trade fairs, yet the quantum of support is grossly inadequate keeping aside the lackadaisical manner in which the support is usually dispensed. It is hardly surprising, therefore, that the scheme generally does not go beyond the urban units, and then, the 'bigger ones' among the small-scale enterprises. The Gupta Committee strongly feels that the scope of participation in domestic trade fairs should be expanded, through the combined efforts of NSIC, SIDBI, the DC (SSI) and SSI Associations. The number of buyer-seller meets must increase. A marketing development authority should be created to disseminate information on product, cost, technology, demand and supply and to deal with the problems of captive marketing, brand and consortium development, and so on. Perhaps, creating a Marketing Development Fund may also help (*ibid*:156-58).

Sub-contracting/ancillarisation offers tremendous opportunities for small rural enterprises to mitigate their marketing problems. It seems, however, that all those elements which could forge vertical linkages along the hierarchical continuum, through ancillarization, subcontracting, common production programmes, etc. has remained largely non-operative; most certainly, these did not go beyond a few specified product lines. Moreover, the success of ancillarization depends upon the availability and dissemination of information, capacity utilization and a precise assessment of technical capabilities of small-scale production units. The DC (SSI) should play a leading role for promoting sub-contracting environment in a wide array of industrial activities, consistent with the base and structure of local industry and the degree of rural-urban interface that exists. Most essentially, there should be specific programmes for technical upgradation of the prospective vendors/sub-contractors to enable them to meet the needed quality standards (*ibid*:158-59).

6.12 Quality of Employment

Quality of employment is a composite concept which encompasses numerous features, not only for the wage-paid workers but for the self-employed also, primarily because in the case of rural industries, a fairly big proportion of workers are un-paid family workers themselves. For the wage-paid workers, facilities such as paid leave, pension and bonus, medical and housing support, accident and disability benefits, insurance cover, etc., are one set of pre-requisites for decent employment. The number of working hours per day, over-time allowance, inflation-indexed wage-rate adjustment, employee-employer relationship including workers' participation in management, etc., make up another set of conditions. In the case of tiny and small rural industries, where wage-paid employees work side by side with the self-employing family workers, including the entrepreneur himself, factors such as adequacy of space, light and cleanliness, availability of heating, cooling, sanitation, drinking water facilities, etc., are close proxies for decent work conditions.

6.12.1 Working Environment

We have adequate evidence that shows poor quality of employment in tiny and small rural industries. To gain a comprehensive view of the prevailing situation, we discuss not only the physical and economic aspects of the working conditions but also the health and occupational hazards usually faced by workers. The most severe economic sufferance nonetheless comes from the low level of productivity which is an unambiguous surrogate of low quality of employment.

6.12.1.1 Working Conditions

We have a plethora of studies that testify to the pathetic working conditions, both physical and economic, in such industries. Generally, physical working conditions affect hired workers quite differently than the employers; in our case, however, both get affected, in varying degree, primarily because both work together and both have to absorb the sting of unwholesome work premises and work techniques. Let us have a glimpse of this 'unwholesomeness'.

6.12.1.I (i) Physical Working Conditions

Recent case studies of bakeries, savouries establishments and fish processing units in Maharashtra throw up highly disturbing signals, practically for each aspect of their existence and operation. Here is a faithful description of what is observed in the bakery units:

> The two Acts applicable to bakeries specify 5 factors relating to health and safety. These are cleanliness, ventilation, sufficient lighting, precautions against fire, and the maintenance of a first aid box... Only one bakery has a fire extinguisher, that too not in a working condition.
> All units except the one recently renovated are dark and dimly lit, only one with an exhaust fan.
> None, of course, has a first aid box, the owners being quite amused when we asked them about it.
> The suffocating heat and smoke of the continuously burning ovens in a room which has little ventilation and a clogged chimney impacts both the quality of the product and the health of workers. In every bakery we

visited we saw the kneader's sweat falling straight into the dough. All workers complained of eye, breathing and 'throat' problems; we ourselves could not bear the smoke for more than a few minutes. The workers spend a not negligible amount every month on eye drops… as well as on tonics to make breathing easier…

No worker is compensated for any injury at work; the Worker's Compensation Act does not apply to bakeries. Burnt and scarred hands and feet have to be tended by the workers themselves. Also, as the workers sleep on the hot floor only on weed mats, they are continuously affected by insect bites and rashes, some even reporting rodent bites. The long hours of work, carried out while standing, result in backaches and varicose veins … (Dewan, 2001).

Anybody familiar with the working of the bakery, sweet-meat and food processing establishments in rural India would subscribe to the truthfulness of every word of what is described above. But then, the malaise is not confined to these branches of production. The working conditions are also reported to be appalling, in varying form and content, in many other industries, such as tanning and leather goods, handloom, powerloom, beedi-, brick-, lime-, soap, paper-, carpet- and match-making industries, saw- and oil-milling, fire works, carpet-making, stone-quarrying, marine-fishing, metal ware industries, and so on.

We have something to add from our own survey also (Table 33). It is distressing to note that nearly 76.0 per cent of the rural and nearly 66.0 per cent of the urban units operate without any heating facility, exposing their workers to hazards of extreme cold and associated medical infirmities. The facility of electric fan is, however, available in a very big majority of such enterprises; it is a different matter nonetheless that the fan may not work for hours together simply because electricity is not available. But then, workers including the family workers, in about 55.0 per cent of the rural and about 30.0 per cent of the urban units are cluttered in closed working premises, which deny them the most crucial pre-requisite of adequate fresh air; that their production efficiency suffers is a foregone outcome. An extremely unpleasing situation is discernible about the space available to the workers for taking rest, when exhausted out of fatigue. On the whole, the physical conditions of work throw up a highly unwholesome and unpleasing situation.

6.12.1.I (ii) Economic Conditions

Conceptually, two sets of indicators are needed to describe economic conditions of people engaged in any production line. For hired workers, facilities such as paid-leave, pension, bonus, etc., are the relevant indicators. For overall economic health of the enterprises, which has a straight bearing on economic conditions of employers as well as employees, productivity performance is the most crucial core indicator.

First, we look at the *economic conditions of wage-paid workers*. Our April-June 2000 survey data throw up a mixed bag of positive and negative features (Section B, Table 33). For example, nearly 54.0 per cent of the rural and about 31.0 per cent of the urban units have no provision of paid-leave. The facility of provident fund, house rent allowance, insurance cover, disability benefits, etc. is nearly conspicuous by its absence in rural as well as urban units; the position about injury allowance is only a shade better. Most crucially, nearly 81.0 per cent of the rural and about 52.0 per cent of the urban units do not observe fixed working hours; that extra work hours are grossly under-paid, and sometimes unpaid, is a fact that needs hardly to be emphasized. Many more depressing features can be added to lend further credence to the unwholesome working conditions of the wage-paid workers. In any case, low wage rates do convey their plight more tellingly than other indicators. In an extensive field survey, around Ahmedabad (Gujarat), conducted in April-June 1998, Unni discovered fairly wide wage rate gaps, for male workers, between formal and informal sectors (e.g. Rs. 57.40/day against Rs. 30.0/day in cotton ginning and pressing, and Rs. 57.70/day against Rs. 37.10/day in electronics industry) (Unni, 2001: 131). Similar wage differentials are also reported by a study on the ceramic-ware industry (Das, 2001: 191)

To a large extent, the unwholesome working conditions in the tiny and small rural enterprises, as sketched out in the preceding analysis, are also responsible for depressing *productivity levels*. The low productivity level in each segment of the rural industrial sector, compared with its urban counterpart, was clearly discernible in Section 6.4. This is, however, not to deny that many other factors, most ostensibly the technology-in-use and indifferent quality of products, are also at work

6.13 WTO Onslaught

It should be absolutely clear to every one that there would be no economic activity in the world which will remain unaffected from the influences of the WTO agreements; one would be living under an illusion if one were to believe that the WTO is to do only with industries or people who are in international trade. For example, even petty farm operators, producing exclusively for the domestic market, may get linked with the international movement of input prices, just as their brethren engaged in tradable commodity production may face more severe earning swings under the new and volatile price regimes. Similarly, even a small scale, family-based industrial enterprise in an Indian village may face a decline in its economic fortune just because the demand for its product is declining now that cheaper substitutes are available through imports, or else, its production efficiency may improve now that raw material costs are lower under the open trade regime or else, it is now ancillarized to an urban-based, modern industrial enterprise, and so on. Impact on people engaged in trade, banking and finance, the wide range of service activities, etc., can likewise be visualised, on short- as well as long-term basis. In sum, "it is as important for farmers, scientists, doctors, singers, writers, etc., as for an industry or a trader or a banker or a sundry service provider" (FISME, 1999: 1).

It is a little pre-mature, at the present juncture, to make a final judgement about the total impact that WTO membership would make on the Indian economy in general, and rural industry in particular, essentially because things have just started evolving. A neat picture will emerge well after all agreements are implemented world-wide, net of neutralizations and modifications that might come off because of the voices being raised by the developing economies, including India, and the countervailing strategies to be unleashed by the vested trade interests, in and outside trade negotiations. Moreover, India herself has just completed the last bit of the opening-up on April 1, 2001. Furthermore, this is hardly the stage at which we can scientifically delineate the effect of a particular agreement, or a specific aspect of the same, on the concerned sector (rural industry, in our case), free of other inter-connections. To attribute all that has gone wrong with the rural industrial sector, in recent years, to the WTO onslaught would undoubtedly be an unpardonable methodological lapse. Perhaps, a detailed in-depth study based on primary surveys, preferably using a 3-digit or 4-digit product classification level, would provide the real answers. But that is for the future. For the time being, the best we can do is to make some conjectures on the basis of what has been going on in the recent past

Disturbing signals regarding the damaging effects of the free flow of imported goods on domestic industry have already started coming in. Although we removed quantitative restrictions on the last batch of 715 items only on April 1, 2001, yet the variety of imports, that have already started coming in, is fairly wide, encompassing a wide range of product lines. Phones, fabrics, electronic goods, sanitary fitting, umbrellas, footwear, bicycles, toys, dry cells, sports shoes, locks, hosiery/woollens, etc. are the items that are offering tough price and quality competition to domestic producers including the dumping reportedly being exercised by China for sometime now. Many more items under threat are crockery, oven polymer, power plant equipment, auto accessories, T.V. parts, industrial sewing needles, and so on. The damage to Indian industry and the tremendous human cost it may entail, have already become matters of excited public debate. The worst affected are reported to be the tiny and small industrial enterprises, most markedly those located in the rural areas where employment levels have started coming down in certain branches of production (Chadha-Sahu, 2002:2014). Here is one of the telling descriptions by a well-informed public analyst:

> Foreign imports have killed off thousands of small and medium industries in India, as many as 400,000 according to an estimate. A number of industries have closed down in Mumbai, Thana-Belapur, Bhiwandi, Aurangabad, Kanpur, Aligarh, Indore and several other towns ...In Bhiwandi 60 per cent of powerlooms are silent. In Aligarh, small firms making locks and other hardware for generations, are downing shutters. In Mumbai, if you motor down Thane-Belapur complex, every other factory is closed. Since everybody cannot be a software engineer and take off for Silicon Valley, thousands if not lakhs of people, have lost their jobs (Dubashi, 2000:10).

In Chapter IV, we did a detailed scrutiny of the changing employment situation under different incarnations of rural industrial groupings (e.g. V.S.I. Sector, tiny/small rural industry, small scale rural industry and organised rural manufacturing). By any objective reckoning, the depressing scenario under the tiny segment (to be more precise, own-account manufacturing enterprises under the unorganised segment) looked so colossal that it could hardly be compensated through small employment increases in rural organised manufacturing. That was enough to evoke a high degree of pessimism. Nonetheless, we have yet one more source (i.e. Economic Census data) to educate us more firmly about the recent happenings on the employment front. Perhaps, the latest available 1998 economic census data lends further credence to the process of employment setbacks that have been observed earlier in the case of unorganized manufacturing. The rate of growth of non-agricultural employment in rural (as well as urban) India witnessed a fairly big decline from 2.53 per cent during 1980-90 to 1.72 per cent during 1990-98 (Table 34).

A more pointed conjecture on WTO's impending impact could perhaps be attempted by looking through the strengths and weaknesses of one of the leading export sectors in which the rural industrial sector has fairly high stakes. Textiles and garments sector is a typical case to go into, both because, production-wise, the rural areas have a fairly substantial share in this industry and fairly big rural employment stakes are involved. It is widely believed that the GATT Agreement on Textiles and Clothing would jeopardize the livelihood of a big army of workers, most notably in the handloom and power-loom sectors, as already hinted by some public analysts (Dubashi, *ibid.*). One could do no better than re-produce the essentials of a SWOT analysis of the sector.

Strengths: One of the largest producers of cotton, jute, silk and manmade fibers; presence of an entire chain of manufacturing e.g., in cotton, from growing, ginning, spinning, weaving, processing to clothing garments/made-ups and also presence of vibrant textiles machinery sector and support institutions as NIFT; availability of cheap skilled labour.

Weaknesses: Low productivity at all levels, from growing to ginning to spinning to weaving (capacity utilization as low as 50 per cent in most of the sub-sectors); poor infrastructure - both externally (basic infrastructure: ports, roads, power, etc) and internally (90 per cent of units being very small or in tiny sector); absence of VAT; too many regulations and controls on dynamic sub-sectors; restrictive import regime and trade policy environment; blatant technological obsolescence; lack of long term strategy.

Opportunities: With the phasing out of restrictive trade policies (Multi Fibre Agreement and other quantitative restrictions), substantial increase expected in size of the foreign markets; besides the developed countries, new markets are likely to be opened up in many developing countries; if ATC obligations are properly observed all across the board, trade in textiles and clothing is expected to rise by US $ 24 billion per year.

Threats: Major benefits of ATC agreement under GATT were not to be available before 2002; although quotas are being removed, yet non-tariff barriers (e.g., in the name of anti-dumping, consumer safety, eco-labelling, etc.) are fast replacing quotas; phasing out of quotas would put further premium on comparative cost advantage; international competition will increase manifold.

Conclusion: The gains are not there for India to go and claim; it would require double the effort to even remain where we are at the moment in textiles and garment exports; apart from evolving and adhering to eco-friendly production processes including the use of chemical and dyes of the approved standards, services in the areas of information, testing eco-quality control, technique assistance, R&D, education and training of workers and environment management system must be strengthened; obviously, much national effort, perhaps for the next 3-4 years is called for; in short, gains could be manifold, but only if the sector gears up to quality, cost and environment-friendly challenges. (FISME, 1999: 27).

7

Recasting Industrialization Strategy

Our analysis throws up many inherent weaknesses of the rural tiny and small enterprises, especially the OAME segment, most visibly in terms of its incapability of sustaining a low-productivity regime during the times that the rural industry has started facing tough competition from its urban counterpart on the one hand, and the more liberal import regime, on the other. What are the directions in which the rural industry in general, and the tiny OAME segment in particular, need to be sailed in years ahead, is a question of great national significance.

It is patently wrong to predict that under the new dispensations, every section of rural industry would suffer growth reverses or, equally serious, job losses. As noted above, the *rural organised manufacturing*, in no major aspect of its functioning, lags behind its urban counterpart. The higher segments of the *rural unorganised manufacturing* too, most noticeably the rural-DMEs, are doing fairly well in relation to their urban counterparts. The real worry is in respect of most segments of the traditional industries under the VSI sector or, looked at from a different perspective, for many of the rural OAME product lines under the unorganised manufacturing. Their weaknesses on technology, productivity and marketing fronts are becoming all too obvious, and many of them have staged a closure primarily because they cannot sustain themselves any more in the open market system.

Our study foresees three possibilities to emerge in the years ahead. First, some categories especially those linked with modern production sectors and capable of absorbing compulsions of competition and related market pressures, are bound to grow. The 'cheap labour' cushion can really take them on to higher growth trajectories with the accompanying benefits of expanding employment and earnings. Second, some others are likely to stay on just because these are a part of a near-static or slowly changing village socio-cultural life. Third, many of the manufacturing and allied activities under the rural-OAME segment, especially those pursued as 'livelihood strategies', in a situation of limited opportunities, largely in conjunction with agrarian pursuits, are likely to face more numerous difficulties; many among them may die a natural death.

What types of policy re-orientations are, therefore, called for at this juncture? Much is already written about the problems of the tiny sector; lack of adequate and timely credit availability, non-availability and/or scarcity of raw materials and other inputs such as power, road and transport network and other infrastructure, unfriendly rules and regulations, wide-spread corruption, restricted market outlets, etc., are the most commonly reported one set of problems. A weak technological base and lack of concern for quality control and market development, largely emanating out of a weak human capital base, make the second set of problems. We have dealt with many of these issues earlier in Chapter VI. In what follows, we touch upon a few more, mainly to emphasize that it is time to recast our strategy of rural industrialization in conformity with the changing economic scenario, both at home and abroad.

7.1 Protection out, Promotion in

Product reservation for the small and tiny industrial sector has been a crucial hallmark of industrial policy in India. The rationale for reserving products for exclusive manufacture by the small-scale sector was that this was the surest way to protect small and tiny units against competition from large enterprises. There is a powerful public opinion that, by and large, the reservation policy has not served its purpose; it crippled the growth of several branches of industry, restricted exports and has not done much even for the promotion of small-scale and tiny industries (Hussain, 1997:75-76). It is not without reasons that, as the time passed, the group of traditional VSI industries as a whole lost tremendously in their share of output but could not 'get away' from providing employment; for example, towards the close of the nineties, the handloom sector had a mere 1.1 per cent share in VSI output against as high as 24.0 per cent share in VSI employment. This uneven-ness in the two shares obviously implied that the handloom sector somehow languished on at low or declining levels of productivity, primarily because some kind of institutional support was forthcoming. Khadi too belongs to the same genre. In total terms, it would not be too wrong to say that, *inter alia*, there has been a pronounced tendency with small and tiny units to stay on as such because, the fear of losing various facilities and incentives in case they move up on the size hierarchy, was too costly to be ignored. The Hussain Committee succinctly points out that:

> the fundamental difficulty with product reservation, as an instrument of policy, is that it does not discriminate between production units on the basis of their efficiency – current or potential. We have no explanation in official documents anywhere how the list of reserved items was selected,

and on what basis additional items have been added. The changes over time give the impression that the choice of products was somewhat arbitrary. Eighty per cent of reserved items are concentrated in 11 three-digit NIC categories. The reminders are spread over 90 three-digit categories. This demonstrates to some extent successful lobbying for reservation by special interest groups. In the absence of a well-defined and rational criterion for product selection, which is impossible in practice, the scope for such lobbying action is large, and the potential for welfare losses to consumers and the economy increases. The reservation policy also adversely affected India's export earnings in a number of product lines like diesel engines, garment finishing, consumer electronics and leather products (Hussain, 1997: 20)

With the changes in the trade policy instituted since 1991, a large variety of consumer goods started coming into the Indian market through imports. This was reinforced by the WTO obligation of completing the process of throwing open the Indian market to imported consumer goods in April 2001; accordingly, imports are moving in freely and it is for sure that very soon more and more items currently reserved for small-scale industries will come from outside, if they have not already started doing so. In other words, a free competition has ensued, and would get intensified before long. It is thus the changed domestic and international contexts that have lent extraordinary weight to the demand for abolition of product reservations. It is contended that small scale and tiny industries would suffer a double disadvantage if de-reservation is not allowed, if the definition of a small scale unit is not revised upwards in terms of investment in plant and machinery in the interest of technological upgrading, if economies of scale are not allowed to operate, if 'a level playing field' is not created, and so on. It is in this context that the government has recently announced de-reservation in some sectors, most notably the textiles and garments.

Dereservation across the board has yet to be put on ground, and we have yet to comprehend its likely consequences. It is claimed by the protagonists of the de-reservation policy that it will pave the way for greater equity participation from large Indian companies and foreign investors. It may also give a boost to the most needed process of sub-contracting, with all its associated benefits of technology upgradation, quality production, price competitiveness, market expansion, and so on. But then, we completely share the Hussain Committee's view that *adequate transitional arrangements* for the small scale and tiny enterprises affected by de-reservation need to be thought over, and put into practice; the committee makes a number of valuable suggestion to lessen the likely degree of economic stress that may befall the tiny units after de-reservation. In particular, the recommendations that (1) the existing units should be given special assistance for expansion, (2) financial institutions and banks should provide equity support, especially to the groups of tiny units which are likely to emerge as big sufferers, (3) the government should create a special multi-purpose fund, to be used for providing one-time support in the form of interest subsidies, technology upgradation (through training and re-training of workers), capacity building of the affected units, etc., need to be scrupulously followed when de-reservation comes into full swing (Hussain, 1997: 77-78). In any case, it must be ensured that the goose is not killed for the egg.

7.2 Sub-Contracting: Tiny Sector's Saviour

At the present juncture of India's rural industrial development, while displacement of workers from non-viable tiny units is a foregone outcome, as already witnessed by us in the case of rural-OAMEs, tremendous opportunities can also be explored for forging sub-contracting and ancilliarisation, especially in product lines that admit of production under putting-out system. As a matter of fact, there are systematic global trends towards decentralised production through sub-contracting and franchising arrangements.

> The element of flexibility applies not just to the spatial dimension, involving a network of widely scattered sub-contractors linked via a parent unit in the production of a complex industrial output, but also a temporal one, where such linkages are continually redefined and reoriented. This also involves a capacity to re-tool and adapt production capabilities of the small-scale and tiny units for acquiring fresh contracts in different product lines that still exploit the specialist skills of these units (Saith, 2000: 56-57).

It really seems that all those elements which could forge vertical linkages along the hierarchical continuum, through ancillarization, subcontracting, common production programmes, etc., remained largely non-operative; most certainly, these did not go beyond a few specified product lines, and were reflective more of pattern-client relationships rather than formal production contracts exposing the small partners to the upcoming demands for new products or new designs or technology hook-ups, etc. For example, common production programme was repeatedly advocated but was never *effectively* introduced (perhaps under pressure from big business lobby) in any industry, thus rupturing the most vital link needed to give the tiny and household based industries a chance for survival. It was natural, therefore, that industrial dualism has been growing between the traditional, cottage and household village industries and modern small-scale sector, on the one hand, and the small and large industries, on the other (Thakur, 1985: 2-3). It is worthwhile looking into the kind of vertical linkages that have evolved in the industrial sector over time; more pointedly, to make a broad assessment of the incidence, nature and benefits of sub-contracting that have accrued, if at all, to rural industry in India.

We have two kinds of experiences to report. The first comes through the 1999-2000 nation-wide NSSO survey of informal manufacturing enterprises in rural (and urban) India. Table 35 shows that nearly 27.0 per cent of rural, and 32.0 per cent of urban enterprises, work under sub-contracting system. The incidence of sub-contracting is relatively larger among the tiny enterprises, compared with larger-sized units (OAMEs and Establishments, respectively, in Table 35). The two most obvious, and surface-view, benefits that accrue to such enterprises are the availability of raw material and product design from the parent company. Supplying of 'improved equipment' by the parent company does not seem to be a common practice; the vendors have to work on their own machinery/equipment which, in most cases, is reflective of a traditional technology. We have thus an interesting mingle of elements of traditional technology operating side by side with those of improved technology. Perhaps, this mingle works much more to the benefit of the so-called 'parent company' inasmuch as the practice of advancing raw material and prescribing product designs in consonance with the changing pulse of the market, has been a well acknowledged feature of a pattern-client type of traditional industrial regime. The benefit of value adding accrues far more proportionately to the 'urban enterprises' or 'trade channels' which, in the present case, seem to be acting as the parent company. In terms of net earnings, the tiny rural enterprises, overwhelmingly concentrated in the informal segment of the manufacturing sector, largely run by traditional and family-trained craftsmen or artisans, end up as mere 'wage earners'; in other words, these are 'industrial enterprises' but only in a highly contrived definitional sense.

Table 36 lends adequate support to what has been characterized above. It is absolutely clear that more than 76.0 per cent of the rural tiny enterprises (OAMEs) are typically household-based ventures, usuallly owned and operated by artisans or craftsmen. More than 95.0 per cent of such household enterprises work under the so-called sub-contracting system. Further, of the household enterprises that work under such a system, more than 92.0 per cent get the supply of raw material, and about 88.0 per cent of them work on the product designs specified by the so-called parent company. Not more than 24.0 per cent of them get machinery/equipment from the contractor/master enterprise. In sum, the type of sub-contracting described above is a living testimony of the exploitation of the home-based rural enterprises by the master enterprise or the contractor, through contrived trade devices. The concrete technological or pecuniary gains do not extend beyond a handful of the village enterprises.

A contrasting experience comes through our own April-June 2000 survey of tiny and small rural enterprises (Table 37). Adequate precaution was exercised to capture only those cases of sub-contracting that typically sustain the modern system of industrial production, and confer concrete technological, commercial and other related benefits on the vendors. For example, only those cases where the link was with a manufacturing unit, rather than with a trading enterprise, were included in our sample. It was this dual character of sub-contracting that put our survey units in a league totally different from those reported by the 1999-2000 NSSO survey.

Our survey data show that around 40.0 per cent of the tiny and small enterprises in rural areas work under the sub-contracting arrangements against 35.0 per cent in urban areas. This sub-contracting encompasses a wide range of production activities/linkages, agreed upon, and renewed from time to time, between the parent company and the vendor. The vendors are expected to share the wisdom of 'feeling the pulse of the market' with the parent company, and update their production technology and design improvement accordingly, often with support from the latter. Nearly 42.0 per cent of the sub-contracting tiny and small enterprises in the rural and 53.0 per cent of those in the urban areas do get raw material from their parent companies. The hassle of ensuring a timely availability of raw material, and tiding over the pecuniary losses that such units usually suffer when purchasing their materials in small quantities, which is a typical weakness of such industrial enterprises, is automatically overcome.

To put the record straight, the kind of technological link reported by our survey is markedly different than the one implied under the 1999-2000 NSSO survey; in the NSSO survey, the linkage between urban trading enterprises and tiny rural units is built to cash on the financial weakness of the rural artisans and craftsmen, usually through piece wage contracts that lead to commercial exploitation of the latter in more ways than one. In our sample, the sub-contracting is reported to have solidified the production and commercial status of many a sub-contractor; a gradual upgradation of the scale of production, or branching off into other associated product lines, or becoming a subsidiary to more than one company in due course of time, etc., are reported by many of the sub-contracting units surveyed by us.

Financial support to the sub-contracting units is not a very common practice with the parent companies; only about one-third of the sub-contracting units get financial accommodation from their parent company. To some extent, it reflects financial stringency on the part of the parent companies and, presumably, for this reason, as we see below, delayed payments to the sub-contracting units is a very common feature of the Indian system of sub-contracting. Most happily, around 94.0 per cent of the sample tiny and small rural sub-contracting units report the benefit of an assured market; this benefit is reported by no fewer than 98.0 per cent of the units located in the semi-urban areas.

We are able to derive some general lessons from our survey. The network of sub-contracting units, which is a wide conglomerate of product lines, spare-parts and component manufacturers, activity specialists (e.g. weaving, dyeing, stitching, bleaching, and packaging) etc., is gradually expanding from urban to semi-urban and/or from semi-urban to rural areas, as also from nearby places to distant locales. It really seems that an hierarchical structure is emerging among the sub-contracting enterprises with units employing as few as one person and doing as simple an activity as stitching or packaging, on the one extreme, and those employing as many as 10 persons, with varying levels of skills and job specializations, being IT-savvy and well informed about technological developments in their trade line, on the other. In conformity with what Saith suggests, a fairly high proportion of the sub-contractors, especially those located in industrial clusters, are graduating themselves upwards to more numerous job activities, and more skill- and technology-intensive jobs, often catering to more than one parent company (Saith, 2000: 56-59). Finally, both competitive and complementary production relationships exist among the sub-contractors.

Sub-contracting has its problems too. For example, more than 93.0 per cent of rural and more than 82.0 per cent of the urban units report delayed payments by the parent company. Happily, an act has already been passed to impose penal interest on the parent company for undue delay in payments. The problems of undue price-cutting, as also an unjustified termination of the contract are reported only by a handful of sub-contracting units. Lastly, a fairly high percentage of rural sub-contracting enterprises (22.0 per cent against only 9.0 per cent for their urban counterparts) complain of 'stringent quality standards'. In a sense, it reflects their inferior standing in terms of quality consciousness which gets rectified through contract-production regimes, and exposure to open market competition that such regimes entail on them; without such contracts, the product quality would need much more to be desired. In any case, sub-contracting is an area that merits a much more concerted policy attention, most ostensibly to ensure survivability and growth of the tiny and small industrial enterprises. The historical experiences, both inside and outside the country, clearly show that sub-contracting acquires much greater chances of success among industrial clusters than otherwise (Kharbanda, 2001:20). This persuades us, once again, to plead for the cluster approach to rural industrial development.

7.3 Cluster Approach

Worldwide, a common characteristic of growth of small and medium-scale enterprises is their agglomeration in clusters. India is not an exception to this. Recently, the government has announced the creation of *new rural industrial clusters* as the key policy instrument under the National Programme of Rural Industrialisation. The Abid Hussain Committee too emphasises the role of industrial clusters in achieving efficient, competitive, export-oriented growth. Industrial clusters thus come across as the flag carriers of the new market-led industrialisation strategy. The cluster approach is basically a sound idea, particularly in the prevailing circumstances under which the whole house of tiny and small industrial enterprises is under threat, both from within and without. But then, India's own working experience with industrial clusters should not be lost sight of when their new incarnations are being advocated.

Theoretically, the local availability of raw materials, of cheap and skilled labour, of good road and rail connections to major towns and markets, favourable climate and adequate availablity of water, etc., are the major incentives that attract prospective entrepreneurs to specific locations. Moreover, an industrial cluster encourages competitive and co-operative interactions, focusing especially on information sharing, cost reduction and market oriented innovation. For such clusters to take off, the government is expected to throw in fiscal incentives and other support. The Indian experience is a mix of successes and failures. A recent UNIDO survey of 138 industrial clusters in India shows that only 13 of these clusters were induced by government policy while the remaining 125 grew spontaneously at the initiative of entrepreneurs themselves (SIDBI, 1999: 57; Hussain, 1997: 79-80). No less than 99 grew in response to market opportunities in the region; only six were attracted by the availability of infrastructure and the rest were drawn by the ready availability of raw material or skilled labour. Moreover, industrial estates developed by the government have been plagued by capacity under-utilization due to wrong choice of locations. A fundamental flaw in the policy has been to believe that the initial burden of cluster development rests squarely on the government, and that, once a cluster comes into existence, government can completely withdraw. In fact, it is at the later stage that such clusters start stagnating when adequate institutional support is not available. It is the creative interface between local entrepreneurs, government agencies, clients and other concerned parties that explains the success stories of, say, Tiruppur industrial estate in Tamil Nadu and Barotiwala industrial estate in Himachal Pradesh, against a not-so-successful rural industrial estate of Bhiwadi of Rajasthan. There is no dearth of success stories from abroad also; the remarkably successful experiences of industrial clusters in Cesena and Ravena regions of Italy, industrial parks and clusters in Brighton-Sussex region of UK, and industrial incubators in Aachen region of Germany, have many features that may be incorporated into India's cluster approach; in particular, strengthening the production base of small and tiny enterprises with infusion of high technologies and constant learning process with the academia, vocational training in tune with the expanding requirements of the industrial sector, co-operation and competition among enterprises, and exploitation of all knowledge resources including international, national and local, through networking with the help of information technologies and learning by doing, have been recognised as the prime factors for lending a competitive edge to such clusters. (Kharbanda, 2001:17-24; Gomes, 2001: 4532)

In brief, industrial clusters can come up but may not survive unless a comprehensive and intensified policy and action programme is initiated. In particular, special importance should be attached to the specific needs of tiny units. The basic elements of such a programme would be technology upgradation, skill enhancement, information dissemination and entrepreneurial competency development. The most restrictive bottleneck is the poor infrastructure, and it is here that the government has to play a leading role (SIDBI, 1999: 58-59; Hussain, 1997: 80; Saith, 2000: 58-59). Even independently of such vertical links, small scale industrial units are seen to enjoy various competitiveness-enhancing advantages through horizontal interactions and collective arrangements that arise when such units exist in the form of an industrial cluster (Saith, 2000: 57).

7.4 Other Miscellaneous Measures

We make a passing reference to a few other measures for revitalization of rural industry in India. For *development* and *strengthening of infrastructure*, many new ideas such as the creation of industrial parks, presumably on the lines of what was done around Seoul-Korea, science and incubation parks where information-intensive, non-polluting labour-using small scale enterprises could be encouraged to come up, government-private sector partnership in vital areas of infrastructure strengthening (e.g. trifurcating electricity boards into generation, transmission and distribution corporations), encouragement to the Jamaican model of telecommunication expansion, expansion of internet facilities, the installation of inland container facilities including customs clearance, etc., are at various stages of adoption and implementation.

Bureaucratic hold over economic matters, unresponsive attitude of public officials, corruption at all levels of government machinery, etc., are the widely accepted 'virtues of India's economy and society' that most of us are now attuned to live with. The rural industry is one of the worst affected victims of such unresponsive attitudes. 'Inspector Raj' has gone *de jure, de facto* it has not. The plethora of outdated rules is still around; inspections are still the means to harass tiny and small enterprises; most crucially, increased *awareness* about the evolving structure of the Indian economy, and the changing pattern of its links with the world outside, on the one hand, and the more stressful time ahead of the tiny and small industries, on the other, has to be created from the top to the bottom. In sum, the economic regime has changed but most of the public institutions and much of the official mindset remain much the same. Under the heightened economic importance that the 73rd Constitutional Amendment lends to *Panchayati Raj* institutions, it is time to evolve a tripartite partnership between rural entrepreneurs, government and panchayat institutions, in the interest of rural economy in general, and rural industrial expansion in particular. It is also the time to re-define and re-demarcate the respective roles of public institutions such as KVIC, district industries centre, cooperative institutions, local governments, and NGOs, so that new economic institutions get evolved, and new norms of people-government relationships get hammered out. We are in complete agreement with the Abid Hussian Committee's view that the district industry centres (DICs) have not succeeded in achieving even the limited objectives assigned to them

> Entrepreneurs still have to shuttle between a variety of departments for clearance of projects. The extension work of DICs has languished as 46 per cent of them were found to have not updated their information. A fair assessment would be that the DICs are unable to cope with administrative overload ... The Expert Group therefore recommends that a completely new look be taken on the functioning of the District Industry Centres in order to make them more promotional rather than regulatory. DICs could acquire additional significance if they can weave a web of linkages with other institutions. They funnction as key conduits for information flowing from a variety of channels with greater efficiency if they can draw on other resources from business (Hussain, 1997: 71).

Also, the role that the *rural community polytechnics* are reported to be playing in promoting improved technologies and work opportunities among the rural people, deserves to be studied in detail for its possible replication to wider areas and activities, including rural industry.

Perhaps, the time has arrived for India to have a thorough review of its educational and training system. Many expert committees have gone into the issue of economic relevance of India's general and technical education programmes and the content of vocational training; in particular, the extremely high and expanding unevenness of educational and training standards in different regions, that somehow stares the nation today in the form of extraordinary digital divides, have been pointed out from time to time. Many solutions have also been recommended. An extremely crucial point that we would like to emphasize in particular is the need for industry-academia interaction. Such an interaction has certainly been on an increase in recent years but, painfully, it has nearly completely bypassed the tiny and small enterprises, most noticeably those located in the rural areas. We can do no better than drawing the attention of policy makers to the extraordinarily successful experiences of small industry-academia interaction through science and technology parks in Cesena and Ravena regions of Italy, industrial clusters of Aachen region in Germany, incubators in Brighton-Sussex regions of UK, and industrial parks in Seoul region of South Korea (Kharbanda, 2001: 24; Gomes, 2001:4532).

This is also the time to have another look at the respective *roles of the central and state governments* in the matter of industrialisation in general, and rural industrial development in particular. Economic expediency demands that small scale industrial development should stay on with the state governments, as of now; the newly emerging problems such *as infrastructural development through foreign direct investment* may also be entrusted to their care, primarily because the decentralised mode of governance meets the flexible needs of rural industrial development, especially in export-linked sectors, in a much more reliable manner.

Lastly, no programme of rural industrialisation in India can, and should, be seen independent of agriculture. In the on-going surge on IT-oriented industrial expansion, the nation's attention is riveted away from agriculture. Perhaps, the claims of agro-processing industries, most expressly in their rightful countryside abode, are getting overlooked. Whatever heights the Indian economy may achieve in the regime of industrialisation in general, and IT-based industrialisation in particular, *agriculture will continue to occupy the central stage,* and with that the importance of agro-based industrialisation needs to be kept up. It is strongly pleaded that policy fixtures may better come out of such aberrations.

It may also be mentioned that the strongest argument for sustaining rural industrialisation, for that matter industrialisation as such, is the existence of tremendous potential demand. This potential has remained latent so far. Perhaps, the issue of *land reforms* needs to be revived, most ostensibly because the much publicised story of rural industrialisation in China, and other East Asian countries, owes itself heavily to this institutional reform.

Bibliography

Acharya, S. and Arup Mitra, *The Potential of Rural Industries and Trade to Provide Decent Work Condition: A Data Reconnaissance in India*, ILO-SAAT, New Delhi, 2000.

Ahmed, G.K. and P.A. Chowdhury, *Rural Industrialisation in Bangladesh*, Bangladesh Institute of Development Studies (BIDS), Dhaka, June 1987.

Anant, T., Sunderam, K., and Tendulkar, S., *Employment and Labour in South Asia*, ILO-SAAT, New Delhi, 1999.

Asher Ramsingh, "Small-Scale and Cottage Industries", in J.S.Uppal (Ed.) *India's Economic Problems*, Tata Mc-Graw Hill, New Delhi, 1983.

Awasthi, D.N., *Regional Pattern of Industrial Growth in India*, Concept Publishing Co., New Delhi, 1981.

Balasubramanian, N., *et al.*, *Structure and Determinants of Non-farm Employment in Rural India*, ILO-SAAT, New Delhi,2000.

Bhalla, G.S. and Chadha, G.K., *The Green Revolution and the Small Peasant*, Concept Publishing Co., New Delhi, 1983.

Bhalla, Sheila, "Globalization, Growth and Employment", in G.S.Bhalla and Manmohan Agarwal (Eds.), *World Economy in Transition - An Indian Perspective*, Har-Anand Publications, New Delhi, 1994.

Bhattacharya, S.N., *Rural Industrialization in India*, B.R. Publishing Co, New Delhi 1980.

Bhattachrya, M and S. Bhattachrya, *Production Efficiency in Small Enterprises*, ILO-SAAT, New Delhi, 1997.

—————, *Environmental Effects of Rural Industrialisation in India*, ILO-SAAT, New Delhi, 2000.

Burra, N., *Child Labour in the Brass-Ware Industries of Moradabad, India*, Working Paper, ILO-ARTEP, New Delhi, 1989.

Cassen Robert, *et al.*, "Stabilization and Structural Reform in India", *Contemporary South Asia*, 2(2), 1993.

Chadha, G.K., "Agricultural Growth and Rural Non-farm Activities: Analysis of Indian Experience", in Yang-Boe Choe and Fu-Chen Lo (Eds.), *Rural Industrialisation and Non-farm Activities of Asian Farmers*, A.P.D.C. Kualalumpur, 1986.

—————, *Technology Improvement in Cottage Industry in India: A Study of Pottery and Rope-making*, ILO/ARTEP Discussion Paper, New Delhi, 1990

—————, "Adoption of Improved Technology in India's Cottage Industries: Constraints and Impact", in Rizwanual Islam (ed.) *Transfer, Adoption and Diffusion of Technology for Small and Cottage Industries*, ILO/ARTEP, 1992.

—————, "Rural Non-farm Employment: An Assessment of Recent Trends", *Indian Journal of Labour Economics*, Vol. 35(3), 1992.

—————, *Non-farm Sector in India's Rural Economy; Policy, Performance and Growth Prospects*, VRF Series No.220, Institute of Developing Economy, Tokyo, 1993.

——————, "Non-farm Employment for Rural Households in India: Evidence and Prognosis", *Indian Journal Labour Economics*, Vol. 36(3), 1993.

——————, *Employment, Earnings and Poverty: A Study of Rural India and Indonesia*, Sage Publications, New Delhi, 1994.

——————, *The Industrialisation Strategy and Growth of Rural Industry in India*, ILO SAAT, Working Papers, New Delhi, 1996.

——————, and Ashwani Saith, *Rural Industrialisation in Post-Reform China*, ILO-SAAT, New Delhi, 1996a.

——————, "Non-farm Employment in Rural Areas: How Well Can Female Workers Compete?" in Papola, T.S. and A.N.Sharma (Eds.) *Gender and Employment in India*, Vikash Publishing House Pvt. Ltd., 1999a.

——————, "Trade, Technology and Employment: Some Missing Links in India's Rural Economy", *The Indian Journal of Labour Economics*, Vol. 42, No. 4, 1999b.

——————, "Informal Sector in the Indian Economy: A Study of Khadi Textiles", Paper Read at *National Workshop on the Strategic Approach to Job Creation in Urban Informal Sector in India*, Surajkund, Haryana, February 17-19, 2000a.

——————, "Economic Reforms and Emerging Demand-Supply Hiatus in India's Rural Labour Market", IEA 82nd Conference Volume, 2000b.

——————, *et al.*, "Education, Skills, and Working Environments of Workers in India's Rural Industry", *International Journal of Occupational and Environmental Health*, Vol. 7, No. 2, 2001a.

——————, *et al.*, "Rural Industry in India and China", An On-going Research Study, J.N.U., New Delhi, 2001b.

——————, *Rural Employment in India: Current Situation, Challenges and Potential for Expansion*, Paper Submitted to ILO-Geneva, 2002a.

——————, and Sahu, P.P., "Post-Reform Setbacks in Rural Employment: Issues That Need Further Scrutiny", *Economic and Political Weekly*, XXXVI, 21, May 25, 2002b.

——————, "Rural Non-Farm Employment in India: What Does Recent Experience Teach Us?", *The Indian Journal of Labour Economics*, Vol. 45, No. 4, Conference Volume, 2002c.

——————, *Rural Non-Farm Sector in Indian Economy: Growth, Challenges and Future Direction*, Paper Read at Collaborative JNU-IFPRI Workshop on "The Dragon and the Elephant: A Comparative Study of Economic and Agricultural Reforms in China and India", 25-28 March 2003.

Chakravarty, Sukhamoy, *Development Planning: The Indian Experience*, Clarendon Press, Oxford, 1987.

Chattopadhya, S., *Industrial Sickness in India*, Sage Publication, New Delhi, 1995

Choe, Yang-Boo and Fu-Chen Lo, (Eds.) *Rural Industrialisation and Non-farm Activities of Asian Farmers*, Asian and Pacific Development Centre, Kuala Lumpur, Malaysia, 1986.

Chuta E. and S.V. Sethuraman (Eds.), *Rural Small-Scale Industries and Employment in Africa and Asia*, International Labour Office, Geneva.

Damodaran, S., "The Urban Informal Sector in India: A Case Study of Leather and Leather Products Industry", Paper Read at *National Workshop on the Strategic Approach to Job Creation in Urban Informal Sector in India*, Surajkund, Haryana, February 17-19, 2000.

Das, K., "Workers and Earnings in Informal Manufacturing: Evidence and Issues in Estimation" in Kundu A., and Sharma, A. N., (Eds.), *Informal Sector in India: Perspectives and Policies*, IHD-IAMR, New Delhi, 2001.

Dewan, R., "Organised Production and Unorganised Producers in the Informal Food Processing Industry", Paper Read at *National Workshop on the Strategic Approach to Job Creation in Urban Informal Sector in India*, Surajkund, Haryana, February 17-19, 2000.

Dubashi, Jay, "Is the Finance Minister Painting an Overly Optimistic Picture of the Economy", *The Sunday Times*, New Delhi, October 22, 2000.

Eapen. M. *Rural Industrialisation in Kerala: Its Dynamic and Linkages*, Copynomie, Erasmus University, Rotterdam, 1999.

Economic and Political Weekly, Bank Credit: Eroding Priority, (Editorial), November 18, 2000.

——————, Current Statistics, September 7, 2002.

Edgren, G. and M.Muqtada, *Strategies for Growth and Employment in Asia: Learning from Within*, ILO/ARTEP Discussion Paper, New Delhi, 1989.

EPW Research Foundation, *Three Years of Economic Reforms in India*, Bombay, 1994.

Federation of Indian Micro and Small and Medium Enterprises, *A Brief Guide to the WTO for Small Businesses*, FISME, New Delhi, 1999.

Gomes, Janina, "SMEs and Industrial Clusters: Lessons for India from Italian Experience", *Economic and Political Weekly*, Vol. 36, No 49, December 2001.

Government of India, *Industrial Policy Resolution*, New Delhi, April 6,1948.

——————, *Industrial Policy Resolution*, New Delhi, April 30, 1956.

——————, *Statement of Industrial Policy, 1977*, New Delhi, December, 1977.

——————, *Statement of Industrial Policy, 1980*, New Delhi, July 23, 1980.

——————, *Text of Industrial Policy, 1990*, New Delhi, May 1990.

——————, *Seminar on Rural Industrialisation, Background Papers, Vol. I and II*, Planning Commission, New Delhi 1984.

——————, *Five Year Plan Documents*, for various plans, Planning Commission, New Delhi,

——————, *Tables with Notes on Survey of Unorganized Manufacture: Non-Directory Establishments and Own-Account Enterprises, July 1984- June 1985, Part-1, All-India*, NSS Report No.363/1, June 1989.

——————, *Tables with Notes on Survey of Unorganised Manufacture: Non-Directory Establishment and Own Account Enterprises*, July 1989 - June 1990, NSS Report No. 396/1 and 2, March 1995.

——————, *Unorganised Manufacturing Sector in India: Its Size, Employment and Some Key Estimates*, July 1994- June 1995, NSS Report No.433, 434 and 435, August 1998.

——————, *Employment and Unemployment in India*, 1993-94, NSS Report No 409, NSSO, New Delhi, 1997.

——————, *Annual Survey of Industries Summary Results for Factory Sector*, Various Issues, CSO, Ministry of Statistics and Programme Implementation, New Delhi.

——————, *Statistical Abstracts of India*, Various Issues, CSO, Ministry of Statistics and Programme Implementation, New Delhi.

——————, *Economic Survey*, Various Issues, Ministry of Finance, New Delhi.

——————, *Report of the Second All-India Census of Small Scale Industrial Units*, Ministry of Industry, August, 1992.

——————, *Report on Sample Survey of Small Scale Industrial Units, 1994-95*, Ministry of SSI & ARI, New Delhi, 2000.

——————, *Comprehensive Policy Package for Small Scale Industries and Tiny Sector*, New Delhi, August 30-31, 2000a.

——————, *Non-Agricultural Enterprises in the Informal Sector in India: 1999-2000*, NSS Report No-456, NSSO, Ministry of Planning, New Delhi, December, 2000b.

——————, *Report of the Study Group on Development of Small Enterprises*, (Chairman: S.P.Gupta), Planning Commission, New Delhi, March 2001.

——————, *Small Scale Industry in India: An Engine of Growth*, Office of the DC SSI, Ministry of SSI, New Delhi, 2002.

——————, *Unorganised Manufacturing Sector in 2000-01*, NSSO Report No 477, June 2002a.

Gupta, D.B., *Rural Industry in India - The Experience of the Punjab Region*, Occasional Paper No. 7, Institute of Economic Growth, New Delhi, 1982.

Haan, H.H.de, *Rural Industrialization in India*, Discussion Paper No.54, Erasmus University, Rotterdam, Sept. 1980.

Harris Nigel, "The Economic Crisis and Planning: Cities and Regions", in K.S. Krishnaswamy *et al.*, (Eds.) *Society and Change: Essays in Honour of Sachin Chaudhuri*, Oxford University Press, 1977.

Hazari, R.K., *Essays on Industrial Policy*, Concept Publishing Company, New Delhi, 1986.

Hazell Peter B.R. and Haggblade Steven, " Rural-Urban Growth Linkages in India", *Indian Journal of Agricultural Economics*, 46/4, Oct.-Dec. 1991.

Ho, Samuel P.A, "The Asian Experience in Rural Non-Agricultural Development and Its Relevance for China", *World Bank Staff Discussion Paper*, No 757, 1986.

Holmstrom, M., "Employment in Small Indian Firms: Choices under Liberalisation", *Economic and Political Weekly*, Vol. 34(9), 1999.

Hussain, A., *Report of the Expert Committee on Small Enterprises*, Ministry of Commerce and Industry, Govt. of India, July 1997.

ILO, S.O.S. "Stress at Work: Costs of Workplace Stress are Rising, with Depression Increasingly Common", *World of Work*, No.37, December 2000.

Inoue, Kyoko, *Industrial Development Policy of India*, I.D.E. Occasional Paper Series No.27, Institute of Developing Economies, Tokyo, 1992.

Ishikawa, S., *Labour Absorption in Asian Agriculture*, ILO/ARTEP, New Delhi, 1986.

Islam, R. (Ed.), *Rural Industrialization and Employment in Asia*, ILO/ARTEP, New Delhi, 1987.

——————, (Ed.), *Transfer, Adoption and Diffusion of Technology for Small and Cottage Industries*, ILO/ARTEP, New Delhi, 1992.   .

Jain, L.C., "Development of Decentralized Industries: A Review and Some Suggestions", *Economic and Political Weekly*, Spl. No., October 1980.

Johanson,Sara and Per Ronnas, *Rural Industrialisation: A Review of Selected Asian Experience*, ILO-SAAT Working Paper, New Delhi, 1996.

Kapoor, J.N. and Saxena, H.C., *Mathematical Statistics*, S.Chand and Co, New Delhi, 1967.

Kashyap, S.P., "Growth of Small-size Enterprises in India: Its Nature and Content", *World Development*, Vol.16, No.6, June 1988.

Khan, N.A., and Haroon, M., "Child Labour in the Lock Industries of Aligarh", IEA Conference Volume, 2000.

Kharbanda, V.P. "Industrial Clusters and Academia-Industry Linkages: Impressions from Italy, Germany and UK", NISTADS NEWS, Vol 3, No 2, October 2001.

Koren, H., *Handbook of Environmental Health and Safety*, Pergamon Press, UK, 1987.

Kulshrestha, A.C., and Singh, G., "Informal Sector in India: Its Coverage and Contributions" in Kundu A., and Sharma, A. N., (Eds.), *Informal Sector in India: Perspectives and Policies*, IHD-IAMR, New Delhi, 2001.

Kurien, C.T., "Small Sector in New Industrial Policy", *Economic and Political Weekly*, March 4, 1978.

Lewis, W.A., "Notes on Unlimited Supplies of Labour", *Manchester School of Economics and Social Studies*, 1958.

Lieten, G.K., "Children, Work and Education", *Economic and Political Weekly*, No.24 and 25, 2000.

Majumdar, A., *et al.*, *Demand for Products of Rural Industries in India*, ILO-SAAT Working Paper, New Delhi, 1996.

Mathur, K.B.L. "State-wise Growth Pattern and Inter-State Inequality in India", in *Regional Dimension of India's Economic Development*, Seminar Proceedings, Planning Commission, 1983.

MAYA, "Child Labour in the Sericulture Sector" Paper Read at *National Seminar on Child Labour: Realities and Policy Dimension*, VVGNLI, Noida, December, 2000.

Mellor, John W., *The New Economics of Growth: A Strategy for India and the Developing World*, Cornell University Press, Ithaca, 1976.

Mukul, "Polluting Industries, Environment and Workers' Health", *Economic and Political Weekly*, August 30, 1997.

Nagaraj R., "Industrial Growth: Further Evidence and Towards an Explanation and Issues", *Economic and Political Weekly*, Oct.13, 1990.

Nihila, M., "Industrial Pollution and Workers' Health: A Case for Intervention", *Economic and Political Weekly*, June 24, 1995.

Oberai, A.S. and Chadha, G.K. "Job Creation in Urban Informal Sector in India: Some Macro-Economic Policy Issues", in A.S. Oberai and G.K. Chadha (Eds.), *Job Creation in Urban Informal Sector in India: Issues and Policy Options*, ILO-SAAT, New Delhi, June 2001

Oshima, H., "Reinterpreting Japan's Post-war Growth", *Economic Development and Cultural Change*, No.31, 1982.

Panchamukhi, V.R., "Trade, Technology and Employment: Profile of Systematic Dilemmas and Paradoxes", *Indian Journal of Labour Economics*, Vol. 34, No.1, Jan-March 2000.

Papola, T.S., *Rural Industrialization: Approaches and Potential*, Himalaya Publishing House, Bombay, 1982.

Paranjape H.K., "Industrial Growth with Justice - India's Strategy", in C.D.Wadhva (Ed.) *Some Problems of India's Economic Policy*, Tata McGraw-Hill, 1977.

Pavlov, V., *et al.*, *India: Social and Economic Development (18th-20th Centuries)*, People's Publishing House, Moscow, 1975.

Ramaswamy, K.V., *Small Scale Manufacturing Industries in India: Some Aspects of Size, Growth and Structure*, Discussion Paper No. 105, Indira Gandhi Institute of Development Research, Bombay, January 1994.

Rani, G. and Fei, J.C.H., "A Theory of Economic Development", *American Economic Review*, 1961.

Rau, S.K., *Rural Industrialization: Policy and Programmes in Four Asian Countries*, Asian Productivity Organization, Tokyo, 1985.

Rosegrant, Mark W. and Hazell, Peter, *Transforming the Rural Asian Economy: The Unfinished Revolution,* Asian Development Bank, 2000.

Roy Choudhury, K.K., "Child Labour in Bidi Industries in Mushridabad: A Micro Study", IEA Conference Volume, 2000.

Saith A., *The Rural Non-farm Economy: Processes and Policies*, ILO, Geneva, 1992.

——————, *Rural Industries in India: Some Policy Perspective*, ILO-SAAT, New Delhi, 2000.

Sandesara J.C., "Small Scale Industrialization: The Indian Experience", *Economic and Political Weekly*, March 26, 1988.

——————, "Modern Small Industry, 1972 and 1987-88: Aspects of Growth and Structural Change", *Economic and Political Weekly*, February 6, 1993.

Sen, Amartya K., *Market, Social Opportunities and Economic Development*, Lakdawala Memorial Lecture, Institute of Social Sciences, New Delhi, June 29, 1994.

Shankar U., "Industrial Policy", in J.S.Uppal (Ed.) *India's Economic Problems*, Tata Mc-Graw Hill, New Delhi, 1983.

Sharma, R., "Child Labour in the Glass Bangle Industry of Firozabad", Paper Read at *National Seminar on Child Labour: Realities and Policy Dimension*, VVGNLI, Noida, December, 2000.

Shirokov, G.K., *Industrialisation of India*, People's Publishing House, New Delhi, 1980.

SIDBI, *SIDBI Report on Small Scale Industries Sector*, 1999 and 2000.

Singh, A.K., "Child Labour in Carpet Industry in UP", IEA Conference Volume, 2000.

Srinivasulu, K, "Handloom Weavers' Struggle for Survival", *Economic and Political Weekly*, No.36, Sept.3, 1994.

Srivastava, G.C., *Rural Industrial Development*, Chugh Publications, Allahabad, 1984.

Suri K.B., (Ed.) *Small Scale Enterprises in Industrial Development: The Indian Experience*, Sage Publications, New Delhi, 1988.

Swamy, Dalip S., *The Political Economy of Industrialization: From Self-reliance to Globalisation*, Sage Publications, New Delhi, 1994.

Thakur, Shrinivas Y., *Rural Industrialization in India: Strategy and Approach*, DERAP Publications, Bergen-Norway, 1985.

The Economic Times, New Delhi, November 3, 2000

United Nations, *Industrialization and Rural Development*, UNIDO, New York, 1978.

Unni, J, "Wages and Employment in Unorganised Sector: Issues in Wage Policy", in Kundu A., and Sharma, A. N., (Eds.), *Informal Sector in India: Perspectives and Policies*, IHD-IAMR, New Delhi, 2001.

Upadhyay, M.N., "District Industries Centres", *Economic and Political Weekly*, Review of Management, May 31, 1980.

Vaidyanathan A., "Labour Use in Rural India: A Study of Spatial and Temporal Variations", *Economic and Political Weekly*, No.52, 1986.

Vani.B.P, *Relative Production Efficiency of Small Scale Industries in India*, ILO -SAAT, New Delhi, 1997.

Vepa, Ram K., *Modern Small Industry in India: Problems and Prospects*, Sage Publications, New Delhi, 1988.

Vijayabaskar,M. "Dimensions of Children's Work in the Cotton Knitwear Industry in Tiruppur", paper read at *National Seminar on Child Labour: Realities and Policy Dimension*, VVGNLI, Noida, December, 2000.

Vyas, V.S. and Mathai, George, "Farm and Non-farm Employment in Rural Areas: A Perspective for Planning", *Economic and Political Weekly*, Annual Number, February 1978.

Vyasulu, Vinod, *et al.*, *Rural Industries in India: Lessons from a Survey*, ILO-SAAT, New Delhi, 2000.

World Bank, *Rural Enterprise and Non-farm Employment*, Washington, D.C., January 1978.

——————, *Small Scale Industry in India: Performance, Evaluation and Agenda for Reforms*, Vol. I and II, Washington, D.C., 1992.

Web Site Browsed: (1) *http://www.laghu-udyog.com*, (2) *http://www.ssi.nic.in*.

TABLE 169

TABLE 1A
Output Expansion in Village and Small Industries (VSI) in India: 1973-74/1998-99 (Rs. in Crores)

Year	TRADITIONAL SECTOR (TS)							MODERN SECTOR (MS)			Total VSI Sector
	Khadi	Village Industries	Hand-loom	Seri-culture	Handi-crafts	Coir	Total TS	Small Scale Industries	Power-loom	Total MS	
1	2	3	4	5	6	7	8	9	10	11	12
Series - I (1979-80 Prices)											
1973-74	50.7	187.4	1290.2	96.8	1635.8	92.2	3353.1	11059.2	3041.3	14100.5	17453.6
1979-80	92.0	348.0	1740.0	131.0	2050.0	86.0	4447.0	21635.0	3250.0	24885.0	29332.0
1984-85	115.9	517.3	1964.2	215.9	2387.0	68.5	5268.9	34454.6	4244.1	38698.7	43967.5
Series - II (1984-85 Prices)											
1984-85	170.0	758.6	2880.0	316.6	3500.0	100.5	7725.7	50520.0	6423.0	56943.0	64668.7
1985-86	164.6	900.4	2589.0	370.0	4100.0	139.5	8263.5	57100.0	7668.5	64768.5	73032.0
1986-87	167.0	1034.0	2759.2	417.0	5100.0	141.0	9618.2	64500.0	8106.3	72606.3	82224.5
1987-88	178.3	1265.2	2806.0	445.0	6150.0	148.7	10993.2	72880.0	8394.0	81274.0	92267.2
1988-89	187.0	1473.8	2773.1	490.0	8250.0	153.2	13327.1	73125.0	9092.0	82217.0	95544.1
1989-90	203.0	1101.0	3377.0	493.0	7067.0	128.0	12369.0	92080.0	9865.0	101945.0	114314.0
Series - III (1993-94 Prices)											
1990-91	349.4	2705.6	3973.2	1011.5	15366.4	161.0	23567.0	210773.4	16073.3	226846.7	250413.7
1991-92	355.8	2698.5	3351.4	925.2	15804.5	167.8	23303.1	190669.8	20961.5	211631.4	234934.5
1992-93	336.5	2733.5	4242.3	1095.4	16847.2	174.7	25429.6	183055.3	23224.6	206279.9	231709.5
1993-94	346.2	3232.0	4421.9	1197.5	18250.0	183.1	27630.7	241650.0	24079.3	265729.3	293360.0
1994-95	301.2	2904.1	5023.4	1185.6	19054.2	186.9	28655.5	261092.4	26187.3	287279.6	315935.1

(Contd. —)

TABLE 1A (Contd.)

Output Expansion in Village and Small Industries (VSI) in India: 1973-74/1998-99 (Rs. in Crores)

Year	TRADITIONAL SECTOR (TS)							MODERN SECTOR (MS)			Total VSI Sector
	Khadi	Village Industries	Hand-loom	Seri-culture	Handi-crafts	Coir	Total TS	Small Scale Industries	Power-loom	Total MS	
1	2	3	4	5	6	7	8	9	10	11	12
1995-96	336.5	2881.6	5854.1	1096.1	20723.7	200.7	31092.7	292938.3	22410.3	315348.6	346441.3
1996-97	355.8	3058.2	6060.6	1113.2	23270.4	210.6	34068.8	324399.4	25212.7	349612.1	383680.9
1997-98	334.0	3226.7	6180.1	1200.7	23585.4	225.8	34752.6	350279.4	27296.0	377575.4	412328.0
1998-99	363.1	3180.5	5520.9	1224.9	24408.8	239.6	34937.9	374964.5	26956.0	401920.4	436858.3
				Compound Growth Rate							
1973-85	7.8	9.7	3.9	7.6	3.5	-2.7	4.2	10.9	3.1	9.6	8.8
1984-90	3.6	7.7	3.2	9.3	15.1	5.0	9.9	12.8	9.0	12.4	12.1
1990-99*	0.1	2.2	7.2	2.5	6.6	5.0	6.0	9.5	5.0	9.2	8.9

Note : Output figures (values in crores of rupees) under Series-I, Series-II and Series-III are at constant prices with Base 1979-80, 1984-85 and 1993-94, respectively. * Growth Rate has been computed through semi-log curve.

Source : 1. Govt. of India, *Seventh Five Year Plan*, 1985-90, Vol.II, p.99 (for figures under Series-I at 1979-80 prices)

2. Govt. of India, *Annual Plan* for 1986-87 (p.151), 1987-88 (p.180), 1988-89 (p.202), 1989-90 (pp.188, 190), 1990-91 (p.180), 1991-92 (p.188), for figures under Series-II at 1984-85 prices.

3. Govt. of India, *Annual Plan* for 1993-94 (pp.290-91), for figures under Series- III at 1993-94 prices.

4. Govt. of India, Indian Planning Experience: A Statistical Profile, January 2001.

5. Govt. of India, *Annual Plan* for 1999-2000 (pp 424-25), for figures under Series- III at 1993-94 prices.

6. Govt. of India, *Annual Plan* for 2000-01 (pp 378-79), for figures under Series- III at 1993-94 prices.

TABLE 171

Table 1B

Employment Expansion in VSI Sector: 1973-74/1998-99

Year	TRADITIONAL SECTOR (TS)							MODERN SECTOR (MS)			Total VSI
	Khadi	Village Industry	Hand-loom	Seri-culture	Handi-crafts	Coir	Total TS	Sm.Scale. Industries	Power-loom	Total MS	
1	2	3	4	5	6	7	8	9	10	11	12
1973-74	8.8	9.3	52.1	12.0	15.0	5.0	102.2	39.7	10.0	49.7	151.9
1979-80	11.2	16.1	61.5	16.0	20.3	5.6	130.7	67.0	11.0	78.0	208.7
1984-85	14.6	22.4	74.7	20.0	27.4	5.9	165.0	90.0	32.2	122.2	287.1
1987-88	14.0	27.8	74.8	57.7	34.9	5.5	214.7	107.0	42.1	149.1	363.8
1989-90	14.1	32.1	76.0	50.0	42.2	5.5	216.9	119.6	45.0	164.6	381.5
1990-91	14.2	34.4	96.9	52.0	43.8	5.5	246.7	124.3	55.0	179.3	426.0
1991-92	14.3	35.4	106.0	54.5	48.3	5.5	263.9	126.0	55.0	181.0	444.9
1992-93	14.5	36.6	106.0	54.8	53.1	5.5	270.4	128.3	60.0	188.3	458.7
1993-94	14.5	39.4	110.0	56.0	58.3	5.0	283.2	139.4	56.0	195.4	478.6
1994-95	15.5	42.0	112.0	60.0	64.0	5.0	298.5	145.0	65.0	210.0	508.5
1995-96	16.7	40.3	128.0	60.0	66.0	5.5	316.1	153.0	68.6	221.0	537.1
1996-97	16.0	45.0	149.0	59.6	70.8	5.5	347.2	160.0	70.8	228.0	575.2
1997-98	14.0	42.5	135.0	60.6	73.0	5.2	330.3	167.0	72.0	239.0	569.3
1998-99	13.9	44.4	160.0	61.4	65.0	5.0	349.7	171.6	70.0	241.6	591.3
Compound Growth Rate											
1973-85	4.7	8.3	3.3	4.8	5.6	1.5	4.5	7.7	11.2	8.5	6.0
1984-90	-0.7	7.5	0.3	3.0	9.0	-1.4	5.6	5.9	6.9	6.1	5.9
1990-99*	0.3	3.4	6.1	2.1	6.0	-0.8	4.6	4.6	3.9	4.4	4.5

Note : Employment figures are in Persons in Lakhs; * Growth Rate has been computed through semi-log curve.

Source : Same as in Table 1A

Table 2

Capital Labour Ratio (Rs.) at Constant 1981-82 Prices in Unorganised Manufacturing in Rural/Urban India: 1984-85/2000-01

NIC Code	Sector Description	Locale	OAMEs			NDMEs			DMEs			All Unorganised		
			84-85	94-95	00-01	84-85	94-95	00-01	84-85	94-95	00-01	84-85	94-95	00-01
1	2	3	4	5	6	7	8	9	10	11	12	13	14	15
20-21	Food Products	R	5760	2695	4899	13522	10215	9933	3982	4671	6205	6753	3847	5634
		U	16077	5184	10416	19023	11030	18512	4948	8222	20653	14954	7661	14921
22	Beverages, etc.	R	1652	504	880	4609	9123	5155	776	6008	2130	1797	1172	1061
		U	1618	1553	1777	7224	1989	16618	3209	2246	8226	2173	1606	2566
23+24+25	Cotton, Wool, Jute etc.	R	3826	2035	3599	9216	5113	7160	2506	6568	9177	3964	3297	4658
		U	5743	5614	7646	4798	16670	17720	2900	13300	20600	4719	10856	14337
26	Textile Products	R	8171	1163	4504	4327	1431	6548	1027	2504	6116	7189	1344	4818
		U	37501	3714	10825	9443	17519	19058	1669	5019	19314	22748	6710	15065
27	Wood Products	R	7213	798	793	5377	3315	3809	3624	2890	6881	7029	967	1055
		U	5564	2140	3194	10102	4348	8671	3105	5087	12518	5982	3356	6758
28	Paper Products	R	1003	1427	6598	5372	6579	12011	11018	7315	16823	3718	3625	9017
		U	2672	5066	8275	19507	9401	19744	7216	17116	20217	9754	10785	16897
29	Leather Products	R	11985	2734	3748	2254	1580	6445	1309	1046	9782	11075	2616	4363
		U	12269	3728	10735	20807	2756	14007	1658	3985	13037	11627	3560	12450
30	Rubber Products	R	2494	1245	967	54044	7755	54089	10159	10123	4648	15086	4731	5009
		U	3530	5248	3608	9508	21775	22345	9240	11811	30613	8390	10247	14436
31	Chemical Products	R	1009	3296	11755	8461	20206	6946	5589	23948	46967	3259	14944	23774
		U	2510	4425	15402	73336	18280	43745	3335	41002	46710	8101	30406	40062
32	Non-metallic Mineral Products	R	5057	1179	1912	5459	4686	6373	1322	2595	8982	4435	1684	5007
		U	1927	3995	4128	6062	5937	18174	1834	6188	19136	2592	5037	12313

(Contd. —)

Table 2 (Contd.)
Capital Labour Ratio (Rs.) at Constant 1981-82 Prices in Unorganised Manufacturing in Rural/Urban India: 1984-85/2000-01

NIC Code	Sector Description	Locale	OAMEs			NDMEs			DMEs			All Unorganised		
			84-85	94-95	00-01	84-85	94-95	00-01	84-85	94-95	00-01	84-85	94-95	00-01
1	2	3	4	5	6	7	8	9	10	11	12	13	14	15
33	Basic Metal Industries	R	1605	1536	5587	20466	12123	6015	11709	27406	13607	7188	10383	8544
		U	5394	5993	11810	5375	7903	18286	5480	13846	39280	5435	9417	24913
34	Metal Products	R	15584	1559	2971	2037	4223	9911	3843	5308	17786	13075	2308	5025
		U	53764	4999	12448	5378	7582	22188	3907	13689	22841	16243	9709	19961
35+36	Machine tool & Elect.	R	31074	2558	5768	7672	4060	20180	1511	8595	19107	14545	3733	9794
		U	2686	10335	28546	20405	21402	34929	7129	20836	36187	9651	20043	34819
37	Transport Equipment	R	3076	4383	7870	13106	5328	7387	6752	25795	23841	6964	10824	12960
		U	10560	10641	26475	32696	15838	57059	6838	17373	39400	12278	15987	44144
38	Other Manufacturing	R	8669	973	3965	4533	3637	6662	1036	3738	2949	7723	1337	4019
		U	8293	9670	14308	9741	11788	20738	1967	15008	15357	6805	11773	16362
39+97+99	Repair Services	R	11371	2598	9035	12116	3070	8854	4892	6415	22347	11346	2685	13769
		U	11779	4533	12812	12016	5899	80269	3220	16157	143198	10869	6414	48332
	All Industries	R	6213	1720	2955	8517	5833	8329	2226	4479	7907	6118	2366	3988
		U	14151	4518	8707	12081	9171	20527	3723	11893	21687	10995	7934	15503

Note: 1. R= Rural and U= Urban
2. Repair Services (NIC 39, 97, 99) are not covered in 56th Round. However, for 2000-01, few industry groups which are not elsewhere classified, are clubbed in industry group 39.

Source: 1. Govt. of India, *Directory Manufacturing Establishments Survey 1984-85: Summary Results*, C.S.O., New Delhi.
2. Govt. of India, N.S.S. Report No. 363/1, June 1989; Report No. 433, September 1997; and Household Level Data (for 2000-01) on CD-ROM, supplied by NSSO New Delhi.

Table 173

Table 2A
Growth of Capital Labour Ratio (%)

NIC Code	Sector Description	Locale	OAMEs		NDMEs		DMEs		All Manufacturing	
			84-85/ 94-95	94-95/ 00-01	84-85/ 94-95	94-95/ 00-01	84-85/ 94-95	94-95/ 00-01	84-85/ 94-95	94-95/ 00-01
1	2	3	4	5	6	7	8	9	10	11
20-21	Food Products	R	-7.32	10.48	-2.77	-0.46	1.61	4.85	-5.47	6.56
		U	-10.70	12.33	-5.30	9.01	5.21	16.59	-6.47	11.75
22	Beverages, etc.	R	-11.20	9.75	7.07	-9.08	22.71	-15.87	-4.19	-1.64
		U	-0.41	2.27	-12.10	42.45	-3.51	24.16	-2.98	8.12
23+24+25	Cotton, Wool, Jute etc.	R	-6.12	9.97	-5.72	5.77	10.11	5.73	-1.83	5.93
		U	-0.23	5.28	13.26	1.02	16.45	7.56	8.69	4.74
26	Textile Products	R	-17.71	25.32	-10.47	28.84	9.32	16.05	-15.44	23.71
		U	-20.64	19.52	6.38	1.41	11.64	25.18	-11.49	14.43
27	Wood Products	R	-19.76	-0.09	-4.72	2.34	-2.24	15.55	-18.00	1.46
		U	-9.11	6.91	-8.09	12.19	5.06	16.19	-5.62	12.38
28	Paper Products	R	3.59	29.08	2.05	10.55	-4.01	14.89	-0.25	16.40
		U	6.61	8.52	-7.04	13.16	9.02	2.81	1.01	7.77
29	Leather Products	R	-13.74	5.40	-3.49	26.40	-2.22	45.14	-13.44	8.90
		U	-11.23	19.28	-18.30	31.12	9.17	21.84	-11.16	23.20
30	Rubber Products	R	-6.71	-4.12	-17.65	38.22	-0.04	-12.17	-10.95	0.95
		U	4.05	-6.05	8.64	0.43	2.48	17.20	2.02	5.88
31	Chemical Products	R	12.56	23.60	9.09	-16.30	15.66	11.88	16.45	8.04
		U	5.84	23.10	-12.97	15.65	28.52	2.20	14.14	4.70

(Contd. —)

TABLE 175

Table 2A (Contd.)
Growth of Capital Labour Ratio (%)

NIC Code	Sector Description	Locale	OAMEs		NDMEs		DMEs		All Manufacturing	
			84-85/ 94-95	94-95/ 00-01	84-85/ 94-95	94-95/ 00-01	84-85/ 94-95	94-95/ 00-01	84-85/ 94-95	94-95/ 00-01
1	2	3	4	5	6	7	8	9	10	11
32	Non-metallic Mineral	R	-13.55	8.38	-1.52	5.26	6.98	22.99	-9.23	19.92
	Products	U	7.56	0.55	-0.21	20.50	12.93	20.70	6.87	16.06
33	Basic Metal Industries	R	-0.43	24.01	-5.10	-11.03	8.88	-11.01	3.75	-3.20
		U	1.06	11.97	3.93	15.01	9.71	18.98	5.65	17.60
34	Metal Products	R	-20.56	11.35	7.56	15.28	3.28	22.33	-15.92	13.84
		U	-21.14	16.42	3.50	19.60	13.36	8.91	-5.02	12.76
35+36	Machine tool & Elect. Machinery	R	-22.10	14.51	-6.17	30.64	18.99	14.24	-12.72	17.44
		U	14.42	18.45	0.48	8.51	11.32	9.64	7.58	9.64
37	Transport Equipment	R	3.60	10.25	-8.61	5.60	14.34	-1.30	4.51	3.05
		U	0.08	16.41	-6.99	23.81	9.77	14.62	2.67	18.44
38	Other Manufacturing	R	-19.65	26.39	-2.18	10.62	13.69	-3.88	-16.09	20.13
		U	1.55	6.75	1.93	9.87	22.53	0.38	5.63	5.64
39+97+99	Repair Services	R	-13.72	23.09	-12.83	19.31	2.75	23.12	-13.42	31.32
		U	-9.11	18.91	-6.87	54.51	17.50	43.86	-5.14	40.02
All	All Industries	R	-12.05	9.44	-3.71	6.11	7.24	9.93	-9.06	9.09
		U	-10.79	11.55	-2.72	14.37	12.31	10.53	-3.21	11.81

Note: The same as in Table 2.
Source: The same as in Table 2.

Table 3

Level of Per Worker Productivity (Rs.) at Constant 1981-82 Prices in Unorganised Manufacturing in Rural/Urban India: 1984-85/2000-01

NIC Code	Sector Description	Locale	OAMEs			NDMEs			DMEs			All Unorganised		
			84-85	94-95	00-01	84-85	94-95	00-01	84-85	94-95	00-01	84-85	94-95	00-01
1	2	3	4	5	6	7	8	9	10	11	12	13	14	15
20-21	Food Products	R	1478	1994	3133	3773	4229	4951	2686	2880	4175	1936	2378	3466
		U	4338	4149	5280	8947	7432	8083	10598	8697	10404	6956	6059	7159
22	Beverages, etc.	R	1462	1096	1211	2186	4334	3066	1631	2741	2167	1535	1323	1322
		U	1528	1969	1385	4423	3544	5135	7664	3543	6824	2231	2121	1712
23+24+25	Cotton, Wool, Jute etc.	R	1082	1730	2336	2349	3811	5207	2873	5290	6673	1253	2686	3169
		U	1974	2897	3580	7291	8621	11029	6247	9225	11580	4093	6528	7931
26	Textile Products	R	1573	1163	3343	2893	2520	5521	2361	3903	6770	1790	1611	3773
		U	2659	2412	4833	4714	5231	9601	5874	7639	11554	3832	5535	7712
27	Wood Products	R	1806	1107	1185	3893	2964	3363	3588	2745	4931	1969	1233	1362
		U	2470	2179	2532	6587	6185	4466	7318	6377	5234	4386	4181	3683
28	Paper Products	R	1012	1039	2547	2845	3877	4219	9639	2208	6256	2915	2193	3360
		U	1937	3138	2419	7706	6132	6210	7424	7669	7951	6207	5777	5808
29	Leather Products	R	3586	2947	3955	3701	5684	6935	4099	6267	6611	3601	3212	4371
		U	5325	5308	5310	6055	5599	8158	11736	7673	11667	7084	6244	8343
30	Rubber Products	R	916	1408	1729	3863	5715	6595	7120	5351	4072	3005	3041	3175
		U	3450	2215	1668	7202	7140	9486	14866	11722	14264	10357	6081	6609
31	Chemical Products	R	1053	1498	3755	5666	7959	14616	6261	13948	15672	3241	7692	11084
		U	1273	6263	7272	17514	12851	16469	6521	14037	23321	4937	12850	18074

(Contd. —)

TABLE 177

Table 3 (Contd.)
Level of Per Worker Productivity (Rs.) at Constant 1981-82 Prices in Unorganised Manufacturing in Rural/Urban India: 1984-85/2000-01

NIC Code	Sector Description	Locale	OAMEs			NDMEs			DMEs			All Unorganised		
			84-85	94-95	00-01	84-85	94-95	00-01	84-85	94-95	00-01	84-85	94-95	00-01
1	2	3	4	5	6	7	8	9	10	11	12	13	14	15
32	Non-metallic Mineral Products	R	1178	1481	2097	1570	3193	7035	2526	4772	6980	1438	2365	4322
		U	2916	2478	2967	5161	4707	10568	3020	4760	7810	3326	3606	6140
33	Basic Metal Industries	R	1741	1629	3703	4960	4546	4062	11704	19824	29211	4520	7202	12987
		U	3935	6575	6358	6366	7401	8348	11664	12673	12361	8768	9056	9458
34	Metal Products	R	1970	2028	2898	3183	4367	7136	6188	4445	8214	2367	2609	3952
		U	5067	4206	5496	9384	6511	8720	15009	8154	10272	10929	6792	8380
35+36	Machine tool & Elect. Machinery	R	4029	2431	3977	4218	5108	7115	1254	8807	12868	2656	3837	5727
		U	2411	5886	8935	7947	9021	13597	11856	15406	17708	9193	12094	15194
37	Transport Equipment	R	4785	3918	4980	3859	4907	6659	5507	7640	23487	4553	5235	11642
		U	8536	4994	7757	193362	13422	13739	38064	12221	15572	66654	11542	14343
38	Other Manufacturing	R	1835	1304	3228	3427	6013	6351	3377	8789	6814	2069	2212	4049
		U	3925	9311	6260	6268	10718	10106	7027	16721	10999	5191	11974	8422
39+97+99	Repair Services	R	2407	3269	2427	4515	3870	4452	6762	6460	6950	2650	3367	4291
		U	6348	5574	5150	6368	5701	32557	7072	10276	53124	6440	6172	18806
	All Industries	R	1554	1761	2548	3227	3974	5542	2839	4310	6156	1802	2227	3227
		U	3139	4119	4235	7578	6943	9090	8778	9285	11043	5673	6392	7427

Note: The same as in Table 2.
Source: The same as in Table 2.

Table 3A
Growth of Per Worker Productivity (%)

NIC Code	Sector Description	Locale	OAMEs		NDMEs		DMEs		All Manufacturing	
			84-85/ 94-95	94-95/ 00-01	84-85/ 94-95	94-95/ 00-01	84-85/ 94-95	94-95/ 00-01	84-85/ 94-95	94-95/ 00-01
1	2	3	4	5	6	7	8	9	10	11
20-21	Food Products	R	3.04	7.82	1.15	2.66	0.70	6.38	2.08	6.48
		U	-0.44	4.10	-1.84	1.41	-1.96	3.03	-1.37	2.82
22	Beverages, etc.	R	-2.84	1.67	7.08	-5.60	5.33	-3.84	-1.47	-0.02
		U	2.57	-5.69	-2.19	6.37	-7.43	11.54	-0.50	-3.51
23+24+25	Cotton, Wool, Jute etc.	R	4.81	5.14	4.96	5.34	6.29	3.95	7.92	2.80
		U	3.91	3.59	1.69	4.19	3.97	3.86	4.78	3.30
26	Textile Products	R	-2.98	19.25	-1.37	13.96	5.15	9.61	-1.05	15.23
		U	-0.97	12.28	1.05	10.65	2.66	7.14	3.75	5.68
27	Wood Products	R	-4.78	1.14	-2.69	2.13	-2.64	10.26	-4.57	1.67
		U	-1.25	2.53	-0.63	-5.28	-1.37	-3.24	-0.48	-2.09
28	Paper Products	R	0.26	16.13	3.14	1.42	-13.70	18.95	-2.80	7.37
		U	4.94	-4.24	-2.26	0.21	0.33	0.60	-0.71	0.09
29	Leather Products	R	-1.94	5.03	4.38	3.37	4.34	0.89	-1.14	5.27
		U	-0.03	0.01	-0.78	6.47	-4.16	7.23	-1.25	4.95
30	Rubber Products	R	4.40	3.48	3.99	2.41	-2.81	-4.45	0.12	0.73
		U	-4.34	-4.62	-0.09	4.85	-2.35	3.33	-5.19	1.40
31	Chemical Products	R	3.59	16.55	3.46	10.66	8.34	1.96	9.03	6.28
		U	17.27	2.52	-3.05	4.22	7.97	8.83	10.04	5.85

(Contd. —)

TABLE 179

Table 3A (Contd.)
Growth of Per Worker Productivity (%)

NIC Code	Sector Description	Locale	OAMEs		NDMEs		DMEs		All Manufacturing	
			84-85/ 94-95	94-95 00-01	84-85/ 94-95	94-95 00-01	84-85/ 94-95	94-95 00-01	84-85/ 94-95	94-95 00-01
1	2	3	4	5	6	7	8	9	10	11
32	Non-metallic Mineral Products	R	2.31	5.97	7.35	14.07	6.57	6.54	5.10	10.57
		U	-1.61	3.05	-0.92	14.43	4.65	8.60	0.81	9.28
33	Basic Metal Ind.	R	-0.66	14.66	-0.87	-1.86	5.41	6.67	4.77	10.33
		U	5.27	-0.56	1.52	2.03	0.83	-0.41	0.32	0.73
34	Metal Products	R	0.29	6.13	3.21	8.53	-3.25	10.78	0.98	7.16
		U	-1.84	4.56	-3.59	4.99	-5.92	3.92	-4.65	3.57
35+36	Machine tool & Elect.Machinery	R	-4.93	8.55	1.93	5.68	21.52	6.52	3.75	6.90
		U	9.34	7.20	1.28	7.08	2.65	2.35	2.78	3.88
37	Transport Equipment	R	-1.98	4.08	2.43	5.22	3.33	20.58	1.41	14.25
		U	-5.22	7.62	-23.41	0.39	-10.74	4.12	-16.08	3.69
38	Other Manufacturing	R	-3.36	16.31	5.78	0.92	10.04	-4.15	0.67	10.60
		U	9.02	-6.40	5.51	-0.97	9.06	-6.74	8.72	-5.70
39+97+99	Repair Services	R	3.11	-4.84	-1.53	2.36	-0.46	1.22	2.43	4.12
		U	-1.29	-1.31	-1.10	33.69	3.81	31.49	-0.42	20.40
	All Industries	R	1.26	6.35	2.11	5.70	4.27	6.12	2.14	6.38
		U	2.75	0.46	-0.87	4.59	0.56	2.93	1.20	2.53

Source: The same as in Table 2.

Table 4

Growth of Employment in Unorganised Manufacturing by Rural-Urban Location and Production Sectors: 1984-85/2000-01

NIC Code	Sector Description	RURAL								URBAN							
		OAMEs		NDMEs		DMEs		All Manufacturing		OAMEs		NDMEs		DMEs		All Manufacturing	
		84-85/ 94-95	94-95/ 00-01	84-85/ 94-95	94-95/ 00-01	84-85/ 94-95	94-95/ 00-01	84-85/ 94-95	94-95/ 00-01	84-85/ 94-95	94-95/ 00-01	84-85/ 94-95	94-95/ 00-01	84-85/ 94-95	94-95/ 00-01	84-85/ 94-95	94-95/ 00-01
1	2	3	4	5	6	7	8	9	10	11	12	13	14	15	16	17	18
20-21	Food Products	-1.68	1.67	-3.90	0.87	2.06	-1.03	-1.56	1.23	-1.61	5.12	-1.06	3.28	-1.55	6.63	-1.43	4.82
22	Beverages, etc.	2.27	6.39	-4.81	-6.30	-3.79	12.39	1.38	6.39	-0.04	6.33	-3.70	-0.63	-7.15	2.76	-0.70	5.86
23+24+25	Cotton, Wool, Jute etc.	-10.33	-0.67	0.73	-4.70	3.19	-9.79	-7.97	-2.65	-5.93	4.08	-0.16	0.38	-1.00	2.05	-3.22	2.59
26	Textile Products	-5.77	12.96	-7.60	14.20	-1.00	-0.95	-5.54	11.87	-10.86	30.71	-12.54	32.07	5.04	7.29	-6.61	21.95
27	Wood Products	0.87	1.88	-1.33	2.46	1.39	-1.40	0.76	1.85	0.12	-0.32	5.46	2.12	-0.68	1.17	1.32	0.74
28	Paper Products	7.31	0.20	13.96	-10.95	-10.42	25.32	7.75	-1.98	4.72	4.27	4.46	8.26	-0.66	6.10	2.41	6.39
29	Leather Products	-8.92	-6.07	-10.83	-1.95	-0.34	11.77	-8.93	-5.08	-2.08	-1.93	2.81	-1.66	5.28	-2.45	1.34	-2.04
30	Rubber Products	11.73	5.58	-2.11	3.96	15.35	19.88	10.99	11.58	15.94	7.08	-2.99	-1.51	-0.93	5.47	3.61	5.27
31	Chemical Products	-8.37	10.32	3.32	15.07	-3.71	11.71	-4.98	11.98	-13.43	7.14	14.76	1.20	2.41	-5.29	-0.04	-1.56
32	Non-metallic Mineral Products	-0.80	-2.13	-4.03	2.96	3.38	11.34	-0.13	2.27	0.12	3.30	2.61	2.17	-0.50	10.39	0.39	5.41
33	Basic Metal Ind.	-4.70	15.53	-6.25	13.93	-1.87	22.40	-4.25	17.48	6.50	-6.73	-1.37	9.43	-4.34	2.53	-0.76	2.08
34	Metal Products	-4.08	5.28	-2.09	7.45	1.26	-3.17	-3.42	5.03	2.90	8.09	8.56	4.97	4.99	-3.39	5.77	2.52
35+36	Machine tool & Elect. Machinery	1.88	10.14	4.16	8.78	-13.57	8.33	-2.95	9.67	-7.43	15.29	2.63	9.80	-2.25	10.82	-1.48	10.92
37	Transport Equipment	-7.84	-4.72	-9.96	7.24	2.03	3.22	-6.62	1.08	10.85	-3.53	8.35	8.49	2.21	6.47	4.57	5.95
38	Other Manufacturing	9.35	-12.09	2.70	5.20	10.11	-3.20	9.13	-10.15	4.60	2.72	5.00	12.57	7.33	-2.90	5.48	3.21
39+97+99	Repair Services	1.71	-65.16	6.03	-62.28	-4.55	-27.03	2.09	-62.07	4.99	-58.59	5.65	-63.40	5.29	-58.10	5.27	-60.04
	All	-2.03	1.18	-2.53	0.92	2.09	2.86	-1.70	1.35	-0.98	3.47	1.40	2.89	1.70	1.73	0.37	2.82

Note: The same as in Table 2.

Source: The same as in Table 2.

Table 4A
Number of Units and Workers in Unorganised Manufacturing Sector: 1984-85/2000-01

(in Lakhs)

Period	Rural			Urban			All Unorganised		
	OAMEs	NDMEs	DMEs	OAMEs	NDMEs	DMEs	Rural	Urban	Total
1	2	3	4	5	6	7	8	9	10
Number of Units									
1984-85	134.4	10.3	1.8	36.5	11.3	3.0	146.4	50.8	197.2
1994-95	95.3	6.7	2.9	27.1	9.3	3.6	105.0	40.1	145.0
2000-01	110.6	6.3	2.5	36.1	10.8	4.0	119.3	50.9	170.2
Increment/Decrement									
94-95/84-85	-39.0	-3.6	1.2	-9.3	-2.0	0.6	-41.5	-10.7	-52.2
00-01/94-95	15.2	-0.4	-0.5	8.9	1.5	0.4	14.4	10.8	25.2
00-01/84-85	-23.8	-4.0	0.7	-0.4	-0.5	1.0	-27.1	0.1	-27.0
Composition of Workers									
1984-85 Full Time	186.6	21.9	19.2	47.7	25.2	26.1	227.8	98.9	326.7
Part Time	32.5	1.7	0.7	5.5	1.4	1.0	34.9	7.9	42.8
Total	219.1	23.6	19.9	53.2	26.6	27.0	262.7	106.8	369.5
1994-95 Full Time	149.6	17.1	23.7	45.2	29.3	31.1	190.3	105.6	295.9
Part Time	28.9	1.2	0.9	3.0	1.2	0.9	31.0	5.1	36.1
Total	178.4	18.3	24.5	48.2	30.6	32.0	221.3	110.8	332.0
2000-01 Full Time	148.7	17.8	27.7	49.3	34.7	34.5	194.1	118.4	312.5
Part Time	42.8	1.6	1.4	9.9	1.6	1.1	45.8	12.5	58.3
Total	191.5	19.3	29.1	59.1	36.3	35.5	239.9	131.0	370.8

TABLE 181

(Contd. —)

Table 4A (Contd.)
Number of Units and Workers in Unorganised Manufacturing Sector: 1984-85/2000-01

(in Lakhs)

Period	Rural			Urban			All Unorganised		
	OAMEs	NDMEs	DMEs	OAMEs	NDMEs	DMEs	Rural	Urban	Total
1	2	3	4	5	6	7	8	9	10
Increment/Decrement									
94-95/84-85 Full Time	-37.1	-4.9	4.4	-2.5	4.2	5.0	-37.5	6.7	-30.8
Part Time	-3.6	-0.5	0.1	-2.5	-0.2	0.0	-3.9	-2.7	-6.7
Total	-40.7	-5.3	4.6	-5.0	4.0	5.0	-41.4	4.0	-37.5
00-01/94-95 Full Time	-0.9	0.7	4.0	4.1	5.4	3.4	3.8	12.8	16.6
Part Time	13.9	0.4	0.5	6.9	0.4	0.1	14.8	7.4	22.2
Total	13.0	1.0	4.5	11.0	5.7	3.5	18.6	20.2	38.8
00-01/84-85 Full Time	-38.0	-4.2	8.5	1.6	9.5	8.4	-33.7	19.5	-14.2
Part Time	10.3	-0.1	0.7	4.4	0.2	0.1	10.9	4.7	15.5
Total	-27.7	-4.3	9.1	6.0	9.7	8.5	-22.8	24.2	1.3

Source: The same as in Table 2.

TABLE 183

TABLE 5

Level of Per Worker Productivity by Location and Employment size Category: April-June 200 Survey

Employment Size (No. of Workers)	Average Productivity (Rs) per annum		Minimum		Maximum		Coefficient of Variation	
	Rural	Urban	Rural	Urban	Rural	Urban	Rural	Urban
1	2	3	4	5	6	7	8	9
upto 2	31767	-**	4200	-**	362500	-**	259	-**
3—4	72026	72725	5000	5975	1650000	855000	402	296
5—6	60522	117556	4510	11017	1920000	800000	555	184
7—8	159659	171210	2571	18900	1774286	1031557	299	173
9—10	174153	252449	17200	38889	2400000	4666667	262	358
above 10	123372	243972	10000	20000	833333	2366000	190	222

Note : ** Figures not estimated because only 2 units fall in this category.

Source : Chadha, G.K., *et al.*, "Rural Industry in India and China", An On-going Research Study, J.N.U., New Delhi, 2001 b.

Table 6
Per Worker Productivity at Constant (1981-82) Prices in Organised and Unorganised Manufacturing Sector by Rural-Urban Location: 2000-01

Manufacturing Segment	Productivity (in Rs. Per Annum)			Rural:Urban Ratio (%)	Organised: Unorganised Ratio (%)		
	Rural	Urban	Total		Rural	Urban	Total
1	2	3	4	5	6	7	8
Unorganised Manufacturing							
OAMEs	2548.6	4235.3	2946.6	60.2	3.6	5.9	4.1
NDMEs	5545.9	9090.6	7858.7	61.0	7.7	12.7	11.0
DMEs	6154.7	11045.5	8844.9	55.7	8.6	15.4	12.4
Total	3227.0	7428.1	4710.6	43.4	4.5	10.4	6.6
Organised Manufacturing*	71659.6	71571.3	71604.4	100.1	-	-	-
Total Manufacturing	9333.6	22236.5	14399.9	42.0	-	-	-

Note: * Latest available data is for the year 1999-2000. For organised segment, per worker productivity is calculated taking Net Value Added, since rural urban break-up is not available for Gross Value Added, whereas for unorganised segment, productivity estimates are based on Gross Value Added.

Source: 1. Govt. of India, *Unorganised Manufacturing Sector in 2000-01*, NSSO Report No- 477, June 2002.
2. Govt. of India, *Annual Survey of Industries: 1999-2000*, Vol. I, CSO, February 2002.

TABLE 185

Table 7

Structural Features of Small Scale Industries in India by Rural-Urban Location: 1987-88 and 1994-95

Area of Location	No. of Units		Employment		Total Production		Fixed Investment		Investment in P+M		Working Capital	
	1987-88	1994-95	1987-88	1994-95	1987-88	1994-95	1987-88	1994-95	1987-88	1994-95	1987-88	1994-95
1	2	3	4	5	6	7	8	9	10	11	12	13
Rural	42.2	42.3	33.3	15.1		17.1	29.4	14.4	28.6	35.2	22.4	29.1
Urban	48.0	48.5	50.4	49.0		48.1	52.0	49.1	51.0	48.9	50.7	54.2
Metropolitan	9.8	9.3	16.3	36.0		34.9	18.6	36.5	20.4	15.9	26.9	16.6
All	100.0	100.0	100.0	100.0		100.0	100.0	100.0	100.0	100.0	100.0	100.0
Backward	62.2	48.3		38.5		38.7	46.6	39.8	45.3	38.7	36.4	36.5
Non-Backward	37.8	51.7		61.5		61.3	53.4	60.2	54.7	61.3	63.6	63.5

Source : 1. Govt. of India, *Report of the Second All-India Census of Small Scale Industrial Units 1987-88*, Ministry of Industry, August, 1992.
2. Govt. of India, *Report on Sample Survey of Small Scale Industrial Units 1994-95*, Ministry of SSI and ARI, 2000.

Table 8

Some Structural Parameters in Small Scale Industrial Sector by Rural-Urban Location: 1987-88 and 1994-95

Per Unit Level (000' Rs.)

Area of Location	Fixed Investment		Investment in P+M		Working Capital		Employment Per Unit	
	1987-88	1994-95	1987-88	1994-95	1987-88	1994-95	1987-88	1994-95
1	2	3	4	5	6	7	8	9
Rural	111	267	65	167	65	481.31	4.97	3.0
Urban	173	313	101	202	130	781.74	6.61	8.5
Metropolitan	302	478	197	342	334	1249.27	10.4	32.7
All	160	309	95	200	123	698.29	6.3	8.5
Backward	120	255	69	160	72	527.7		6.7
Non-Backward	225	360	138	238	206	857.8		10.1

Source: The same as in Table 7.

TABLE 187

Table 9

Location-wise Distribution of No. of Units and Production in Major Branches of Small Scale Industrial Sector: 1987-88 and 1994-95

Area of Location		Percentage Share Within Production Location											
		Mfg/Assembling Only		Processing		Job Work		Repairing/Services		Combined		Overall	
		1987-88	1994-95	1987-88	1994-95	1987-88	1994-95	1987-88	1994-95	1987-88	1994-95	1987-88	1994-95
1		2	3	4	5	6	7	8	9	10	11	12	13
Rural	A	44.00	46.41	21.20	14.69	11.10	19.62	15.50	14.87	8.20	4.41	100.00	100.00
	B	70.70	75.98	20.80	10.23	2.40	0.69	1.20	0.76	4.90	12.34	100.00	100.00
Urban	A	52.70	52.73	11.50	8.52	12.90	18.01	15.10	15.56	7.80	5.18	100.00	100.00
	B	78.50	77.60	11.30	4.84	2.00	13.12	1.30	0.84	6.90	3.59	100.00	100.00
Metropolitan	A	64.20	62.98	8.30	5.79	12.40	19.59	4.70	6.50	10.40	5.14	100.00	100.00
	B	78.50	90.81	7.40	4.02	2.30	1.74	0.90	0.69	10.90	2.74	100.00	100.00
All	A	50.20	51.01	15.20	10.87	12.10	18.84	14.30	14.43	8.20	4.85	100.00	100.00
	B	76.40	79.29	13.00	6.58	2.10	6.85	1.20	0.79	7.30	6.50	100.00	100.00
Backward	A	46.10	46.07	17.40	13.85	12.00	18.37	16.20	16.75	8.30	4.96	100.00	100.00
	B	73.60	76.33	17.50	10.65	1.60	1.04	1.70	0.71	5.60	11.28	100.00	100.00
Non-Backward	A	57.00	55.63	11.70	8.08	12.30	19.27	11.00	12.26	8.00	4.75	100.00	100.00
	B	78.50	81.15	9.70	4.01	2.50	10.51	0.80	0.84	8.50	3.48	100.00	100.00

Note : A = Share in Units   B = Share in output

Source : The same as in Table 7.

Table 10

Distribution of No. of Units and Output in Major Branches of Small Scale Industrial Sector by Location: 1987-88 and 1994-95

Area of Location		Percentage Share Within Production Location											
		Mfg/Assembling Only		Processing		Job Work		Repairing/Services		Combined		Overall	
		1987-88	1994-95	1987-88	1994-95	1987-88	1994-95	1987-88	1994-95	1987-88	1994-95	1987-88	1994-95
1		2	3	4	5	6	7	8	9	10	11	12	13
Rural	A	37.00	38.40	58.60	57.10	38.60	44.00	45.90	43.50	42.20	38.40	42.20	42.20
	B	24.80	33.40	43.00	54.20	30.50	3.50	27.50	33.70	18.00	66.30	26.80	34.90
Urban	A	50.40	50.10	36.00	38.00	51.30	46.30	50.80	52.30	45.30	51.80	48.00	48.50
	B	52.30	47.00	44.30	35.40	45.00	92.10	56.20	51.40	48.60	26.50	50.90	48.10
Metropolitan	A	12.60	11.50	5.40	5.00	10.10	9.70	3.30	4.20	12.50	9.80	9.80	9.30
	B	22.90	19.50	12.70	10.40	24.50	4.30	16.30	14.90	33.40	7.20	22.30	17.00
All	A	100.00	100.00	100.00	100.00	100.00	100.00	100.00	100.00	100.00	100.00	100.00	100.00
	B	100.00	100.00	100.00	100.00	100.00	100.00	100.00	100.00	100.00	100.00	100.00	100.00
Backward	A	57.10	43.60	71.00	61.60	61.60	47.10	70.50	56.10	63.30	49.40	62.20	48.30
	B	40.70	37.20	56.90	62.60	32.50	5.90	60.00	34.70	32.40	67.10	42.20	38.70
Non-Backward	A	42.90	56.40	29.00	38.40	38.40	52.90	29.50	43.90	36.70	50.60	37.80	51.70
	B	59.30	62.80	43.10	37.40	67.50	94.10	40.00	65.30	67.60	32.90	57.80	61.30

Note   : A = Share in Units   B = Share in output
Source : The same as in Table 7.

TABLE 189

Table 11

Percent Share of Rural Areas in Production Units, Employment, Production and Fixed Investment in Small Scale Industrial Sector by Major Industry Group: 1987-88 and 1994-95

Broad Industry Group	Percentage Share of Rural Areas								Percentage Share of Urban and Metropolitan							
	No. of Units		Employment		Production		Fixed Investment*		No. of Units		Employment		Production		Fixed Investment*	
	1987-88	1994-95	1987-88	1994-95	1987-88	1994-95	1987-88	1994-95	1987-88	1994-95	1987-88	1994-95	1987-88	1994-95	1987-88	1994-95
1	2	3	4	5	6	7	8	9	10	11	12	13	14	15	16	17
Food Products (20–21)	63.2	61.9	53.5	50.8	42.9	36.4	48.5	-	36.8	38.1	46.5	49.2	57.1	63.6	51.5	-
Beverages(22)	48.4	45.6	19.9	30.6	14.0	20.4	32.1	-	51.6	54.4	80.1	69.4	86.0	79.6	67.9	-
Cotton Textiles (23)	27.3	36.7	22.2	32.2	19.9	4.1	25.2	-	72.7	63.3	77.8	67.8	80.1	95.9	74.8	-
Wool, Synthetic, (24)	38.4	35.3	20.4	28.5	8.1	37.4	18.3	-	61.6	64.7	79.6	71.5	91.9	62.6	81.7	-
Jute, Mesta, (25)	25.6	37.9	29.8	27.6	11.3	7.0	36.1	-	74.4	62.1	70.2	72.4	88.7	93.0	63.9	-
Textile Products (26)	54.1	51.0	23.4	21.8	7.0	37.5	15.3	-	45.9	49.0	76.6	78.2	93.0	62.5	84.7	-
Wood/Products (27)	55.6	54.8	46.9	49.0	35.5	11.9	42.7	-	44.4	45.2	53.1	51.0	64.5	88.1	57.3	-
Paper/Products (28)	16.4	21.4	15.2	20.9	12.8	19.5	16.8	-	83.6	78.6	84.8	79.1	87.2	80.5	83.2	-
Leather/Products (29)	58.0	47.8	31.0	30.3	33.4	84.9	29.2	-	42.0	52.2	69.0	69.7	66.6	15.1	70.8	-

(Contd. —)

Table 11 (Contd.)

Percent Share of Rural Areas in Production Units, Employment, Production and Fixed Investment in Small Scale Industrial Sector by Major Industry Group: 1987-88 and 1994-95

Broad Industry Group	Percentage Share of Rural Areas								Percentage Share of Urban and Metropolitan							
	No. of Units		Employment		Production		Fixed Investment*		No. of Units		Employment		Production		Fixed Investment*	
	1987-88	1994-95	1987-88	1994-95	1987-88	1994-95	1987-88	1994-95	1987-88	1994-95	1987-88	1994-95	1987-88	1994-95	1987-88	1994-95
1	2	3	4	5	6	7	8	9	10	11	12	13	14	15	16	17
Chemicals/Products (30)	25.8	34.3	26.0	37.6	23.1	41.3	29.0	-	74.2	65.7	74.0	62.4	76.9	58.7	71.0	-
Rubber, Plastic, Coal, Pet. (31)	29.3	37.2	34.0	40.0	28.0	29.6	30.4	-	70.7	62.8	66.0	60.0	72.0	70.4	69.6	-
Non-Met.Min. Prodts (32)	55.3	57.8	62.1	58.6	56.1	12.5	54.4	-	44.7	42.2	37.9	41.4	43.9	87.5	45.6	-
Basic Metal (33)	14.0	22.4	19.8	34.8	21.3	47.3	22.4	-	86.0	77.6	80.2	65.2	78.7	52.7	77.6	-
Metal Products (34)	34.2	33.9	23.7	26.6	23.8	9.3	20.5	-	65.8	66.1	76.3	73.4	76.2	90.7	79.5	-
Non-Electrical Machinery (35)	17.9	24.2	13.0	21.0	10.3	12.5	14.3	-	82.1	75.8	87.0	79.0	89.7	87.5	85.7	-
Electrical Machinery (36)	12.0	21.2	11.5	20.9	11.8	24.6	14.7	-	88.0	78.8	88.5	79.1	88.2	75.4	85.3	-
Transport Equip. (37)	26.0	30.6	16.0	22.8	12.9	83.7	17.9	-	74.0	69.4	84.0	77.2	87.1	16.3	82.1	-
Other Manufacturing Ind. (38)	22.6	23.6	17.1	22.2	11.2	7.7	16.3	-	77.4	76.4	82.9	77.8	88.8	92.3	83.7	-
All manufacturing	42.2	42.2	33.3	34.4	26.8	34.9	29.4	-	57.8	57.8	66.7	65.6	73.2	65.1	70.6	-

* For 1994-95 rural-urban break-up of fixed investment by broad industry group is not available.

Source : The same as in Table 7.

TABLE 191

Table 12

Annual Compound Growth Rate of Employment, Productivity and Associated Variables in Organised Manufacturing: 1987-88/1997-98 (1981-82 Prices)

Manufacturing Group	Locale	Workers	Technical Personnel	K:L Ratio	Productivity	NVA	Real Wage**	Fixed Capital
				Rate of Growth * (in %)				
1	2	3	4	5	6	7	8	9
Food Products (20+21)	R	3.85	4.26	10.39	4.78	8.81	6.11	14.64
	U	1.12	1.78	8.31	7.28	8.48	2.85	9.52
	T	2.79	3.07	9.50	5.71	8.66	4.56	12.56
Beverages(22)	R	1.73	3.17	15.31	7.92	9.77	3.80	17.30
	U	3.55	1.23	4.16	2.79	6.43	4.06	7.85
	T	3.09	2.48	8.72	4.15	7.37	3.98	12.08
Cotton Textiles (23)	R	5.40	7.74	15.69	6.94	12.71	5.68	21.93
	U	-2.41	-0.29	9.26	0.56	-1.86	-2.97	6.63
	T	0.01	1.95	13.48	3.13	3.12	-0.07	13.47
Wool, Synthetic, (24)	R	9.85	13.95	13.84	9.35	20.12	10.30	25.05
	U	-0.75	0.89	-0.62	3.73	2.95	-0.18	-1.37
	T	2.24	4.41	12.48	6.00	8.38	3.13	15.00
Jute, Mesta, (25)	R	-3.88	-4.08	9.30	0.28	-3.61	-6.70	5.06
	U	1.77	-0.11	-0.69	1.55	3.34	3.58	1.07
	T	0.98	-0.07	0.59	1.58	2.58	2.40	1.58
1987-88/92-93	R	-19.67	-14.53	14.09	4.03	-16.43	-23.97	-8.35
	U	3.25	3.15	-0.07	-0.90	2.32	4.92	3.18
	T	0.17	0.40	1.85	0.02	0.19	1.54	2.02

(Contd. —)

Table 12 (Contd.)

Annual Compound Growth Rate of Employment, Productivity and Associated Variables in Organised Manufacturing: 1987-88/1997-98 (1981-82 Prices)

Manufacturing Group	Locale	Workers	Technical Personnel	K:L Ratio	Productivity	NVA	Real Wage**	Fixed Capital
1	2	3	4	5	6	7	8	9
1992-93/97-98	R	19.64	9.88	4.19	-1.55	17.81	23.03	24.66
	U	2.20	-1.06	-0.11	2.09	4.34	3.95	2.09
	T	3.76	0.20	0.60	1.51	5.33	5.07	4.39
Textile Products(26)	R	13.08	11.17	3.40	0.96	14.16	9.76	16.92
	U	12.72	11.05	7.52	2.97	16.07	13.68	21.20
	T	12.81	11.09	6.55	2.80	15.97	13.26	20.20
Wood/Products(27)	R	3.23	3.74	-0.37	0.44	3.68	3.20	2.85
	U	-1.47	-2.28	6.23	-3.00	-4.42	-0.10	4.66
	T	0.82	0.10	3.12	-1.83	-1.03	0.86	3.97
Paper/Products(28)	R	5.47	6.15	9.18	6.20	12.01	7.49	15.16
	U	0.92	1.76	5.59	6.19	7.17	2.76	6.56
	T	2.13	2.74	8.38	6.10	8.35	3.76	10.69
Leather/Products(29)	R	3.32	5.17	10.31	5.63	9.14	4.79	13.97
	U	5.02	6.20	13.00	7.82	13.23	4.11	18.69
	T	4.47	5.94	11.69	7.53	12.34	4.33	16.68
Agro-Processing (20-29)	R	4.35	5.53	13.35	6.66	11.30	5.85	18.29
	U	1.53	2.02	5.82	4.16	5.75	1.55	7.44
	T	2.56	3.32	10.29	5.04	7.73	2.81	13.11

Rate of Growth * (in %)

(Contd. —)

TABLE 193

Table 12 (Contd.)

Annual Compound Growth Rate of Employment, Productivity and Associated Variables in Organised Manufacturing: 1987-88/1997-98 (1981-82 Prices)

Manufacturing Group	Locale	Workers	Technical Personnel	K:L Ratio	Productivity	NVA	Real Wage**	Fixed Capital
				Rate of Growth * (in %)				
1	2	3	4	5	6	7	8	9
Chemicals/Products(30)	R	16.82	17.84	9.90	11.12	29.81	18.36	28.35
	U	8.93	12.44	8.32	6.61	16.13	11.24	17.99
	T	11.61	14.00	9.68	7.80	20.31	13.16	22.41
Rubber, Plastic, Coal, Pet. (31)	R	0.38	-0.22	12.02	18.71	19.15	1.03	12.44
	U	-3.05	-5.14	9.29	4.67	1.48	-3.51	5.96
	T	-1.91	-3.65	11.24	11.63	9.74	-2.27	9.12
Non-Met.Min.Prodts (32)	R	2.32	4.17	6.59	9.35	11.89	5.07	9.06
	U	-1.97	0.37	10.35	8.77	6.64	0.83	8.18
	T	0.34	2.27	8.41	8.77	9.14	4.69	8.78
Basic Metal (33)	R	5.67	6.32	11.97	10.42	17.44	6.85	18.32
	U	-0.03	0.75	9.36	9.82	9.77	2.84	9.32
	T	1.01	1.82	10.62	9.80	10.91	3.30	11.74
Metal Products(34)	R	4.18	4.65	13.68	4.98	9.38	5.48	18.44
	U	2.92	3.79	10.79	3.73	6.77	3.82	14.03
	T	3.22	3.97	11.72	3.96	7.30	4.14	15.32
Machine Tools, etc. (35+36)	R	5.96	5.26	6.15	4.94	11.19	7.12	12.49
	U	0.69	1.42	7.72	6.28	7.01	2.35	8.47
	T	1.59	2.03	7.84	6.03	7.71	3.01	9.55

(Contd. —)

Table 12 (Contd.)

Annual Compound Growth Rate of Employment, Productivity and Associated Variables in Organised Manufacturing: 1987-88/1997-98 (1981-82 Prices)

Manufacturing Group	Locale	Rate of Growth * (in %)						
		Workers	Technical Personnel	K:L Ratio	Productivity	NVA	Real Wage**	Fixed Capital
1	2	3	4	5	6	7	8	9
Transport Equip. (37)	R	6.27	3.11	5.55	10.24	17.14	6.23	12.15
	U	1.22	2.93	9.01	9.83	11.18	2.76	10.34
	T	2.00	2.95	8.77	9.75	11.94	3.18	10.94
Other Manufacturing Ind. (38)	R	7.10	7.84	10.12	9.58	17.35	9.81	17.94
	U	6.94	6.62	10.90	10.20	17.84	7.15	18.60
	T	6.95	6.84	10.68	10.13	17.79	6.54	18.37
Repair of Capital Goods (39)$	R	13.82	10.54	10.17	4.18	18.58	15.34	25.39
	U	8.31	10.58	8.14	6.19	15.01	8.64	17.11
	T	8.90	10.61	9.15	5.96	15.40	9.07	18.86
Repair Services (97)	R	-7.79	-6.24	16.31	11.38	2.70	-7.61	7.25
	U	-10.42	-4.30	20.27	9.72	-1.73	-11.34	7.73
	T	-10.18	-4.45	19.45	9.76	-1.42	-11.02	7.29
1989-90/92-93	R	-21.33	-19.34	-32.42	16.33	-8.48	-24.19	-46.85
	U	-12.34	-7.25	12.92	-6.22	-17.80	-13.77	-1.01
	T	-13.18	-8.12	1.98	-5.03	-17.54	-14.57	-11.45
1992-93/97-98	R	10.49	15.68	42.76	13.42	30.86	14.91	57.72
	U	1.95	7.20	28.44	13.14	15.34	3.09	30.95
	T	2.76	7.84	29.87	13.42	16.55	4.04	33.44

(Contd. —)

TABLE 195

Table 12 (Contd.)

Annual Compound Growth Rate of Employment, Productivity and Associated Variables in Organised Manufacturing: 1987-88/1997-98 (1981-82 Prices)

Manufacturing Group	Locale	Rate of Growth * (in %)						
		Workers	Technical Personnel	K:L Ratio	Productivity	NVA	Real Wage**	Fixed Capital
1	2	3	4	5	6	7	8	9
Non-Agrobased Manufacturing	R	5.64	5.98	10.27	11.96	18.28	7.38	16.50
	U	1.59	2.43	8.82	7.89	9.62	3.23	10.55
	T	2.61	3.24	9.99	8.95	11.80	3.96	12.86
All manufacturing	R	4.86	5.76	11.57	10.40	15.77	8.05	16.99
	U	1.56	2.30	8.23	6.95	8.62	3.08	9.92
	T	2.58	3.27	10.07	7.84	10.63	0.77	12.91
Electricity (40)	R	-5.83	0.37	23.12	24.78	17.49	-2.33	15.94
	U	2.68	3.88	4.90	10.80	13.76	3.91	7.71
	T	2.09	3.56	6.35	12.20	14.55	4.32	8.57
Gas & Steam Generation (41)	R	5.90	7.77	5.15	54.53	67.07	9.20	11.36
	U	-0.23	-0.28	28.26	35.99	37.44	1.25	27.97
	T	2.18	3.00	16.58	59.18	64.25	3.83	19.12
Water Works & Supply (42)	R	6.80	5.39	-2.29	12.53	20.17	8.39	4.35
	U	5.57	7.37	9.65	8.04	14.05	9.23	15.74
	T	5.75	7.05	5.96	9.32	15.58	9.09	12.05
Non-Conventional Energy (43)	R	-0.97	9.67	72.35	84.29	82.52	9.32	70.69
	U	14.33	11.12	39.19	31.73	56.53	17.75	59.15
	T	8.38	4.98	53.64	65.62	79.47	11.35	66.49

(Contd. —)

Table 12 (Contd.)

Annual Compound Growth Rate of Employment, Productivity and Associated Variables in Organised Manufacturing: 1987-88/1997-98 (1981-82 Prices)

Manufacturing Group	Locale	Rate of Growth * (in %)							
		Workers	Technical Personnel	K:L Ratio	Productivity	NVA	Real Wage**	Fixed Capital
1	2	3	4	5	6	7	8	9
Storage & WH Services (74)	R	7.78	6.54	3.76	10.64	19.26	7.73	11.84
	U	3.16	3.97	4.98	15.00	18.63	5.39	8.29
	T	5.73	5.17	4.19	12.93	19.40	6.73	10.15
All	R	4.65	5.53	10.46	9.42	14.50	6.19	15.60
	U	1.72	2.61	5.25	6.10	7.92	3.02	7.06
	T	2.56	3.33	6.88	6.90	9.62	3.66	9.61

Note : R = Rural; U = Urban;   T = Total; NVA = Net Value Added;

* = Rate of Growth has been estimated through fitting semi-log curve;

** Money wages have been deflated by using CPI number for industrial workers at the constant (1982) prices to arrive at real wages;

$ Rate of growth of manufacturing group (39) has been estimated for the period 1989-90 to 1997-98, since information for 1987-88 and 1988-89 is not available for this group.

Source : 1. Govt. of India, Annual Survey of Industries Results for Factory Sector, Various Issues, CSO, Dept. of Statistics, Ministry of Planning.

2. Govt. of India, Statistical Abstract India 1998, CSO, Dept. of Statistics, Ministry of Planning, p. 346

TABLE 197

Table 13

Capital Labour Ratio and Labour Productivity in Orgnised Manufacturing by Production Sector and Rural Urban Locale: 1987-88/1997-98 (1981-82 Prices)

Manufacturing Group	Locale	Capital : Labour Ratio (in Rs. Thousand)					Productivity (in Rs. Thousand)				
		1987-88	1990-91	1992-93	1994-95	1997-98	1987-88	1990-91	1992-93	1994-95	1997-98
1	2	3	4	5	6	7	8	9	10	11	12
Food Products (20+21)	R	24.52	37.06	37.79	50.14	64.64	16.69	23.23	18.31	31.56	26.73
	U	26.06	32.27	38.55	49.40	60.18	23.48	26.03	30.94	42.05	48.47
	T	25.15	34.99	38.07	49.86	63.09	19.45	24.44	22.98	35.57	34.30
Beverages (22)	R	12.95	8.70	11.55	20.46	37.02	11.52	9.92	10.56	14.26	18.11
	U	6.52	7.20	8.04	9.46	8.33	10.77	12.83	12.76	14.57	14.50
	T	8.13	7.66	8.99	12.01	16.18	10.96	11.94	12.17	14.50	15.49
Cotton Textiles (23)	R	34.42	38.25	53.43	81.13	122.56	14.82	25.95	26.20	31.01	29.97
	U	21.75	23.27	24.96	38.87	52.97	17.01	22.73	16.32	25.83	18.09
	T	24.75	27.25	33.81	52.55	82.73	16.49	23.58	19.39	27.51	23.17
Wool, Synthetic, (24)	R	98.23	129.44	202.95	210.31	314.35	23.86	51.97	62.33	89.29	84.46
	U	57.44	77.41	83.79	115.74	125.33	33.71	50.75	37.76	62.12	48.56
	T	67.52	88.53	119.11	148.10	202.46	31.28	51.01	45.04	71.42	63.21
Jute, Mesta, (25)	R	5.28	7.23	9.66	9.61	11.50	7.48	9.06	9.05	9.13	11.14
	U	8.09	9.45	8.74	9.31	8.87	10.91	9.10	10.47	12.04	13.68
	T	7.59	9.24	8.81	9.33	9.20	10.30	9.10	10.37	11.85	13.36
Textile Products (26)	R	57.14	49.63	53.49	59.80	51.90	21.64	29.09	25.56	26.83	23.21
	U	18.97	16.84	22.32	27.47	33.94	22.71	33.27	39.94	40.20	29.45
	T	23.73	20.49	24.78	30.41	36.76	22.58	32.81	38.81	38.98	28.47
Wood/Products (27)	R	21.99	26.43	15.73	21.92	20.90	9.39	22.96	12.57	14.75	9.29
	U	13.33	23.38	13.47	14.08	30.48	16.49	22.36	11.06	10.55	14.38
	T	16.90	24.85	14.57	18.17	24.93	13.57	22.65	11.79	12.74	11.43

(Contd. —)

Table 13 (Contd.)

Capital Labour Ratio and Labour Productivity in Orgnised Manufacturing by Production Sector and Rural Urban Locale: 1987-88/1997-98 (1981-82 Prices)

Manufacturing Group	Locale	Capital : Labour Ratio (in Rs. Thousand)					Productivity (in Rs. Thousand)				
1	2	1987-88	1990-91	1992-93	1994-95	1997-98	1987-88	1990-91	1992-93	1994-95	1997-98
		3	4	5	6	7	8	9	10	11	12
Paper/Products (28)	R	106.82	118.99	91.87	296.99	203.19	19.52	35.02	26.69	48.19	34.10
	U	44.32	50.87	47.24	64.14	92.59	24.46	33.24	30.85	42.13	40.09
	T	59.10	66.81	58.13	130.65	128.64	23.29	33.65	29.83	43.86	38.14
Leather/Products (29)	R	26.78	25.47	30.20	36.78	48.01	16.32	21.22	22.87	23.07	20.80
	U	13.37	18.79	26.50	33.95	37.56	22.48	23.29	32.49	32.29	46.62
	T	17.76	21.08	27.79	34.92	40.81	20.47	22.58	29.13	29.14	38.59
Agro-Processing (20-29)	R	34.27	41.20	49.42	77.45	98.14	16.00	23.75	21.93	33.90	30.46
	U	24.18	28.26	29.40	39.09	47.55	19.44	24.90	23.09	31.36	29.01
	T	27.59	32.69	36.85	53.02	68.79	18.27	24.51	22.66	32.29	29.62
Chemicals/Products (30)	R	210.17	410.31	364.58	445.24	526.19	69.60	109.10	140.57	171.53	163.04
	U	134.34	219.23	213.90	265.66	388.80	123.10	108.23	122.64	140.26	153.91
	T	154.51	284.93	263.04	331.27	451.81	108.87	108.53	128.49	151.68	158.10
Rubber, Plastic, Coal, Pet. (31)	R	204.02	299.54	310.67	325.90	530.09	67.54	152.00	218.99	237.40	256.25
	U	118.37	140.08	187.48	247.37	283.13	69.45	102.47	104.76	122.97	42.96
	T	144.97	191.82	224.30	272.61	375.21	68.86	118.54	138.90	159.75	122.48
Non-Met.Min.Prodts (32)	R	91.10	109.69	118.54	155.13	199.11	18.12	33.12	32.89	40.73	40.60
	U	55.51	58.47	58.69	89.25	137.46	25.14	35.54	28.08	36.33	54.62
	T	73.77	84.29	90.30	124.91	174.55	21.54	34.32	30.62	38.71	46.19
Basic Metal (33)	R	220.78	166.82	309.95	331.56	572.61	33.79	47.90	88.58	75.86	83.40
	U	127.93	219.52	250.19	310.72	269.75	35.53	55.93	42.98	74.98	123.05
	T	140.97	211.51	259.88	314.38	345.63	35.29	54.71	50.37	75.13	113.11

(Contd. —)

Table 13 (Contd.)

Capital Labour Ratio and Labour Productivity in Orgnised Manufacturing by Production Sector and Rural Urban Locale: 1987-88/1997-98 (1981-82 Prices)

Manufacturing Group	Locale	Capital : Labour Ratio (in Rs. Thousand)					Productivity (in Rs. Thousand)				
1	2	1987-88	1990-91	1992-93	1994-95	1997-98	1987-88	1990-91	1992-93	1994-95	1997-98
		3	4	5	6	7	8	9	10	11	12
Metal Products(34)	R	48.90	50.73	78.77	97.28	111.14	30.56	28.18	33.88	45.79	42.09
	U	26.72	33.65	38.22	54.02	76.62	32.83	28.51	29.13	39.77	43.53
	T	30.82	36.87	44.97	61.46	85.23	32.41	28.44	29.92	40.81	43.17
Machine Tools etc. (35+36)	R	96.02	130.70	147.06	154.89	192.19	56.61	82.06	95.33	97.34	93.78
	U	51.88	61.32	71.51	86.10	107.64	57.42	67.24	70.56	92.86	104.37
	T	57.72	72.69	83.86	98.21	127.19	57.31	69.67	74.61	93.65	101.92
Transport Equip. (37)	R	120.07	119.02	134.65	140.56	183.67	27.59	73.15	39.88	64.36	67.98
	U	55.47	55.35	69.91	77.76	124.44	39.53	53.26	54.21	65.76	94.03
	T	64.08	64.08	78.47	88.35	136.82	37.94	55.99	52.32	65.53	88.59
Other Manufacturing Ind. (38)	R	108.82	141.78	179.82	227.77	338.31	63.23	79.40	89.70	105.71	106.89
	U	42.45	59.62	85.73	91.76	108.59	49.53	49.59	74.23	94.69	121.61
	T	54.72	76.02	105.04	117.95	154.91	52.06	55.54	77.40	96.81	118.65
Repair of Capital Goods (39)	R	NA	26.21	31.79	36.95	71.37	NA	29.76	38.83	34.28	35.41
	U	NA	13.49	18.45	16.71	35.26	NA	34.81	35.84	41.01	51.72
	T	NA	14.47	19.61	18.52	39.01	NA	34.42	36.10	40.41	50.02
Repair Services (97)	R	15.22	19.54	16.41	58.71	79.93	22.13	28.77	27.66	28.88	85.31
	U	11.03	18.97	16.82	42.42	73.28	27.16	40.57	45.41	58.14	86.22
	T	11.35	19.03	16.78	44.20	74.10	26.78	39.37	44.03	54.94	86.11
Non-Agrobased Manufacturing	R	137.77	194.13	211.49	250.23	349.56	40.85	72.01	88.89	103.71	107.59
	U	76.79	107.80	123.06	151.27	177.25	49.13	61.71	63.18	81.90	95.68
	T	90.17	128.09	143.79	176.27	230.32	47.32	64.13	69.21	87.41	99.35

(Contd. —)

TABLE 199

Table 13 (Contd.)

Capital Labour Ratio and Labour Productivity in Orgnised Manufacturing by Production Sector and Rural Urban Locale: 1987-88/1997-98 (1981-82 Prices)

Manufacturing Group	Locale	Capital : Labour Ratio (in Rs. Thousand)					Productivity (in Rs. Thousand)				
		1987-88	1990-91	1992-93	1994-95	1997-98	1987-88	1990-91	1992-93	1994-95	1997-98
1	2	3	4	5	6	7	8	9	10	11	12
All manufacturing	R	73.32	100.48	109.50	144.64	199.67	25.37	42.46	46.75	61.05	61.61
	U	51.75	69.44	79.32	97.17	115.50	35.00	43.96	44.45	57.53	63.94
	T	57.81	78.47	88.54	111.91	146.32	32.30	43.52	45.16	58.63	63.09
Electricity (40)	R	1668.04	605.64	2257.34	2000.53	6126.65	303.88	164.56	393.64	324.20	2013.00
	U	494.21	769.27	847.56	775.74	788.75	57.29	98.69	138.51	124.86	161.19
	T	515.64	754.99	925.59	846.97	928.20	61.79	104.44	152.63	136.45	209.57
Gas & Steam Generation (41)	R	861.57	1520.84	1060.26	1392.14	821.95	61.86	14.14	309.93	348.95	1028.76
	U	254.92	204.19	147.19	544.75	1674.68	97.47	69.96	38.91	218.67	1168.37
	T	400.66	710.06	456.10	1029.82	1237.02	88.92	48.52	130.60	293.25	1096.71
Water Works & Supply (42)	R	144.96	135.84	59.59	94.64	102.76	23.62	45.56	118.04	153.81	67.82
	U	34.74	56.40	47.41	65.16	82.89	27.12	24.02	33.19	40.15	61.89
	T	52.70	71.87	49.57	69.69	86.57	26.55	28.22	48.26	57.62	62.99
Non-Conventional Energy (43)	R	NA	250.87	285.18	357.03	7215.43	NA	22.24	31.52	44.05	1504.02
	U	NA	20.50	733.33	846.90	162.22	NA	20.50	-23.16	456.60	67.66
	T	NA	164.21	450.29	653.92	1513.73	NA	21.59	11.38	294.08	342.89
Storage & WH Services (74)	R	105.26	116.73	83.82	105.30	139.34	13.20	24.90	46.53	29.75	26.77
	U	80.45	123.12	103.40	123.25	127.41	17.54	33.18	32.80	52.60	59.32
	T	93.09	119.69	93.05	112.04	134.48	15.33	28.74	40.06	38.34	40.02
All	R	83.96	103.98	126.58	159.81	212.24	27.01	42.46	47.66	59.38	64.88
	U	96.73	120.39	129.36	143.53	155.72	36.05	45.51	47.43	57.34	64.44
	T	93.47	115.92	128.57	148.19	174.58	33.75	44.68	47.50	57.92	64.59

TABLE 201

Table 13 (Contd.)

Capital Labour Ratio and Labour Productivity in Orgnised Manufacturing by Production Sector and Rural Urban Locale: 1987-88/1997-98 (1981-82 Prices)

	1987-88	1990-91	1992-93	1994-95	1997-98
1	2	3	4	5	6
Rural Share in Total Organised Manufacturing					
i) Number of Factories	26.38	27.50	28.92	29.32	33.70
ii) Number of Workers	25.50	27.24	28.42	28.64	32.30
iii) Number of Technical Personnel	21.49	23.46	25.01	24.33	28.93
iv) Fixed Capital	22.91	24.44	27.98	30.88	40.60
v) Net Value Added	20.41	25.89	28.52	29.36	33.50

Note ˙: R = Rural, U = Urban, T = Total, NA = Figures not available

Source : Govt. of India, *Annual Survey of Industries*, Various Issues, CSO, Dept. of Statistics, Ministry of Planning.

Table 14

Percent Share of Rural Areas in Employment in Small Scale and Organised Manufacturing Sector by Major Industry Group

Broad Industry Group	Percent share of Rural areas in			
	SSI		Org. mfg.	
	1987-88	1994-95	1987-88	1994-95
1	2	3	4	5
Food Products (20+21)	53.5	50.8	59.4	63.1
Beverages (22)	19.9	30.6	25.0	27.0
Cotton Textiles (23)	22.2	32.2	23.7	31.1
Wool, Synthetic, (24)	20.4	28.5	24.7	29.6
Jute, Mesta, (25)	29.8	27.6	17.8	6.9
Textile Products (26)	23.4	21.8	12.5	7.9
Wood/Products (27)	46.9	49.0	41.2	48.5
Paper/Products (28)	15.2	20.9	23.7	24.4
Leather/Products (29)	31.0	30.3	32.7	34.9
Chemicals/Products (30)	26.0	37.6	26.6	32.6
Rubber, Plastic, Coal, Pet. (31)	34.0	40.0	31.1	29.9
Non-Met.Min.Prodts (32)	62.1	58.6	51.3	52.8
Basic Metal (33)	19.8	34.8	14.0	16.2
Metal Products (34)	23.7	26.6	18.5	16.6
Machine Tools Etc. (35+36)	12.3	21.0	13.2	16.3
Transport Equip. (37)	16.0	22.8	13.3	13.2
Other Manufacturing Ind. (38)	17.1	22.2	18.5	20.5
Repair of Capital Goods (39)	33.5	—	—	8.8
All manufacturing	33.3	34.4	28.1	30.6

Source: 1. Govt. of India, *Annual Survey of Industries Results for Factory Sector*,   Various Issues, CSO, Dept. of Statistics, Ministry of Planning.

   2. Govt. of India,.*Report of the Second All-India Census of Small Scale Industrial Units 1987-88,* Ministry of Industry, August, 1992.

   3. Govt. of India, *Report on Sample Survey of Small Scale Industrial Units* 1994-95, Ministry of SSI and ARI, 2000.

TABLE 203

Table 15 A
Share of Individual States in the Three Layers of Rural Unorganised Manufacturing Enterprises: 1984-85/2000-01

States	OAMEs			NDMEs			DMEs			Total			Chi-Square Test							
													1984-85/1994-95				1994-95/2000-01			
	84-85	94-95	00-01	84-85	94-95	00-01	84-85	94-95	00-01	84-85	94-95	00-01	OAMEs	NDMEs	DMEs	Total	OAMEs	NDMEs	DMEs	Total
1	2	3	4	5	6	7	8	9	10	11	12	13	14	15	16	17	18	19	20	21
Andhra Pradesh	7.75	8.81	10.19	7.64	14.42	10.24	10.64	15.59	10.15	7.78	9.36	10.19	0.15	6.02	2.30	0.32	0.22	1.22	1.89	0.08
Assam	1.39	2.61	2.05	2.42	4.52	2.42	0.86	0.27	0.57	1.46	2.67	2.04	1.06	1.83	0.41	1.00	0.12	0.98	0.33	0.15
Bihar	8.75	11.78	9.61	8.78	6.05	5.23	2.59	2.20	2.73	8.68	11.15	9.24	1.05	0.85	0.06	0.70	0.40	0.11	0.12	0.33
Gujarat	1.38	2.23	2.03	2.65	1.93	1.73	3.51	5.71	5.48	1.49	2.31	2.09	0.52	0.19	1.38	0.45	0.02	0.02	0.01	0.02
Haryana	1.04	0.74	0.82	0.84	0.96	1.58	0.92	0.56	0.53	1.03	0.75	0.85	0.09	0.02	0.14	0.08	0.01	0.39	0.00	0.01
Him.Pradesh	0.50	0.88	0.76	0.77	0.68	1.00	0.38	0.10	0.70	0.51	0.85	0.77	0.30	0.01	0.21	0.21	0.02	0.15	3.60	0.01
Jammu & Kashmir	0.84	0.34	1.21	1.12	0.30	0.98	1.55	0.12	0.46	0.87	0.33	1.18	0.30	0.60	1.32	0.33	2.20	1.52	0.95	2.16
Karnataka	3.29	5.33	5.61	3.62	5.32	6.64	11.27	24.56	13.13	3.41	5.86	5.82	1.26	0.79	15.65	1.77	0.01	0.33	5.32	0.00
Kerala	2.58	1.93	3.00	5.17	6.87	12.19	8.51	3.32	7.26	2.83	2.28	3.57	0.16	0.56	3.17	0.11	0.59	4.13	4.68	0.72
Madhya Pradesh	5.85	4.56	6.34	2.53	3.10	2.56	4.77	1.44	2.96	5.61	4.38	6.07	0.28	0.13	2.32	0.27	0.70	0.09	1.60	0.65
Maharashtra	5.85	4.16	5.64	6.55	4.57	5.33	6.67	6.12	7.31	5.91	4.24	5.66	0.49	0.60	0.04	0.47	0.53	0.13	0.23	0.48
Orissa	5.26	13.79	8.21	4.52	3.82	2.80	1.55	1.68	1.79	5.16	12.82	7.79	13.82	0.11	0.01	11.35	2.26	0.27	0.01	1.97
Punjab	1.24	1.14	1.52	0.18	1.96	2.90	0.75	0.38	1.09	1.16	1.17	1.58	0.01	18.04	0.18	0.00	0.13	0.45	1.32	0.15
Rajasthan	3.56	3.06	3.41	2.64	2.20	2.27	2.19	0.92	1.61	3.48	2.94	3.32	0.07	0.07	0.74	0.08	0.04	0.00	0.53	0.05
Tamilnadu	5.97	5.82	6.89	12.26	9.98	10.41	14.90	11.49	11.43	6.51	6.24	7.17	0.00	0.42	0.78	0.01	0.20	0.02	0.00	0.14
Uttar Pradesh	33.79	17.63	14.43	25.23	20.38	16.95	17.31	17.78	19.55	33.01	17.81	14.67	7.73	0.93	0.01	7.00	0.58	0.58	0.18	0.55
West Bengal	10.94	15.20	18.29	13.09	12.93	14.78	11.62	7.76	13.24	11.10	14.85	18.00	1.66	0.00	1.28	1.27	0.63	0.26	3.86	0.67

Source: The same as in Table 2.

Table 15 B

Share of Individual States in Employment among the Three Layers of Rural Unorganised Manufacturing: 1984-85/2000-01

States	OAMEs			NDMEs			DMEs			Total			Chi-Square Test							
													1984-85/1994-95				1994-95/2000-01			
	84-85	94-95	00-01	84-85	94-95	00-01	84-85	94-95	00-01	84-85	94-95	00-01	OAMEs	NDMEs	DMEs	Total	OAMEs	NDMEs	DMEs	Total
1	2	3	4	5	6	7	8	9	10	11	12	13	14	15	16	17	18	19	20	21
Andhra Pradesh	7.43	8.90	10.28	6.51	7.84	8.77	9.57	7.46	9.39	7.50	8.65	10.04	0.29	0.27	0.47	0.18	0.21	0.11	0.50	0.22
Assam	1.28	2.62	1.88	2.45	4.34	17.62	1.07	0.27	0.56	1.37	2.50	3.23	1.41	1.46	0.59	0.94	0.21	40.71	0.32	0.21
Bihar	9.00	10.87	10.02	10.04	6.28	4.18	2.41	4.32	2.83	8.61	9.77	8.70	0.39	1.40	1.52	0.16	0.07	0.70	0.51	0.12
Gujarat	0.52	1.93	1.89	2.39	2.13	1.45	3.68	7.75	6.74	0.92	2.59	2.37	3.81	0.03	4.49	3.00	0.00	0.22	0.13	0.02
Haryana	1.07	0.66	0.67	0.89	1.04	1.17	0.72	1.37	0.95	1.02	0.77	0.75	0.16	0.02	0.59	0.06	0.00	0.02	0.13	0.02
Him.Pradesh	0.37	0.60	0.54	0.84	0.64	0.77	0.35	0.37	0.65	0.41	0.58	0.58	0.14	0.04	0.00	0.07	0.00	0.03	0.21	0.00
Jammu & Kashmir	0.45	0.25	1.43	0.87	0.25	0.71	2.66	0.12	0.72	0.65	0.24	1.28	0.09	0.43	2.43	0.26	5.49	0.82	3.06	4.62
Karnataka	2.78	4.64	4.50	3.37	5.07	5.87	12.94	16.60	11.32	3.58	5.99	5.36	1.24	0.85	1.03	1.62	0.00	0.13	1.68	0.07
Kerala	2.29	1.59	2.28	6.28	7.65	10.52	11.30	5.14	7.06	3.31	2.47	3.57	0.21	0.30	3.36	0.21	0.30	1.08	0.72	0.49
Madhya Pradesh	3.30	4.33	6.29	1.62	2.75	2.04	3.95	1.33	3.65	3.20	3.87	5.60	0.32	0.78	1.74	0.14	0.89	0.18	4.02	0.78
Maharashtra	4.94	3.87	4.93	5.59	4.81	4.53	5.94	7.52	8.03	5.07	4.34	5.22	0.23	0.11	0.42	0.10	0.29	0.02	0.04	0.18
Orissa	6.75	16.15	10.42	4.93	3.79	2.07	1.60	1.81	1.59	6.21	13.56	8.68	13.11	0.26	0.03	8.72	2.04	0.78	0.03	1.76
Punjab	1.07	0.87	1.18	1.72	1.90	2.16	0.68	1.07	2.34	1.10	0.98	1.40	0.04	0.02	0.22	0.01	0.11	0.04	1.49	0.18
Rajasthan	3.35	2.64	3.00	2.54	2.13	2.05	1.68	0.87	1.57	3.15	2.40	2.75	0.15	0.06	0.39	0.18	0.05	0.00	0.57	0.05
Tamilnadu	6.15	5.19	6.16	15.72	12.07	9.42	14.87	13.86	11.45	7.66	6.70	7.04	0.15	0.84	0.07	0.12	0.18	0.58	0.42	0.02
Uttar Pradesh	37.24	18.45	14.65	19.22	23.21	13.95	15.93	20.71	29.72	34.04	19.09	16.20	9.48	0.83	1.44	6.57	0.78	3.70	3.92	0.43
West Bengal	12.01	16.46	19.88	15.06	14.10	12.73	10.66	9.44	1.42	12.19	15.49	17.22	1.65	0.06	0.14	0.90	0.71	0.13	6.81	0.19

Source: The same as in Table 2.

TABLE 205

Table 15 C

Inter-State Concentration Index for the Three Layers of Rural Unorganised Manufacturing Enterprises: 1984-85/2000-01

States	OAMEs			NDMEs			DMEs			Total			Chi-Square Test							
													1984-85/1994-95				1994-95/2000-01			
	84-85	94-95	00-01	84-85	94-95	00-01	84-85	94-95	00-01	84-85	94-95	00-01	OAMEs	NDMEs	DMEs	Total	OAMEs	NDMEs	DMEs	Total
1	2	3	4	5	6	7	8	9	10	11	12	13	14	15	16	17	18	19	20	21
Andhra Pradesh	0.96	1.01	1.01	0.85	0.54	0.86	0.90	0.48	0.92	0.96	0.92	0.98	0.00	0.11	0.20	0.00	0.00	0.18	0.42	0.00
Assam	0.92	1.00	0.92	1.01	0.96	7.29	1.24	1.01	0.99	0.94	0.94	1.58	0.01	0.00	0.04	0.00	0.01	41.72	0.00	0.44
Bihar	1.03	0.92	1.04	1.14	1.04	0.80	0.93	1.96	1.04	0.99	0.88	0.94	0.01	0.01	1.14	0.01	0.02	0.05	0.44	0.00
Gujarat	0.38	0.86	0.93	0.90	1.10	0.84	1.05	1.36	1.23	0.62	1.12	1.14	0.63	0.04	0.09	0.41	0.01	0.06	0.01	0.00
Haryana	1.02	0.89	0.82	1.06	1.08	0.74	0.78	2.43	1.78	1.00	1.03	0.88	0.02	0.00	3.51	0.00	0.01	0.10	0.17	0.02
Him.Pradesh	0.75	0.68	0.72	1.09	0.94	0.77	0.92	3.73	0.94	0.80	0.68	0.75	0.01	0.02	8.51	0.02	0.00	0.03	2.09	0.01
Jammu & Kashmir	0.54	0.74	1.18	0.77	0.84	0.73	1.71	0.98	1.57	0.75	0.71	1.09	0.07	0.01	0.31	0.00	0.27	0.02	0.35	0.20
Karnataka	0.85	0.87	0.80	0.93	0.95	0.88	1.15	0.68	0.86	1.05	1.02	0.92	0.00	0.00	0.19	0.00	0.01	0.01	0.05	0.01
Kerala	0.89	0.82	0.76	1.21	1.11	0.86	1.33	1.55	0.97	1.17	1.08	1.00	0.00	0.01	0.04	0.01	0.00	0.06	0.21	0.01
Madhya Pradesh	0.56	0.95	0.99	0.64	0.89	0.79	0.83	0.92	1.23	0.57	0.88	0.92	0.26	0.09	0.01	0.17	0.00	0.01	0.10	0.00
Maharashtra	0.84	0.93	0.87	0.85	1.05	0.85	0.89	1.23	1.10	0.86	1.03	0.92	0.01	0.05	0.13	0.03	0.00	0.04	0.01	0.01
Orissa	1.28	1.17	1.27	1.09	0.99	0.74	1.03	1.08	0.89	1.20	1.06	1.11	0.01	0.01	0.00	0.02	0.01	0.06	0.03	0.00
Punjab	0.86	0.77	0.78	9.75	0.97	0.75	0.91	2.82	2.14	0.95	0.84	0.89	0.01	7.91	3.98	0.01	0.00	0.05	0.16	0.00
Rajasthan	0.94	0.86	0.88	0.96	0.97	0.90	0.77	0.95	0.97	0.90	0.82	0.83	0.01	0.00	0.04	0.01	0.00	0.00	0.00	0.00
Tamilnadu	1.03	0.89	0.89	1.28	1.21	0.91	1.00	1.21	1.00	1.18	1.07	0.98	0.02	0.00	0.04	0.01	0.00	0.08	0.03	0.01
Uttar Pradesh	1.10	1.05	1.02	0.76	1.14	0.82	0.92	1.17	1.52	1.03	1.07	1.10	0.00	0.19	0.07	0.00	0.00	0.09	0.11	0.00
West Bengal	1.10	1.08	1.09	1.15	1.09	0.86	0.92	1.22	0.11	1.10	1.04	0.96	0.00	0.00	0.10	0.00	0.00	0.05	1.01	0.01

Source: The same as in Table 2.

Table 16A
State-wise Growth Rate of Employment in Unorganised Manufacturing Sector (%): 1984-85/2000-01

States	RURAL								URBAN							
	1984-85/1994-95				1994-95/2000-01				1984-85/1994-95				1994-95/2000-01			
	OAMEs	NDMEs	DMEs	Total	OAMEs	NDMEs	DMEs	Total	OAMEs	NDMEs	DMEs	Total	OAMEs	NDMEs	DMEs	Total
1	2	3	4	5	6	7	8	9	10	11	12	13	14	15	16	17
Andhra Pradesh	-0.50	-1.16	-0.39	-0.54	3.73	5.94	5.02	4.03	-4.56	-3.54	-2.73	-4.06	5.57	2.63	8.90	5.36
Assam	4.98	2.74	-10.95	4.14	-4.20	31.35	14.21	5.86	0.48	2.77	-2.37	1.07	4.00	0.91	0.49	2.04
Bihar	-0.42	-7.42	8.27	-0.70	-0.09	-2.84	-5.81	-0.47	3.10	-0.64	0.25	1.59	-0.86	-4.79	-8.48	-2.59
Gujarat	11.39	-4.09	10.01	8.70	0.92	-2.51	-1.26	0.01	23.21	8.55	8.58	11.95	-7.51	1.97	-6.73	-4.91
Haryana	-6.86	-1.50	8.96	-4.73	1.65	6.05	-4.89	1.09	-3.42	-0.86	1.40	-1.40	6.37	5.95	6.62	6.29
Him.Pradesh	2.52	-5.51	2.66	1.42	-0.30	7.28	11.05	1.52	-4.45	-7.31	-10.94	-7.02	-8.53	-0.49	-1.50	-4.12
Jammu & Kashmir	-7.86	-14.21	-25.27	-11.38	35.22	23.46	36.69	34.47	-17.84	-12.96	-21.00	-16.10	66.06	18.76	42.95	46.14
Karnataka	2.84	1.05	4.70	3.23	0.77	6.54	-5.18	-0.37	-1.43	-0.68	-5.65	-2.32	7.23	1.22	6.59	5.63
Kerala	-5.79	-1.04	-5.61	-4.77	7.54	9.65	6.56	7.87	-13.33	-13.58	-9.20	-12.53	5.59	8.46	9.30	7.58
Madhya Pradesh	0.40	2.26	-8.41	-0.06	7.77	-1.08	19.54	7.94	-4.69	2.56	0.29	-2.34	6.00	-1.43	3.18	3.60
Maharashtra	-4.64	-4.43	4.56	-3.45	5.45	2.94	2.19	4.65	1.78	8.41	5.74	5.09	6.28	1.45	0.74	2.61
Orissa	6.63	-5.50	3.37	6.03	-5.88	-6.01	-1.05	-5.80	1.15	0.46	-1.65	0.56	-0.97	-1.12	1.04	-0.72
Punjab	-4.28	-1.99	6.84	-3.11	6.53	6.21	15.06	7.71	0.12	2.51	6.02	2.49	1.69	4.35	3.90	3.33
Rajasthan	-4.57	-4.66	-4.37	-4.57	3.42	3.28	11.56	3.80	-1.68	-1.91	-2.95	-1.89	5.71	2.04	13.96	5.90
Tamilnadu	-3.94	-5.51	1.41	-3.25	4.21	-0.23	-2.10	2.30	-6.01	-3.43	-1.11	-4.07	3.04	6.20	2.55	3.69
Uttar Pradesh	-8.91	-1.13	4.84	-7.46	-2.55	-4.49	7.34	-1.25	0.96	2.08	1.42	1.32	-0.05	-0.42	0.36	-0.07
West Bengal	0.85	-3.62	0.89	0.43	4.50	2.22	-26.30	3.28	-3.07	-2.21	-3.73	-2.97	8.88	2.82	5.85	6.24
All India	-2.03	-2.53	2.09	-1.70	1.18	0.93	2.87	1.35	-0.98	1.40	1.70	0.37	3.48	2.90	1.74	2.83

Source: The same as in Table 2.

TABLE 207

Table 16B

State-wise Growth Rate of Per Worker Productivity in Unorganised Manufacturing Sector (%): 1984-85/2000-01

States	RURAL								URBAN							
	1984-85/1994-95				1994-95/2000-01				1984-85/1994-95				1994-95/2000-01			
	OAMEs	NDMEs	DMEs	Total	OAMEs	NDMEs	DMEs	Total	OAMEs	NDMEs	DMEs	Total	OAMEs	NDMEs	DMEs	Total
1	2	3	4	5	6	7	8	9	10	11	12	13	14	15	16	17
Andhra Pradesh	-0.49	5.01	7.28	1.36	8.81	-2.62	6.60	6.80	3.54	2.07	-9.10	-0.72	3.30	6.40	5.56	4.86
Assam	-1.75	0.01	4.95	-1.64	13.19	-23.87	21.56	2.98	3.17	2.39	0.00	2.18	2.26	3.35	5.24	3.04
Bihar	-2.83	2.44	-6.12	-2.50	7.88	11.60	29.75	9.52	3.06	-0.42	-13.38	-2.97	0.56	6.06	6.75	2.55
Gujarat	-6.70	1.14	5.97	-1.09	4.25	8.24	-1.34	1.48	-4.29	-0.26	-0.56	-1.58	1.07	8.95	5.56	5.59
Haryana	6.17	5.78	-3.21	6.88	4.94	1.74	-7.87	-0.07	12.57	-7.27	-3.14	-1.72	-2.28	-0.62	-3.66	-2.24
Him.Pradesh	1.14	-1.88	-5.23	-0.81	4.47	21.28	24.03	13.41	-12.49	-0.34	12.01	-4.55	8.93	8.35	12.25	10.55
Jammu & Kashmir	-5.71	-4.08	0.02	-4.95	19.86	19.96	22.26	19.69	2.92	1.64	5.33	2.75	-1.64	8.13	6.03	0.54
Karnataka	0.97	-0.19	2.42	1.11	6.80	10.94	8.80	8.24	1.50	5.09	3.25	2.52	2.30	3.38	1.80	1.99
Kerala	2.58	5.11	5.76	4.79	5.92	3.01	12.35	6.86	-8.69	-1.89	3.27	-2.98	8.71	10.76	7.73	9.91
Madhya Pradesh	-1.16	4.77	-0.93	-0.28	0.41	-4.70	3.18	-0.71	3.83	2.36	9.19	6.04	-4.20	-8.40	-2.15	-6.50
Maharashtra	2.34	5.58	0.21	3.03	6.64	-2.81	10.79	5.37	0.75	-4.67	2.54	0.70	0.04	3.77	0.40	0.51
Orissa	-2.61	6.76	-0.33	-2.39	8.54	2.80	6.02	8.16	5.02	1.44	-1.79	1.93	-1.58	4.07	6.53	2.03
Punjab	3.87	32.67	4.35	6.68	1.48	3.56	6.63	4.02	6.02	-2.35	-10.00	-3.23	-1.50	9.10	5.27	4.95
Rajasthan	6.70	6.09	12.20	7.11	4.88	8.28	-1.91	4.96	4.53	4.05	-1.66	2.92	0.58	5.71	5.82	3.55
Tamilnadu	7.10	8.65	8.35	8.30	0.57	2.96	3.73	0.98	5.28	1.91	5.62	5.62	1.12	5.89	0.68	2.16
Uttar Pradesh	4.79	-2.10	5.66	5.72	2.39	5.55	-0.11	3.40	2.49	0.88	-5.01	-0.55	0.69	4.58	2.80	2.52
West Bengal	1.46	3.59	2.26	1.59	6.81	4.17	64.19	8.96	3.06	2.61	-3.37	0.12	0.44	4.15	6.21	3.16
All India	1.26	2.11	4.27	2.14	6.35	5.70	6.12	6.38	2.75	-0.87	0.56	1.20	0.46	4.60	2.94	2.54

Source: The same as in Table 2.

Table 17

Inter-State Rank Correlation Coefficient in Respect of Per Worker Productivity (1) between 84-85 and 94- 95 and 94-95 and 2000-01 for Rural and Urban Areas, and (2) between Rural and Urban Areas, for 84-85, 94-95 and 00-01, by Enterprise Type

Rank Correlation between Productivity Levels of 84-85 and 94-95 and 00-01 for Rural/Urban Areas

	Correlation Coefficients		Z Value	
1	84-85/94-95	94-95/00-01	84-85/94-95	94-95/00-01
	2	3	4	5
Rural				
OAMEs	0.502	0.637	-7.838	-7.085
NDMEs	0.208	0.212	-9.113	-9.097
DMEs	0.554	0.417	-7.568	-8.241
Total	0.471	0.730	-7.990	-6.428
Urban				
OAMEs	0.485	0.841	-7.922	-5.321
NDMEs	0.765	0.520	-6.131	-7.746
DMEs	0.120	0.762	-9.452	-6.158
Total	0.536	0.637	-7.663	-7.085

Rank Correlation for Productivity Levels between Rural and Urban Areas for 1984-85, 1994-95 and 2000-01

	Correlation Coefficient	Z Value
6	7	8
1984-85		
OAMEs	0.679	-6.808
NDMEs	0.419	-8.232
DMEs	0.311	-8.699
Total	0.694	-6.701
1994-95		
OAMEs	0.571	-7.475
NDMEs	0.559	-7.541
DMEs	0.279	-8.831
Total	0.635	-7.098
2000-01		
OAMEs	0.848	-5.230
NDMEs	0.765	-6.131
DMEs	0.199	-9.148
Total	0.767	-6.113

TABLE 209

Table 18
Level and Growth Rate of Productivity Per worker in the Unorganised Manufacturing Sector in Individual States: 1984-85/2000-01

(at constant 1981-82 Prices)

Productivity Range	1984-85		1994-95		Growth Rate of Per Worker Productivity 1984-85/94-95	Growth Rate of Employment 1984-85/94-95	2000-01		Growth Rate of Per Worker Productivity 94-95/00-01	Growth Rate of Employment 94-95/00-01
1	2	3	4	5	6	7	8	9	10	11
Rural Low Level (up to Rs. 1750)	Orissa		Orissa		-2.39	6.03	Orissa		8.16	-5.80
	Andhra Pradesh									
	Karnataka									
	Tamil Nadu									
	Uttar Pradesh									
	West Bengal									
Share of	Employment	71.18		13.56				8.68		
	Enterprises	66.97		12.82				7.79		
	Value Added	59.32		5.31				3.78		
	Fixed Asset	22.54		5.05				2.64		
Medium Level (Rs 1751 to Rs 3000)			Bihar		-2.50	-0.70	Madhya Pradesh		-0.71	7.94
			H.P.		-0.81	1.42	Assam		2.98	5.86
			Madhya Pradesh		-0.28	-0.06	Andhra Pradesh		6.80	4.03
			Assam		-1.64	4.14	Uttar Pradesh		3.40	-1.25
			Andhra Pradesh		1.36	-0.54				
			Jammu & Kashmir		-4.95	-11.38				
			Karnataka		1.11	3.23				
			Uttar Pradesh		5.72	-7.46				
			West Bengal		1.59	0.43				

(Contd. —)

Table 18 (Contd.)
Level and Growth Rate of Productivity Per worker in the Unorganised Manufacturing Sector in Individual States: 1984-85/2000-01

(at constant 1981-82 Prices)

Productivity Range	1984-85		1994-95		Growth Rate of Per Worker Productivity 1984-85/94-95	Growth Rate of Employment 1984-85/94-95	2000-01		Growth Rate of Per Worker Productivity 94-95/00-01	Growth Rate of Employment 94-95/00-01
1	2	3	4	5	6	7	8	9	10	11
Share of	Employment	27.24		66.18				35.07		
	Enterprises	30.67		67.26				32.97		
	Value Added	36.80		61.80				29.51		
	Fixed Asset	76.00		57.17				31.12		
High Level (More than Rs. 3000)	Jammu & Kashmir		Gujarat		-1.09	8.70	Karnataka		8.24	-0.37
			Haryana		6.88	-4.73	West Bengal		8.96	3.28
			Kerala		4.79	-4.77	Bihar		9.52	-0.47
			Punjab		6.68	-3.11	Tamil Nadu		0.98	2.30
			Rajasthan		7.11	-4.57	Maharashtra		5.37	4.65
			Tamil Nadu		8.30	-3.25	Kerala		6.86	7.87
			Maharashtra		3.03	-3.45	Rajasthan		4.96	3.80
							Punjab		4.02	7.71
							Gujarat		1.48	0.01
							Haryana		-0.07	1.09
							Himachal Pradesh		13.41	11.05
							Jammu & Kashmir		19.69	34.47
Share of	Employment	1.57		20.25				56.24		
	Enterprises	2.36		19.93				59.25		
	Value Added	3.89		32.89				66.07		
	Fixed Asset	1.48		37.78				66.25		

(Contd. —)

TABLE 211

Table 18 (Contd.)
Level and Growth Rate of Productivity Per worker in the Unorganised Manufacturing Sector in Individual States: 1984-85/2000-01

(at constant 1981-82 Prices)

Productivity Range	1984-85		1994-95		Growth Rate of Per Worker Productivity 1984-85/94-95	Growth Rate of Employment 1984-85/94-95	2000-01		Growth Rate of Per Worker Productivity 94-95/00-01	Growth Rate of Employment 94-95/00-01
1	2	3	4	5	6	7	8	9	10	11
Urban Productivity Range										
Low Level (up to Rs. 5000)	Andhra Pradesh		Andhra Pradesh		-0.72	-4.06	Orissa		2.03	-0.72
	Orissa		Orissa		-3.23	0.56				
	Assam		Uttar Pradesh		-0.55	1.32				
	West Bengal		West Bengal		0.12	-2.97				
	Jammu & Kashmir		Bihar		-2.97	1.59				
	Karnataka		Kerala		-2.98	-12.53				
	Madhya Pradesh									
	Rajasthan									
	Tamil Nadu									
Share of	Employment	60.61		40.26				1.14		
	Enterprises	59.25		43.23				1.33		
	Value Added	46.34		29.78				0.71		
	Fixed Asset	24.71		22.33				0.60		

(Contd. —)

Table 18 (Contd.)
Level and Growth Rate of Productivity Per worker in the Unorganised Manufacturing Sector in Individual States: 1984-85/2000-01

(at constant 1981-82 Prices)

Productivity Range	1984-85		1994-95		Growth Rate of Per Worker Productivity 1984-85/94-95	Growth Rate of Employment 1984-85/94-95	2000-01		Growth Rate of Per Worker Productivity 94-95/00-01	Growth Rate of Employment 94-95/00-01
1	2	3	4	5	6	7	8	9	10	11
Medium Level (Rs 5001 to Rs 8000)	Bihar		Gujarat		-1.58	11.95	Madhya Pradesh		-6.50	3.60
	Kerala		Himachal Pradesh		-4.55	-7.20	Andhra Pradesh		4.86	5.36
	Uttar Pradesh		Jammu & Kashmir		2.75	-16.10	Uttar Pradesh		2.52	-0.07
			Karnataka		2.52	-2.32	Bihar		2.55	-2.59
			Madhya Pradesh		6.04	-2.34	West Bengal		3.16	6.24
			Rajasthan		2.92	-1.89	Karnataka		1.99	5.63
			Tamil Nadu		5.62	-4.07	Jammu & Kashmir		0.54	46.14
			Assam		2.18	1.07	Tamil Nadu		2.16	3.69
							Rajasthan		3.55	5.90
							Assam		3.04	2.04
Share of	Employment	22.68		40.47				69.43		
	Enterprises	22.60		40.53				73.56		
	Value Added	23.66		41.63				58.38		
	Fixed Asset	61.98		36.47				53.47		

(Contd. —)

TABLE 213

Table 18 (Contd.)
Level and Growth Rate of Productivity Per worker in the Unorganised Manufacturing Sector in Individual States: 1984-85/2000-01

(at constant 1981-82 Prices)

Productivity Range	1984-85		1994-95		Growth Rate of Per Worker Productivity 1984-85/94-95	Growth Rate of Employment 1984-85/94-95	2000-01		Growth Rate of Per Worker Productivity 94-95/00-01	Growth Rate of Employment 94-95/00-01
1	2	3	4	5	6	7	8	9	10	11
High Level (More than Rs. 8000)	Maharasthra		Maharasthra		0.70	5.09	Kerala		9.91	.7.58
	Haryana		Haryana		-1.72	-1.40	Haryana		-2.24	6.29
	Punjab		Punjab		-3.23	2.49	Maharasthra		0.51	2.61
	Gujarat						Punjab		4.95	3.33
	Himachal Pradesh						Gujarat		5.59	-4.91
							Himachal Pradesh		10.55	-4.12
Share of	Employment	16.70		19.27				29.43		
	Enterprises	18.14		16.24				25.12		
	Value Added	30.00		28.59				40.91		
	Fixed Asset	13.31		41.20				45.93		

Source: The same as in Table 2.

Table 19
Hirschman-Herfindahl Index (%)

	RURAL				URBAN				All Un-organised
	OAMEs	NDMEs	DMEs	TOTAL	OAMEs	NDMEs	DMEs	TOTAL	
1	2	3	4	5	6	7	8	9	10
Enterprises									
1984-85	15.40	11.43	10.05	14.90	10.12	8.74	9.99	9.63	12.49
1994-95	10.39	10.29	13.88	10.16	9.54	8.69	11.05	9.14	9.20
2000-01	9.70	9.63	11.13	9.59	9.16	7.95	9.23	8.70	8.89
Employment									
1984-85	18.52	11.59	10.05	16.37	12.35	11.19	10.38	11.02	13.50
1994-95	11.39	10.82	11.57	10.63	10.19	8.70	11.10	9.34	9.22
2000-01	10.51	14.00	11.01	9.70	9.37	7.95	9.53	8.59	8.64
Fixed Asset									
1984-85	36.10	20.74	8.51	32.07	39.49	34.17	10.15	32.53	18.73
1994-95	9.76	9.82	10.83	8.75	9.60	11.85	18.95	12.59	9.33
2000-01	8.32	8.81	11.37	8.40	7.80	7.13	8.96	7.75	7.26
Value Added									
1984-85	13.35	11.28	8.18	11.89	8.55	6.87	10.33	8.14	8.87
1994-95	9.88	10.60	12.62	9.75	9.42	8.30	13.27	9.68	8.66
2000-01	9.25	8.41	11.08	8.92	8.16	7.44	9.69	8.08	7.61

Source: The same as in Table 2.

TABLE 215

TABLE 20

Major Problems Faced by Informal Manufacturing Enterprises by Enterprise Category and Place of Location: 1999-2000 NSS Data

Enterprise Category	% of Enterprises Reporting one or more Problems	Shortage of Capital	Lack of Infrastructure	Competition from Larger Units	Non-Recovery of Service Charges	Local Problems	Lighting or Power Problem
1	2	3	4	5	6	7	8
OAMEs							
Rural	71.1	36.6	19.0	10.6	8.8	17.0	6.4
Urban	68.1	40.4	15.3	19.6	5.7	14.2	5.3
Combined	70.3	37.6	18.0	13.1	7.9	16.3	6.1
Establishments							
Rural	74.7	40.1	15.2	18.0	8.5	14.9	16.5
Urban	74.7	37.2	15.7	9.6	8.1	13.6	14.6
Combined	74.7	38.1	15.5	25.9	8.3	14.0	15.2
All Enterprises							
Rural	71.3	36.8	18.8	11.1	8.8	16.9	7.1
Urban	70.0	39.5	15.4	22.4	6.4	14.1	7.8
Combined	70.9	37.7	17.7	14.8	8.0	16.0	7.4

Note: Columns 3-8 under heading "Proportion of Enterprises Reporting".

Source : Govt. of India, Non-Agricultural Enterprises in the Informal Manufacturing Sector in India, Key Results, NSS 55th Round, (July 1999-June 2000), NSS Report No. 456, 2000b: 70-75.

Table 21

Institutional Support in Setting up and Running of Tiny and Small Enterprises: April-June 2000 Survey

Item	Percentage of Units Benefiting from Formal/Informal Institutions					
	Rural-Located Units		Urban-Located Units		All Units	
	Formal	Informal*	Formal	Informal*	Formal	Iinformal*
1	2	3	4	5	6	7
Training	23	77	42	58	32	68
Finance	34	66	53	47	43	57
Supply of Raw Material	18	82	21	79	19	81
Market Intelligence	12	88	18	82	14	86
Product Sale	13	87	20	80	16	84

Note   : * includes friends and relatives, fellow entrepreneurs, and self-effort.

Source : The same as in Table 5.

TABLE 217

Table 22
Percentage of Sample Units Having Specified Infrastructural Facilities:
April-June 2000 Survey

		% of Sample Units		
		Rural	Urban	Total
1		2	3	4
A.	**Common to the Area**			
(i)	**Paved Road**			
	Not Available	2.79	2.72	2.76
	0 to 1 K.M.	79.53	90.22	84.46
	1 to 5 K.M.	15.81	7.07	11.78
	5 K.M. & above	1.86	0.00	1.00
(ii)	**Railway Station**			
	Not Available	38.14	20.11	29.82
	0 to 1 K.M.	1.86	3.80	2.76
	1 to 5 K.M.	25.58	35.87	30.33
	5 K.M. & above	34.42	40.22	37.09
(iii)	**Information Centre**			
	Not Available	62.79	46.20	55.14
	0 to 1 K.M.	0.93	1.63	1.25
	1 to 5 K.M.	10.23	39.13	23.56
	5 K.M. & above	26.05	13.04	20.05
(iv)	**Product Designing Centre**			
	Not Available	76.74	66.30	71.93
	0 to 1 K.M.	0.00	1.63	0.75
	1 to 5 K.M.	7.44	18.48	12.53
	5 K.M. & above	15.81	13.59	14.79
(v)	**Training Centre**			
	Not Available	56.28	45.11	51.13
	0 to 1 K.M.	0.00	2.17	1.00
	1 to 5 K.M.	9.30	20.11	14.29
	5 K.M. & above	34.42	32.61	33.58
(vi)	**Repair Workshop**			
	Not Available	54.42	37.50	46.62
	0 to 1 K.M.	13.95	11.96	13.03
	1 to 5 K.M.	24.65	39.13	31.33
	5 K.M. & above	6.98	11.41	9.02
(vii)	**Market Centre**			
	Not Available	22.79	5.43	14.79
	0 to 1 K.M.	7.91	14.13	10.78
	1 to 5 K.M.	30.70	22.83	27.07
	5 K.M. & above	38.60	57.61	47.37

(Contd. —)

Table 22 (Contd.)
Percentage of Sample Units Having Specified Infrastructural Facilities: April-June 2000 Survey

		% of Sample Units	
	Rural	Urban	Total
1	2	3	4
(viii) Bank			
Not Available	4.19	0.54	2.51
0 to 1 K.M.	17.21	16.30	16.79
1 to 5 K.M.	59.07	71.20	64.66
5 K.M. & above	19.53	11.96	16.04
B. Attached to the Unit			
(i) Electricity	93.49	98.91	95.99
(ii) Water	85.12	97.28	90.73
(iii) Sewerage	31.16	41.85	36.09
(iv) Telephone	55.35	84.24	68.67
(v) Fax	7.44	20.11	13.28
(vi) Computer	15.35	32.07	23.06

Source: The same as in Table 5.

TABLE *219*

Table 23

Knowledge and Adoption of Different Components of Technological Change by Pottery Units: 1990 Survey in Rural Haryana

Component of Technology	% of Pottery Units Knowing/Adopting the Technological Component		
	Units Which Knew	Units Which Knew And Adopted	Adopters out of Total Units
1	2	3	4
1. Brick Klin*	96	21.0	20.1
2. Electrical Wheel*	93	3.2	3.0
3. Jigger Jolly*	13	4.6	0.6
4. New Products**	89	26.1	23.2
5. New Design**	77	25.0	19.5

Note : * Reference period is the preceeding 10 years

      ** Reference period is the preceeding 5 years.

Source : Chadha, G.K., "Adoption of Improved Technology in India's Cottage Industries: Constraints and Impact", in Rizwanual Islam *(ed.)*, *Transfer, Adoption and Diffusion of Technology for Small and Cottage Industries*, ILO/ARTEP, 1992.

Table 24A

Knowledge and Adoption of Different Components of Technological Change by an Assorted Group of Rural Industries: April-June 2000 Survey

Component of Technology	% of Industrial Units Knowing and Adopting the Technology Component								
	Rural			Urban			Total		
	Units Which Knew	Units Which Knew and Adopted	Adopters out of Total Units	Units Which Knew	Units Which Knew and Adopted	Adopters out of Total Units	Units Which Knew	Units Which Knew and Adopted	Adopters out of Total Units
1	2	3	4	5	6	7	8	9	10
1. Improved Machinery	49.7	50.5	25.1	64.1	62.7	40.2	56.4	56.9	32.1
2. New Products	25.1	96.3	24.2	44.6	90.2	40.2	34.1	92.6	31.6
3. New Raw Material	12.1	92.3	11.2	23.9	93.2	22.3	17.5	92.9	16.3
4. New Design	38.6	97.6	37.7	39.1	94.4	36.9	38.8	96.1	37.3

Note : Reference period for each form of technology component is the preceding 5 years.

Source : The same as in Table 5.

TABLE 221

Table 24B

Sources of Acquisition of Different Components of Technological Change by Rural Industries: April-June 2000 Survey

Component of Technology	Own Employees	Fellow Entrepreneur	Open Market	Govt. Agency	Training Institute	Parent Co(s)	Total
1	2	3	4	5	6	7	8
1. Improved Machinery							
Rural	5.56	0.00	90.74	1.85	0.00	1.85	100.00
Urban	13.51	2.70	82.43	0.00	1.35	0.00	100.00
Total	10.16	1.56	85.94	0.78	0.78	0.78	100.00
2. New Products							
Rural	42.31	0.00	19.23	0.00	0.00	38.46	100.00
Urban	37.84	5.41	36.49	0.00	0.00	20.27	100.00
Total	39.68	3.17	29.37	0.00	0.00	27.78	100.00
3. New Raw Material							
Rural	8.33	0.00	79.17	0.00	0.00	12.50	100.00
Urban	24.39	2.44	53.66	0.00	0.00	19.51	100.00
Total	18.46	1.54	63.08	0.00	0.00	16.92	100.00
4. New Designs							
Rural	53.09	0.00	18.52	0.00	0.00	28.40	100.00
Urban	35.29	4.41	33.82	0.00	1.47	25.00	100.00
Total	44.97	2.01	25.50	0.00	0.67	26.85	100.00

Note : Reference period for each form of technology component is the preceding 5 years.

Source : The same as in Table 5.

Table 24C

Source of Finance Available to Rural Industry for Adopting Technological Improvements: April-June 2000 Survey

Component of Technology	Own Savings	Borrowings from Friends /Relatives	Loan from Govt. Agency	Loan from Bank	Others*	Total
1	2	3	4	5	6	7
1. Improved Machinery						
Rural	40.74	5.56	9.26	40.74	3.70	100.00
Urban	59.46	0.00	5.41	33.78	1.35	100.00
Total	51.56	2.34	7.03	36.72	2.34	100.00
2. New Products						
Rural	80.77	1.92	1.92	15.38	0.00	100.00
Urban	77.03	0.00	2.70	17.57	2.70	100.00
Total	78.57	0.79	2.38	16.67	1.59	100.00
3. New Raw Material						
Rural	79.17	0.00	4.17	16.67	0.00	100.00
Urban	63.41	0.00	19.51	17.07	0.00	100.00
Total	69.23	0.00	13.85	16.92	0.00	100.00
4. New Designs						
Rural	91.36	0.00	0.00	8.64	0.00	100.00
Urban	82.35	0.00	4.41	11.76	1.47	100.00
Total	87.25	0.00	2.01	10.07	0.67	100.00

Note   : 1. * = village money lenders, cooperative society, etc.
          2. Reference period for each form of technology component is the preceding 5 years.
Source : The same as in Table 5.

TABLE 223

Table 25

Educational Background of Rural Workers in Indian States: NSS Data 1983/1999-00

State	Year	Rural Male				Rural Female				Rural Persons			
		Not Literate	Upto Primary	Middle	Secondary & Above	Not Literate	Upto Primary	Middle	Secondary & Above	Not Literate	Upto Primary	Middle	Secondary & Above
1	2	3	4	5	6	7	8	9	10	11	12	13	14
Andhra Pradesh	1983	62.4	23.1	7.4	7.0	86.1	10.3	2.2	1.4	-	-	-	-
	1993-94	54.7	29.4	8.3	7.5	75.2	19.5	3.4	1.9	65.0	24.4	5.8	4.7
	1999-00	49.1	31.0	9.6	10.3	66.5	24.1	5.4	4.0	57.8	27.5	7.5	7.1
Assam	1983	33.4	37.9	17.8	10.8	62.6	24.5	9.8	3.1	-	-	-	-
	1993-94	32.9	40.4	16.2	10.4	47.9	35.4	11.3	5.3	39.8	38.2	13.9	8.0
	1999-00	31.6	39.6	17.2	11.6	46.3	34.1	13.2	6.2	38.6	37.0	15.3	9.0
Bihar	1983	58.4	17.8	14.5	9.3	90.2	5.6	3.2	0.9	-	-	-	-
	1993-94	54.0	25.5	9.9	10.4	80.3	14.1	3.4	2.2	66.5	20.1	6.8	6.5
	1999-00	54.4	26.2	9.0	10.3	76.3	17.0	4.0	2.7	64.9	21.7	6.6	6.7
Gujarat	1983	45.3	32.8	12.2	9.5	74.2	18.1	4.9	2.7	-	-	-	-
	1993-94	39.5	39.1	9.0	12.3	63.9	26.0	5.1	5.1	51.2	32.8	7.1	8.8
	1999-00	34.6	36.4	16.1	12.9	57.0	28.4	8.8	5.8	45.7	32.4	12.5	9.4
Haryana	1983	47.6	21.0	18.0	13.4	88.2	8.1	1.7	2.1	-	-	-	-
	1993-94	41.3	36.2	8.1	14.3	66.0	25.8	4.4	3.9	52.9	31.3	6.3	9.4
	1999-00	33.7	37.1	10.6	18.5	55.4	30.8	7.2	6.4	43.9	34.1	9.0	12.8
Himachal Pradesh	1983	43.1	29.3	12.8	14.9	68.4	20.3	6.4	4.8	-	-	-	-
	1993-94	32.4	41.3	11.0	15.4	48.9	37.1	6.5	7.4	40.9	39.1	8.7	11.2
	1999-00	26.9	38.9	13.3	20.8	41.4	36.9	9.1	12.6	34.3	37.9	11.2	16.6
Jammu & Kashmir	1983	61.4	16.2	13.6	8.7	87.3	6.9	3.5	2.3	-	-	-	-
	1993-94	40.7	34.5	13.9	10.9	61.3	26.5	7.4	4.7	50.9	30.5	10.7	7.9
	1999-00	36.3	34.9	14.2	14.4	59.3	23.5	9.6	7.4	47.3	29.6	12.0	11.1

(Contd. —)

Table 25 (Contd.)

Educational Background of Rural Workers in Indian States: NSS Data 1983/1999-00

State	Year	Rural Male				Rural Female				Rural Persons			
		Not Literate	Upto Primary	Middle	Secondary & Above	Not Literate	Upto Primary	Middle	Secondary & Above	Not Literate	Upto Primary	Middle	Secondary & Above
1	2	3	4	5	6	7	8	9	10	11	12	13	14
Karnataka	1983	51.7	27.4	11.9	9.0	79.4	13.6	4.4	2.6	-	-	-	-
	1993-94	46.5	32.2	11.0	10.3	66.0	23.1	7.1	3.8	56.2	27.7	9.1	7.0
	1999-00	42.8	29.8	13.7	13.3	60.7	24.5	9.1	5.4	51.8	27.3	11.4	9.4
Kerala	1983	13.1	45.7	26.4	14.8	26.8	41.1	20.2	11.8	-	-	-	-
	1993-94	14.5	41.0	27.4	17.1	18.3	40.6	25.9	15.2	16.5	40.8	26.6	16.1
	1999-00	15.2	36.4	27.6	20.5	21.3	35.4	24.5	18.8	18.4	35.9	26.0	19.7
Madhya Pradesh	1983	57.4	29.7	8.1	4.7	89.3	8.4	1.7	0.6	-	-	-	-
	1993-94	52.5	34.3	6.4	5.8	77.9	18.9	1.8	1.4	64.7	26.9	4.2	4.2
	1999-00	44.8	39.0	8.6	7.4	68.3	26.2	3.3	2.1	56.1	32.9	6.0	5.0
Maharashtra	1983	41.4	35.1	14.7	8.7	76.8	16.3	4.9	2.0	-	-	-	-
	1993-94	37.1	36.0	15.6	11.3	60.3	27.1	8.8	3.8	48.5	31.6	12.2	7.6
	1999-00	32.2	35.7	17.3	14.5	51.4	30.1	12.2	6.2	41.6	33.0	14.8	10.5
Orissa	1983	47.7	34.4	12.1	5.9	79.9	14.2	4.3	1.5	-	-	-	-
	1993-94	47.8	33.7	12.2	6.2	69.5	22.4	5.8	2.3	58.6	28.1	9.0	4.3
	1999-00	43.3	35.1	13.1	8.4	62.9	25.3	7.9	3.8	53.2	30.2	10.5	6.1
Punjab	1983	51.3	24.6	11.3	12.6	71.1	17.5	5.9	5.4	-	-	-	-
	1993-94	43.5	32.1	10.2	14.2	56.1	28.5	6.8	8.6	49.5	30.4	8.6	11.5
	1999-00	37.6	34.5	10.5	17.4	47.2	33.8	7.2	11.6	42.2	34.0	8.9	14.6
Rajasthan	1983	63.9	21.5	8.8	5.6	93.1	5.3	0.8	0.7	-	-	-	-
	1993-94	52.7	32.9	8.2	6.2	85.0	12.4	1.7	1.0	68.2	23.1	5.0	3.7
	1999-00	44.8	37.2	10.2	8.0	76.0	19.5	2.8	1.7	59.9	28.7	6.6	4.9

(Contd. —)

TABLE 225

Table 25 (Contd.)

Educational Background of Rural Workers in Indian States: NSS Data 1983/1999-00

State	Year	Rural Male				Rural Female				Rural Persons			
		Not Literate	Upto Primary	Middle	Secondary & Above	Not Literate	Upto Primary	Middle	Secondary & Above	Not Literate	Upto Primary	Middle	Secondary & Above
1	2	3	4	5	6	7	8	9	10	11	12	13	14
Tamil Nadu	1983	40.4	37.7	13.8	8.1	73.2	18.8	5.1	2.8	-	-	-	-
	1993-94	35.0	41.5	11.7	11.8	57.2	30.8	6.4	5.5	46.2	36.1	9.0	8.6
	1999-00	32.1	39.1	14.2	14.4	49.7	31.4	10.8	8.0	40.8	35.4	12.5	11.1
Uttar Pradesh	1983	55.8	22.4	12.4	9.2	88.1	8.5	2.0	1.3	-	-	-	-
	1993-94	50.4	29.5	10.3	9.7	77.1	17.1	3.3	2.5	63.1	23.6	7.0	6.3
	1999-00	44.8	31.4	11.9	11.6	69.3	21.9	4.6	4.0	56.7	26.9	8.4	7.8
West Bengal	1983	38.6	37.7	12.3	11.3	72.0	20.1	5.3	2.5	-	-	-	-
	1993-94	41.4	40.4	10.5	7.7	59.3	32.2	6.1	2.3	50.1	36.4	8.3	5.1
	1999-00	37.2	40.2	13.4	9.2	54.7	32.9	9.0	3.3	45.8	36.5	11.2	6.3
India	1983	49.7	28.5	12.7	9.0	79.8	13.6	4.3	2.3	-	-	-	-
	1993-94	45.5	33.7	10.9	9.8	67.9	23.0	5.6	3.4	56.4	28.5	8.3	6.7
	1999-00	41.2	34.2	12.6	11.7	61.5	26.0	7.5	5.0	51.1	30.2	10.1	8.3

Note : 1983 figures are corresponding proportion of persons of age 15 years and above.

Source : 1. Govt. of India, *SARVEKSHANA*, Vol. XI, No 4, April 1988: 19-21.

2. Govt. of India, *Key Results on Employment and Unemployment*, NSS Reort No 406, June, 1996: 52-57.

3. Govt. of India, *Employment and Unemployment Situation in India, 1999-2000, Part I*, NSS Report No. 458, May 2001: 54-57.

Table 26

Distribution of Educated Rural Workers Staying Back in Agriculture and those Moving out to Non-Agricultural Jobs by Workers' Sex: 1983/1999-2000

Worker Category	Year/ Period	Proportion of Educated Workers Engaged in		Proportion of Incremental Educated Workers Engaged in		Growth Rate of Employment (Annual Compound: %)						Share of Educated Workers among Total Workers	
						Agriculture		Non-agriculture		All Sectors			
		Agr.	Non-agr.	Agr.	Non-agr.	Educated Workers	All Workers	Educated Workers	All Workers	Educated Workers	All Workers	Agr.	Non-agr.
1	2	3	4	5	6	7	8	9	10	11	12	13	14
Rural Male	1983	45.45	54.55									4.91	19.99
	1993-94	51.53	48.47									8.96	23.38
	1999-00	52.79	47.21									12.17	26.69
	1983/93-94			56.90	43.10	9.26	0.05	6.62	1.99	7.89	0.51		
	93-94/99-00			55.62	44.38	6.91	0.32	6.00	2.62	6.47	0.94		
Rural Female	1983	26.93	73.07									0.32	5.43
	1993-94	34.32	65.68									1.04	11.37
	1999-00	46.86	53.14									2.15	13.06
	1983/93-94			38.17	61.83	13.60	-0.15	9.76	1.18	10.92	0.02		
	93-94/99-00			63.30	36.70	15.87	-0.02	6.11	1.21	9.94	0.15		
Rural Persons	1983	44.38	55.62									2.92	14.72
	1993-94	50.18	49.82									6.46	21.25
	1999-00	52.26	47.74									8.84	24.17
	1983/93-94			55.23	44.77	9.43	-0.03	6.92	1.79	8.10	0.33		
	93-94/99-00			56.54	43.46	7.44	0.18	5.95	2.31	6.71	0.66		

Source : 1. Govt. of India, SARVEKSHANA, Vol. XIV, No 1 & 2 Oct-Dec. 1990.
2. 1993-94 and 1999-00 data are extracted from household level data on CD-ROM supplied by NSSO, Govt. of India.

TABLE 227

Table 27

Educational and Training Background of Family and Hired Workers Engaged in Tiny and Small Enterprises in India: April-June 2000 Survey

1	Family Worker						Hired Worker						Total Worker					
	Rural	%age	Urban	%age	Total	%age	Rural	%age	Urban	%age	Total	%age	Rural	%age	Urban	%age	Total	%age
	2	3	4	5	6	7	8	9	10	11	12	13	14	15	16	17	18	19
General Education																		
Illiterate	51	12.72	11	3.53	62	8.70	153	14.77	84	6.41	237	10.10	204	14.20	95	5.85	299	9.77
Upto Primary	66	16.46	11	3.53	77	10.80	254	24.52	343	26.16	597	25.44	320	22.27	354	21.81	674	22.03
Upto Middle	67	16.71	41	13.14	108	15.15	332	32.05	423	32.27	755	32.17	399	27.77	464	28.59	863	28.20
Upto Matric	101	25.19	79	25.32	180	25.25	280	27.03	382	29.14	662	28.21	381	26.51	461	28.40	842	27.52
Upto Graduate	110	27.43	150	48.08	260	36.47	16	1.54	73	5.57	89	3.79	126	8.77	223	13.74	349	11.41
Upto P.G.	6	1.50	19	6.09	25	3.51	1	0.10	5	0.38	6	0.26	7	0.49	24	1.48	31	1.01
Others	0	0.00	1	0.32	1	0.14	0	0.00	1	0.08	1	0.04	0	0.00	2	0.12	2	0.07
Total	401	100.00	312	100.00	713	100.00	1036	100.00	1311	100.00	2347	100.00	1437	100.00	1623	100.00	3060	100.00
Technical Education*																		
ITI	15	3.74	9	2.88	24	3.37	49	4.73	66	5.03	115	4.90	64	4.45	75	4.62	139	4.54
Polytechnic	7	1.75	6	1.92	13	1.82	1	0.10	12	0.92	13	0.55	8	0.56	18	1.11	26	0.85
Engineering	24	5.99	47	15.06	71	9.96	2	0.19	12	0.92	14	0.60	26	1.81	59	3.64	85	2.78
MBA	5	1.25	5	1.60	10	1.40	0	0.00	0	0.00	0	0.00	5	0.35	5	0.31	10	0.33
Others	5	1.25	13	4.17	18	2.52	1	0.10	0	0.00	1	0.04	6	0.42	13	0.80	19	0.62
Total	56	13.97	80	25.64	136	19.07	53	5.12	90	6.86	143	6.09	109	7.59	170	10.47	279	9.12
Training																		
On the Job	200	49.88	171	54.81	371	52.03	980	94.59	1222	93.21	2202	93.82	1180	82.12	1393	85.83	2573	84.08
Family	150	37.41	83	26.60	233	32.68	5	0.48	5	0.38	10	0.43	155	10.79	88	5.42	243	7.94
Govt. Agency	51	12.72	58	18.59	109	15.29	51	4.92	84	6.41	135	5.75	102	7.10	142	8.75	244	7.97
Total	401	100.00	312	100.00	713	100.00	1036	100.00	1311	100.00	2347	100.00	1437	100.00	1623	100.00	3060	100.00

Note   : * In the case of Technical Education, the percentages are share to total workers.
Source : The same as in Table 5.

Table 28

Distribution of Persons (Age 5 Years and Above) by Status of Current Attendance in Educational Institutions for Different Age Groups in Rural and Urban India: 1993-94/1999-2000

Age Group (Years)	Current Status on Attending Educational Institutions	Rural Areas						Urban Areas					
		Male		Female		Persons		Male		Female		Persons	
		93-94	99-00	93-94	99-00	93-94	99-00	93-94	99-00	93-94	99-00	93-94	99-00
1	2	3	4	5	6	7	8	9	10	11	12	14	15
5-9	Not Attending	33.5	29.2	44.0	36.9	38.5	32.8	16.2	16.1	20.3	19.0	18.1	17.5
	Pre-Primary Schooling	15.4	18.8	12.6	16.7	14.0	17.8	22.0	25.7	19.0	25.5	20.7	25.6
	Primary Schooling	48.4	50.3	41.2	44.9	45.0	47.8	58.0	55.1	56.9	52.6	57.5	53.9
	Middle & Higher Levels	2.6	1.7	2.2	1.5	2.4	1.6	3.6	3.1	3.8	2.9	3.7	3.0
10-14	Not Attending	24.0	21.6	44.2	35.2	33.2	27.9	13.2	12.9	18.4	18.4	15.6	15.5
	Pre-Primary to Primary	34.0	36.2	25.6	30.1	30.2	33.2	28.6	30.4	24.7	27.3	25.7	28.9
	Middle Level Schooling	33.9	35.1	23.9	29.0	29.3	32.2	44.5	45.6	43.2	42.6	43.9	44.2
	Secondary & Higher Levels	8.2	7.1	6.2	5.7	7.3	6.7	13.8	11.1	13.5	11.7	13.7	11.4
15-19	Not Attending	58.7	56.0	79.2	73.4	68.0	64.0	43.0	41.1	50.2	48.0	46.3	44.2
	Up to Middle Level	9.4	11.5	5.2	7.0	7.5	9.5	7.6	8.4	5.7	7.1	6.7	7.8
	Secondary & HigherLevels	26.3	29.3	13.1	17.3	20.3	29.8	34.5	39.9	30.9	34.0	32.8	37.2
	Technical Degree and Diploma	5.6	3.2	2.5	2.3	4.4	2.7	14.8	10.6	13.2	10.9	14.1	10.8
20-24	Not Attending	89.2	89.3	97.1	96.2	93.2	93.0	77.3	76.6	86.6	83.2	81.8	79.7
	Higher Secondary & Higher Levels	4.1	4.3	1.4	1.5	2.8	2.8	4.6	5.1	2.5	2.9	3.6	4.2
	Technical Degree	4.8	4.6	1.1	1.7	2.9	3.1	11.7	12.9	7.3	10.3	9.6	11.5
	Technical Diploma	1.8	1.8	0.4	0.6	1.1	1.1	6.2	5.4	3.5	3.6	4.9	4.6

Source : 1. For 1993-94, Govt. of India, N.S.S. Report No. 409, March 1997: A79-A84.
2. For 1999-2000, Govt. of India, NSS Report No. 458 (Part I), May 2001: A119-A124.

TABLE 229

Table 29

Percentage of Child Workers among Total Workers by Farm and Non-Farm Sector and Place of Residence: 1987-88/1997-98.

Age Group (in Years)	1987-88			1993-94			1997-98		
	5-9	10-14	5-14	5-9	10-14	5-14	5-9	10-14	5-14
1	2	3	4	5	6	7	8	9	10
Rural									
Farm	2.2	16.1	8.7	1.1	11.7	6.1	0.5	8.2	4.2
Non-farm	0.1	2.6	1.3	0.2	1.2	1.2	0.1	1.1	0.5
Total	2.3	18.7	9.9	1.3	14.0	7.3	0.6	9.3	4.8
Urban									
Farm	0.1	1.8	0.9	0.1	1.0	0.6	0.2	1.0	0.6
Non-farm	0.3	5.8	3.0	0.3	4.6	2.5	0.2	3.7	2.0
Total	0.4	7.6	3.9	0.4	5.6	3.1	0.4	4.7	2.7

Source: 1. For 1987-88, SARVEKSHANA, Special Number, Sept. 1990: S190-S193.

2. For 1993-94, Govt. of India, NSS Report No. 409, March 1997: A114-A117.

3. For 1998, Govt. of India, NSS Report No. 448, June 1999: A20-A23.

Table 30
Proportion of Enterprises Located Inside the Residential Premises: 2000-01 NSS Data

NIC Code	Sector Description	Rural				Urban			
		OAMEs	NDMEs	DMEs	Total	OAMEs	NDMEs	DMEs	Total
1	2	3	4	5	6	7	8	9	10
01405	Cotton ginning, cleaning and baling	22.9	0.0	7.6	20.0	61.1	10.0	0.0	52.4
15	Food Products and Beverages	64.1	32.8	30.9	60.6	53.9	24.2	19.8	44.6
16	Tobacco Products	99.1	39.7	24.9	97.9	97.4	44.0	43.8	96.9
17	Textiles	95.7	74.9	55.0	93.5	90.7	47.0	32.0	76.7
18	Wearing Apparel; Dressing & Dyeing Fur	76.6	16.0	23.5	72.0	71.5	12.7	19.5	58.0
19	Tanning & Dressing of Leather	71.8	40.8	8.6	70.3	56.1	38.0	33.8	48.8
20	Wood & Wood Products	78.7	29.8	27.7	77.5	46.5	20.3	16.6	40.3
21	Paper & Paper Products	98.0	42.5	4.6	95.0	91.3	27.1	16.9	70.5
36	Furniture	66.8	8.1	56.9	46.7	42.4	17.1	19.9	26.6
22	Publishing, Printing etc.	30.0	8.0	0.0	16.8	28.7	3.0	0.0	10.8
23	Coke, Refined Petroleum Products	97.5	28.7	4.5	83.4	98.5	25.3	25.2	87.6
24	Chemical and Chemical Products	87.1	38.8	29.4	72.1	71.5	14.7	13.1	37.6
25	Rubber & Plastic Products	77.9	33.8	7.1	69.7	80.2	26.8	10.6	61.7
26	Non-Metallic Mineral Products	36.6	48.2	0.8	34.5	48.7	27.4	10.5	32.2
27	Basic Metal	59.4	24.1	27.7	55.2	45.4	19.0	13.6	29.5
28	Fabricated Metal Products	74.7	38.5	21.9	70.7	22.7	11.6	7.8	14.2
29	Machinery & Equipment	0.0	0.0	0.0	0.0	0.0	0.0	0.0	0.6
30	Office, Accounting & Computing Machinery	61.3	58.5	10.3	58.1	37.9	0.8	5.9	20.1
31	Electrical Machinery and Apparatus	64.3	81.8	0.0	54.9	80.7	19.3	34.1	42.0
32	Radio, TV & Communication Equipment	28.8	47.6	6.2	32.6	30.2	34.4	2.3	18.7
33	Medical, Precision & Optical Instruments, Clocks etc.	0.0	12.4	5.4	2.9	13.3	13.0	9.1	8.3
34	Motor Vehicles, Trailers, and Semi-Trailers	32.9	28.4	0.0	29.7	30.2	6.3	18.0	27.5
35	Other Transport Equipment	63.9	32.9	16.8	60.6	49.6	33.4	13.8	40.6
37	Recycling	41.1	42.2	25.0	41.0	60.0	20.0	28.1	52.6
	All Industries	79.6	35.0	26.1	76.2	69.5	47.6	19.7	55.5

Source: Govt. of India, *Unorgnised Manufacturing Sector in India, 2000-01: Characteristics of Enterprises*, Report No-478, NSSO, September 2002:A103-A110.

TABLE 231

Table 31

Proportion of Small-Scale Closed Units by Industry Group and Rural Urban Location: 1987-88 and 1994-95

Industry Division	Proportion of Closed Units to the Total Units				Share of Closed Units in Each Industrial Group to Total			
	1987-88			1994-95	1987-88			1994-95
	Rural	Urban	Total	Total	Rural	Urban	Total	Total
1	2	3	4	5	6	7	8	9
Food Products (20+21)	21.23	33.06	25.89	27.91	15.20	10.70	11.39	12.30
Beverages(22)	35.76	35.85	35.80	37.65	0.90	0.60	0.69	0.97
Cotton Textiles (23)	36.94	37.51	37.34	36.29	0.20	0.40	0.30	0.54
Wool, Synthetic, (24)	29.25	42.35	37.17	44.26	0.20	0.30	0.22	0.54
Jute, Mesta, (25)	42.27	50.59	48.29	40.82	0.00	0.10	0.08	0.15
Textile Products(26)	36.22	39.84	37.77	33.36	11.30	6.50	8.36	7.53
Wood/Products(27)	27.47	32.53	29.69	27.94	10.70	6.90	7.82	6.96
Paper/Products(28)	25.07	27.08	26.67	29.23	1.70	4.90	4.41	4.55
Leather/Products(29)	33.08	36.26	34.35	36.70	6.40	3.20	4.42	3.60
Chemicals/Products(30)	42.02	44.99	44.07	39.02	4.50	7.40	6.67	6.09
Rubber, Plastic, Coal, Pet.(31)	46.92	47.43	47.25	40.43	6.20	7.90	7.65	6.86
Non-Met.Min.Prodts (32)	38.00	39.91	38.82	34.66	9.90	5.50	6.74	5.87
Basic Metal (33)	39.28	39.11	39.14	36.16	1.30	4.00	3.17	3.71
Metal Products(34)	33.77	40.90	38.32	34.47	10.70	15.90	13.85	9.80
Machinery and its Parts (35)	31.17	32.25	32.02	30.58	3.10	8.00	6.64	7.44
Machine Tools (36)	40.24	38.69	38.98	42.03	0.90	2.70	2.51	4.42
Transport Equip. (37)	29.11	36.09	34.03	39.12	1.10	2.30	1.95	2.41
Other Manufacturing (38)	39.01	39.65	39.47	42.71	1.20	2.20	1.91	3.29
Repair and Other Services (97,99)	27.58	26.13	26.81	27.10	14.30	10.50	11.22	12.98
Total	30.48	35.65	33.33	32.52	100.00	100.00	100.00	100.00

Source : 1. Govt. of India, *Report of the Second All-India Census of Small Scale Industrial Units 1987-88*, Ministry of Industry, August, 1992.
2. Govt. of India, *Report on Sample Survey of Small Scale Industrial Units 1994-95*, Ministry of SSI and ARI, 2000.

Table 32
Net Earning from Rope-making by Marketing
Arrangement and Level of Technology

Marketing System	Type of Technology Used		
	Hand-Operated	Pedal-Operated	Power-Operated
1	2	3	4
Net Total Earnings			
1. Through Trade Intermediary	7410.20	4586.00	5358.40
2. Independently	7554.68	14867.11	16780.60
Per Day Net Earning			
1. Through Trade Intermediary	14.30	9.67	11.01
2. Independently	17.08	32.54	48.76

Source: Chadha, 1992: 240.

TABLE 233

Table 33
Percentage of Sample Units Which Do Not Have the Basic Facilities

Item	% of Sample Units which do not have the Specified Facilities		
	Rural	Urban	Total
1	2	3	4
A. Working Environment			
(i) Heater	76.11	65.91	71.07
(ii) Fresh Air Fan	55.00	28.98	42.13
(iii) Fan	20.56	17.61	19.10
(iv) Toilet	25.56	7.39	16.57
(v) Adequate Working Space	10.56	5.11	7.87
B. Working Condition			
(i) Paid Leave	53.89	31.25	42.70
(ii) Provident Fund	90.56	89.20	89.89
(iii) Pension	97.22	94.89	96.06
(iv) House Rent Allowance	91.67	86.93	89.33
(v) Insurance Policy	95.00	86.93	91.01
(vi) Disability Benefits	97.22	91.48	94.38
(vi) Injury Allowance	67.22	46.02	56.74
(vii) Fixed Working Hours	80.56	51.70	66.29

Source: The same as in Table 5.

Table 34

Employment in Non-Crop Agricultural Activities and Non-Agricultural Sector by Rural-Urban Location: (Economic Census Data) 1980, 1990 and 1998.

1	2	Activities Allied to Agriculture* 3	Non-Agricultural Activities 4	Total 5
Rural				
	1980	2433018	21793510	24226528
	%	10.04	89.96	100.00
	1990	4206566	27969200	32175766
	%	13.07	86.93	100.00
	1998	6081232	32051302	38132534
	%	15.95	84.05	100.00
Absolute Change				
	1980/1990	1773548	6175690	7949238
	1990/1998	1874666	4082102	5956768
	1980/1998	3648214	10257792	13906006
Annual Compound Growth Rate (%)				
	1980/1990	5.63	2.53	2.88
	1990/1998	4.71	1.72	2.15
	1980/1998	5.22	2.17	2.55
Urban				
	1980	394866	28557279	28952145
	%	1.36	98.64	100.00
	1990	525847	37684600	38210447
	%	1.38	98.62	100.00
	1998	609229	41889478	42498707
	%	1.43	98.57	100.00
Absolute Change				
	1980/1990	130981	9127321	9258302

(Contd. —)

Table 34 (Contd.)

Employment in Non-Crop Agricultural Activities and Non-Agricultural Sector by Rural-Urban Location: (Economic Census Data) 1980, 1990 and 1998.

1	2	Activities Allied to Agriculture*	Non-Agricultural Activities	Total
		3	4	5
	1990/1998	83382	4204878	4288260
	1980/1998	214363	13332199	13546562
Annual Compound Growth Rate (%)				
	1980/1990	2.91	2.81	2.81
	1990/1998	1.86	1.33	1.34
	1980/1998	2.44	2.15	2.16
Total	1980	2827884	50350789	53178673
	%	5.32	94.68	100.00
	1990	4732413	65653800	70386213
	%	6.72	93.28	100.00
	1998	6690461	73940780	80631241
	%	8.30	91.70	100.00
Absolute Change				
	1980/1990	1904529	15303011	17207540
	1990/1998	1958048	8286980	10245028
	1980/1998	3862577	23589991	27452568
Annual Compound Growth Rate (%)				
	1980/1990	5.28	2.69	2.84
	1990/1998	4.42	1.50	1.71
	1980/1998	4.90	2.16	2.34

Note : (1) Figures exclude Assam and Jammu & Kashmir; (2) * includes activities (other than crop production and plantations) such as live-stock, agricultural services, hunting, trapping, forestry and logging, fishing etc.

Source : Govt.of India, *Economic Census* 1980, 1990 and 1998, CSO. (**http://www.nic.in/stat/stat_act.htm**)

TABLE 235

Table 35

Sub-Contracting in the Unorganized Manufacturing Sector in India by Place of Location and Enterprise category: 1999-2000 NSS Data

Enterprise Category	Percentage of Enterprises			
	Working Under Contract	Getting Raw Material from Parent Co(s)	Working on Design by Parent Co(s)	Working with Equipment Supplied by Parent Co(s)
1	2	3	4	5
OAMEs				
Rural	27.8	91.5	92.6	23.9
Urban	33.8	86.8	91.8	25.9
Combined	29.4	90.1	92.4	24.5
Establishment				
Rural	19.8	75.7	89.1	22.0
Urban	25.8	67.8	88.7	18.6
Combined	23.9	69.9	88.8	19.5
All Enterprises				
Rural	27.3	90.8	92.5	23.8
Urban	31.5	82.4	91.1	24.2
Combined	28.7	87.8	92.0	23.9

Note : Own Account Enterprise (OAME) is an enterprise run by household labour, usually without any hired worker employed on a 'fairly regular basis'.

Establishment is an enterprise, which has got at least one hired worker on a 'fairly regular' basis.

Source : Govt. of India, *Non-Agricultural Enterprises in the Informal Manufacturing Sector in India, Key Results, NSS 55th Round, (July 1999-June 2000),* NSS Report No. 456, 2000b: 52-57

TABLE 237

Table 36

Percentage of Household Enterprises in the Informal/Unorganised Manufacturing Sector of Indian Economy Working under Contract System by Place of Location and Enterprise Category: 1999-2000 NSS Data

Enterprise Category	% of Households to Total Informal Manufacturing Enterprises	Households Enterprises Working under Contract System (%)	% of Household Enterprises Working under Contract System that		
			Receive Raw Material from Parent Cos.	Work on Design Specified by Parent Cos.	Work With Own Equipment
1	2	3	4	5	6
OAMEs					
Rural	76.3	95.3	92.3	87.8	76.0
Urban	62.7	94.3	90.0	87.5	69.3
Combined	72.6	95.2	91.8	89.4	74.0
Establishment					
Rural	28.5	87.2	79.8	80.8	65.4
Urban	17.2	87.8	77.0	82.4	73.4
Combined	20.8	87.6	78.3	81.7	69.7
All Enterprises					
Rural	73.3	95.2	92.1	89.7	75.5
Urban	49.9	93.8	89.1	87.2	69.6
Combined	65.6	94.7	91.1	89.0	73.7

Note : The same as in Table 35.

Source : Govt. of India, Non-Agricultural Enterprises in the Informal Manufacturing Sector in India, Key Results, NSS 55th Round, (July 1999-June 2000), NSS Report No. 456, 2000b: 46-50, 64-69.

Table 37

Benefits and Problems Associated with Subcontracting among the Tiny and Small Industry of India by Rural – Urban Location: April-June 2000 Survey

	Rural	Urban	Total
1	2	3	4
A. Proportion of Enterprises Working under Sub-contracting Arrangement	38.6	35.9	37.3
B. *Benefits*			
Receive Raw Material	42.17	53.03	46.98
Financial Support	33.73	27.27	30.87
Technological Up-gradation	46.99	31.82	40.27
Assured Market	93.98	100.00	96.64
C. *Problems*			
Dilatory Tactics	92.77	81.82	87.92
Unjustified Termination	6.02	4.55	5.37
Undue Price Cutting	9.64	9.09	9.40
Stringent Quality Standards	21.69	9.09	16.11

Source: The same as in Table 5.

www.ingramcontent.com/pod-product-compliance
Lightning Source LLC
Chambersburg PA
CBHW070359270326
41926CB00014B/2616